THE ROSE OF BEING

THE ROSE OF BEING

Jung, Consciousness, Myth and Metaphor

GERRY ANNE LENHART, Ph.D.

Alive Book Publishing

The Rose of Being
Jung, Consciousness, Myth, and Metaphor
Copyright © 2025 by Gerry Anne Lenhart, Ph.D.

All rights reserved. No part of this book may be reproduced or transmitted in any form or by any means without written permission from the publisher and author.

Additional copies may be ordered from the publisher for educational, business, promotional or premium use. For information, contact ALIVE Book Publishing at: alivebookpublishing.com, or call (925) 837-7303.

Book Design by Alex Johnson
Technical Advisor: Scott Lenhart
ISBN 13
978-1-63132-263-1

Library of Congress Control Number: 2025917351
Library of Congress Cataloging-in-Publication Data is available upon request.

First Edition

Published in the United States of America by ALIVE Book Publishing
an imprint of Advanced Publishing LLC
3200 A Danville Blvd., Suite 204, Alamo, California 94507
alivebookpublishing.com

PRINTED IN THE UNITED STATES OF AMERICA

10 9 8 7 6 5 4 3 2 1

FOR THE MEMORY OF MY MOTHER
Frances West Brown Aeh

Beauty knows itself by mirrored grace
If Love and Death are the twin wings
That take a good Soul to Heaven
She sleeps and wakes
Tonight
In the company
Of Angels

and

THE MEMORY OF MY FATHER
Clyde Lowell Brown

Hermes personified
Peter Pan
And the Pied Piper
Rolled into One
A Trinity
Whose gift
Was divine laughter

and

THE MEMORY OF MY DAUGHTER
Laura Lee Lenhart
A Band of Angels sing your praise
God Bless the Child
Angel on Earth

ACKNOWLEDGMENTS

The seeds of this book were planted many years ago. The third "Jungian" book I read was Psychological Types, which became my happy obsession. Many years later, I would like to thank all the people whose help along the way was invaluable. Much appreciation, to my son Scott, whose talent in photography was amazing, as well as his technical ability. I would like to thank my son Mark for his many years of encouragement and technical support when I was ready to give up trying to master the elusive machine. Both sons appeared to inherit all the technical ability that I was definitely not blessed. I would also like to thank my husband Lawrence who listened with great patience over the years as I shared my enthusiasm over new discoveries of Psychological Types. He truly was my captive audience. Many thanks to Eric and the wonderful staff at Alive publishing for all their help in making my book possible.

CONTENTS

Chapter 1. Introduction — 15

    Jung and the Four Psychological Functions — 15

    The Genesis Model — 20

    The Irrational Functions of Intuition and Sensation — 33

    The Rational Functions of Feeling and Thinking — 41

    Aspects of Jung's Four Psychological Functions and their Relationship to One Another before and after Birth — 46

    The Womb Archetype and the Psychology of the Child in the Womb as Metaphors — 58

    Eros, Thanatos, and the Desire for Paradise — 61

Chapter 2. Michael Fordham — 69

    Michael Fordham and Jungian Developmental Psychology — 69

    Fordham on the Child in the Womb — 70

    Fordham on Cosmogonic Myths and the Womb as Paradise — 76

    Archetypes, the Unconscious, and Mandalas — 85

    More on Mandala Symbolism — 88

    Primary Narcissism or Primary Love? — 91

    The Self, Ego and Individuation — 96

    Fordham, Jung, and the Genesis Hypothesis — 102

Chapter 3. First Prelude to Genesis: Antecedent Archetypes That Describe Basic Psychic Energy and the Four Functions — 113

    Sumerian Archetypes and Symbols as Personifications of Archetypal Energy Patterns — 114

    The Fall of the Divine Child/Angel, Lucifer: The Serpent Archetype and the Four Psychological Functions — 128

Moses as Divine and Human Child: The Hero Archetype, Confidant
of Angels   138

Chapter 4. Second Prelude to Genesis: The Four Archangels of Michael, Uriel, Raphael, & Gabriel as Personifications of Neutral or Undifferentiated Psychic Energy   147

Disinterest and the High Indifference: Two Concepts Describing Neutral
or Undifferentiated Psychic Energy   148

The Archangel Michael as Archetype for the Psychological Function of
Neutral or Undifferentiated Intuition   151

The Archangel Uriel as Archetype for the Psychological Function of
Neutral or Undifferentiated Sensation   154

The Archangel Raphael as Archetype for the Psychological Function of
Neutral or Undifferentiated Feeling   160

The Archangel Gabriel as Archetype for the Psychological Function of
Neutral or Undifferentiated Thinking   166

Chapter 5. The Myth of Genesis as a Metaphor for the Divine Child, the Psychological Child, and the Biological Child: Mythological Origins of Consciousness and Jung's Four Psychological Functions   171

The Mythological Level: Creation of the Divine Child from the First
Divine Syzygy in Genesis   172

The Divine Syzygy of the Spirit and Water in Genesis: Archetypes for
the Creation of the Divine Child, the Psychological Child, and the
Biological Child   181

The Father God, the Serpent, Eve and Adam as Primary Archetypes in
Genesis: Personifications of the Four Psychological Functions   189

The Serpent in Genesis as the Function of Unconscious Sensation
(Intuition) or the Divine Child Archetype: The Serpent in Eden as the
Archetype of Conscious Sensation   192

Eve or the Feeling Function as the Bone (Beginning) of Adam or the
Thinking Function   197

Adam as Divine Child, Image of God: Archetype for the Psychological
Function of Undifferentiated Thinking   203

Chapter 6. Symbols and Archetypes from Divergent Mythologies that Express Psychic Energy Related to Genesis, the Self, and the Four Psychological Functions   **219**

    The Rope Image of the Hindu *Bhagavad Gita*: An Eastern Three-In-One Motif   219

    A Comparison of the Wind and Water Symbolism in Genesis with the Great Serpent Mound: Tokchi'i, Guardian of the East   220

    The Symbolism in the Tenth Picture of the Rosarium Philosophorum: Three Serpents Contained by One Chalice   223

    Psyche and Eros: Symbols of Transformation Leading to the *Coniunctio* and Birth of a Divine Girl/Child Named Joy: Archetype for the Self   227

    Mythology and Biological Psychology as a Function of the Human Nervous System: The Left/Right Brain Metaphor   234

Chapter 7. Conclusion   **247**

List of Figures   **259**

This is the Mother-Love
Which is one of the most moving
And unforgettable
Memories of our lives,
The mysterious root of all
growth and change;
the love that means
homecoming, shelter, and
the long silence.
From which everything begins
And which everything ends.

C.G. Jung
From <u>Archetypes of the Collective Unconscious</u>

Before I formed thee in the belly I knew thee; and before thou camest forth out of the womb I sanctified thee, *and* **I ordained thee a prophet unto the nations.**

JEREMIAH 1:5

Chapter 1
Introduction

<u>Jung and the Four Psychological Functions</u>

In <u>Psychological Types</u>, Jung (1971/1921) describes four basic psychic functions that are capable of becoming conscious: intuition, sensation, feeling, and thinking:

> Under sensation I include all perceptions by means of the sense organs; by thinking, I mean the function of intellectual cognition and the forming of logical conclusions; feeling is a function of subjective evaluation; intuition I take as perception by way of the unconscious, or perception of unconscious events (p. 518).

Jung goes on to explain that, in his experience, there are only four basic functions, a fact that seems to be self-evident if one inquires into the possibilities. These psychic functions are the methods employed by humans to acquire knowledge of themselves and the surrounding world; cognition is not restricted to one function, and each function provides its own kind of knowledge.

Of equal importance in Jung's typology are the attitude types of introversion and extraversion, which he (1971/1921) describes as:

> distinguished by their attitude to the object. The introvert's attitude is an abstracting one… he is always intent on withdrawing libido from the object, as though he had to prevent the object from gaining power over him. The extravert, on the contrary, has a positive relation to the object. He affirms its importance to such an extent that his subjective attitude is constantly related to and oriented by the object (p. 330).

These brief explications of his major topics, namely, the eight variations of personality and the attitude types of introversion and extraversion, are later described as having this purpose:

> To provide a critical psychology which will make a methodical investigation and presentation of the empirical material possible. First, and foremost, it is a critical tool for the research worker, who needs definite points of view and guidelines if he is to reduce the chaotic profusion of individual experiences to any kind of order (1971/1921, p. 555).

Jung (1971/1921) said of his typology, "It is not a physiognomy and not an anthropological system, but a critical psychology dealing with the organization and delimitation of psychic processes that can be shown to be typical" (p. xv). Here Jung makes it clear that he was not concerned with the origins of the psychological functions, but used them as a tool in organizing empirical material. It was Jung's purpose to describe individual types of the human personality, to explain and explore individual differences of cognition and various methods of expression in the personality by using the psychic functions of intuition, sensation, feeling, and thinking, along with the attitudinal types of introversion and extraversion.

Jung (1971/1921) states: "Since every man, as a relatively stable being possesses all the basic psychological functions, it would be a psychological necessity with a view to perfect adaptation that he should also employ them in equal measure" (p. 19). Here Jung confirms the possibility of all four functions working in equal measure in the psyche of one person. Throughout his writing, he describes what happens when one function is superior and conscious and another function is inferior and unconscious. When one conscious position is extreme, the position of the other extreme will exist in the unconscious, causing a neurosis or a maladaptation to consciousness.

The interplay of conscious and unconscious opposites, as well as opposites in general, is prevalent in Jung's thinking and writing, and appears to be the foundation for his theory of opposites or the transcendent function. He (1971/1921) describes this as follows:

> The "function" being here understood not as a basic function but as a complex function made up of other functions, and "transcendent" not as denoting a metaphysical quality but merely the fact that this function facilitates a transition from one state to another. The raw material shaped by thesis and antithesis, and in the shaping of which the opposites are united, is the living symbol (p. 480).

This definition describes the importance that Jung gave to the symbol as a means for uniting the opposites, and also describes the complex relationship of the symbol with the four psychological functions.

An expanded individual consciousness was not seen as important only to the person who obtains the limits of personal potential, but equally important to the society to which he belongs. Jung (1953/1943) makes this clear when he says that "development of individuality is simultaneously a development of society. Suppression of individuality through the predominance of collective ideals and organizations is a moral defeat for society" (p. 303).

Fordham (1972) writes:

> The subtitle of the first English translation of Psychological Types reads or *The psychology of individuation,* an addition to the first Swiss edition and not added to later ones in German; it is omitted from the recent edition in the Collected works. The addition is curious because there is no mention of individuation in the text until its definition at the end of the book (p. 112).

This is literally true, but not quite reflective of the spirit of the text, which I understand as significantly related to the individuation process. Meier (1986), however, appears to share my conviction concerning typology:

"Jung's most important contribution to psychology was the discovery and practice of the process of individuation. In spite of the supremacy of this concept, its origins in terms of chronology are far from being as clear as they should be, and in this respect not even Jung's memoirs yield the needed biographical information."

But before I give you the prehistory, history and an account of the survival of the concept of individuation, I shall ask you to remember: *Individuation begins and ends with typology* (emphasis Meier's, p. 242).

I completely agree with Meier that individuation begins and ends with typology and that individuation was Jung's most important contribution to psychology. I would describe Jung's monumental work on psychological types as an attempt to take apart the human psyche and describe how the parts work. All of this work appears to revolve around the process of individuation, and the most important concept for achieving this end is the transcendent function, which is the symbol that unites the opposites.

Jung (1971/1921) describes and links his work on psychological functions with the concept of individuation in an important way:

> The concept of individuation plays a large role in our psychology. In general, it is the process by which individual beings are formed and differentiated; in particular, it is the development of the psychological individual as a being distinct from the general, collective psychology. Individuation, therefore, is a process of differentiation having for its goal the development of the individual personality (p. 448).

The above definition succinctly describes Jung's purpose in attempting to provide a theoretical model of psychological types or functions. Individuation appears to me to be the primary goal of this work and Jung's multitudinous insights are, as he described them, "critical tools" for further research.

Newborn
Oil on Canvas

Passage indeed O soul to primal thought,
Not lands and seas alone, thy own clear freshness,
The young maturity of brood and bloom,
To realms of budding Bibles.

O soul, repressless, I with thee and thou with me,
Thy circumnavigation of the world begin,
Of man, the voyage of his mind's return,
To reason's early paradise,
Back, back to wisdom's birth, to innocent intuitions,
Again with fair creation.

Walt Whitman
Leaves of Grass, Passage to India, verse 7
1981, p. 383

The Genesis Model

Since individuation was a major reason for Jung's differentiation and explication of the four functions and the attitudinal types of introversion and extraversion, and since Jung did not describe a model of how these functions would look in the beginning psyche of one individual, such a model would contribute to psychology's understanding of the individuation process, especially concerning aspects associated with the beginning of human life, which is seen here as beginning in the womb rather than at birth. Many myths and stories can be said to contain the same information and I have included some of these variations in this book. Genesis, however, is the most important myth of our Western culture. Seen as a metaphor, it contains new and astoundingly beautiful truths. Using the psychological functions as Jung described them enables us to use a psychological method to interpret mythology, psychology and religion in a new and meaningful way.

My emphasis in this book is primarily concerned with the four psychological functions as psychic energy that contains opposites. These first appear in undifferentiated form, and eventually become differentiated. Jung calls this the process of differentiation. Implicit in this model is the idea that the human experience of being in the womb and human birth are described metaphorically in the cosmological myth of Genesis. This is not simply to reduce the myth and the archetypes to psychic energy, but to suggest that the first or literal level of the Genesis myth, which could be called the divine level, describes a second level, which is the psychological level. It is also to suggest that contained within these first two levels is a third level that is a synthesis of the first two levels, which can be seen as the biological or physical nature of humanity. Finally, it is to suggest that a fourth level exists, where differences that can readily be seen can also be dissolved and where all levels can be seen as identical. The four levels of the cosmological myth can be seen as occurring in the reverse order of the functions as they appear in the human child. The Divine Child level is the synthesis of the depth or instinctual level, personified by the Father God archetype.

Levels of meaning are also described by Joseph Campbell (1990a) who says that "mythology is psychology, misread as cosmology, history, and biography" (p. 33). While I agree with the important statement that mythology contains psychology, I would suggest that the misreading only occurs when the literal level is taken as an absolute, ignoring the other levels of interpretation as erroneous. I would also suggest that the reverse is possible: Mythology is not only psychology misread; it contains cosmology, history, and biography, as well as other subject matter, within its parameters expressed in layers that can be identified. To interpret the myth as only psychology is to make the same error as interpreting it as having no meaning beyond the literal. It appears necessary to identify the multifarious levels of meaning that converge to express a single meaning.

Joseph Campbell (1990d) describes the metaphor in myth as "twofold in its connotation, first it is psychological and second it is universal and it is connotative of both at the same time." I would suggest that this is true of the Genesis myth, which is metaphysical, psychological and physical and is connotative of all three at the same time. In addition, when all three levels are seen, a fourth level is created that contains the first three levels.

Developmental psychology appears to be mainly concerned with the second or psychological level, and the third or biological level, and this is the beginning focus of this research. The myth of creation and the myth of Paradise in Genesis will be discussed later in detail, with the suggestion that the first two chapters in Genesis are a metaphor for both the psychological and the biological levels.

Questions I have asked concerning developmental psychology are the following:

- If psychological functions exist, is there an implicit order in the development of the four functions in the individual human psyche?
- What is the order?
- If an order exists, at what point in human development does each function appear?
- What is the relationship of the irrational functions of intuition and sensation to one another and why are they opposed?
- What is the relationship of the rational functions of feeling and thinking to one another and why are they opposed?
- Which function or functions address(es) the soul complex?
- How are all functions related to the ego complex?
- How do the four functions work together to produce psychological wholeness?
- How are they related to the transcendent function?
- If an order to the psychological functions does exist, what would the implications inherent in this order suggest?

It is my objective to assume the following hypothesis, which is true in my opinion. There is an implicit order in the development of the four psychological functions, as described by Carl Jung. The order in which they occur in individual human development is the following: intuition, sensation, feeling, and thinking.

This model can be best viewed as a spiral or circular image although many other images are possible. In the essay "Father: Saturn and Senex" (included in A Blue Fire, 1991) Hillman describes quite well the idea that I wish to pursue, namely, that two kinds of consciousness exist after birth and continue throughout life. Hillman (1991), in a description of creation myths, discusses a process that is quite similar to the model that I propose. He states:

> The need for a "second beginning" is often put in creation myths. The first start is wiped out, and the world begins again, after the flood. Gods and heroes have a second birth (Osiris, Dionysus) or two tales are told of their origin, and mystical man is born. Psychology has taken this ontological image about two levels of being and two structures of consciousness and laid it out in terms of progressive time: first half and second half of life. But these "halves" are less biological or psychological fact as they are *a mythical description of the two levels on which we live.* Some men live from a "twice-born" state early in their youth; others go through a midlife crisis moving from one to another; others may repeatedly live now one, now the other in alternations. *First half and second half* pertain to kinds of consciousness, not to periods (emphasis Hillman's, p. 214).

Jung maintained that one type of consciousness (soul) was put aside for the development of the other (ego) and later (midlife) needed to be resumed, facilitating the individuation process. I agree with Hillman that two "levels of being and two structures of consciousness" can be lived simultaneously by many people. However, one type of consciousness can be forsaken for the growth of the other, which is Jung's usual description. It is, of course, the later type that one might find in therapy or analysis; sometimes it is not the reclaiming of soul that is necessary, but a higher development of ego consciousness. The psyche could be said to be out of balance in either case. Jung was not necessarily wrong in his concept of "progressive time"; what he perhaps failed to realize was the important interplay between these two types of consciousness from the beginning of life.

Despite these differences, I think Hillman's statement concerning two kinds of consciousness is important and applicable to the model that I propose. The two types of consciousness that he describes are what I would call two major archetypes: soul and ego. I believe that the unity of soul and ego is what Jung called the Self. Cosmological myths are particularly well suited to describe the relationship between these complexes because they purport to describe the beginning of life and the universe.

Jung (1971/1921) says that "the four functions therefore form, when arranged diagrammatically, a cross with a rational axis at right angles to an irrational axis" (p. 554). I have used various diagrams to describe the process of individuation. One model employs the cross (at right angles) symbolism; others include the circle or mandala symbol. I have also used numerous diagrams to describe the splitting and uniting of opposites, utilizing the wheel or cross diagram, or both, with the functions not at right angles, but in clock formation, indicating the symbolism of movement and time. The symbol of a circle, divided into four equal parts, with the irrational functions on the right of the page, the rational functions on the left, and intuition at the top right side, as the beginning place, adequately depicts this wheel or clock model.

I have also indicated a beginning place, which was a possibility not addressed by Jung. It is suggested that the beginning place occurs in the psychological function of intuition. But intuition is also the ending place that is represented in mythological literature as the return to Paradise. In psychology, this has often been described as the desire to return to the womb, the mother, or the feminine. I see intuition as the beginning place which can be called Paradise and it is in the mother's womb. The return to Paradise is also Intuition but with this difference. "East of Eden" is the return to Paradise and one is conscious of this experience unlike the first experience of being in the womb.

A developmental model that begins not only at birth, but with conception and the experience of the child in the womb, can be constructed that reflects and extends the psychological concepts of Carl Jung, based on his theories of the four psychological functions and on his theory of the transcendent function. This model would include not only the beginning of ego development, but the development of the soul complex and its origin in human consciousness.

Jung did not construct a developmental model defining the origins of human consciousness. A model that defines and reflects his concepts in a developmental theory that begins with the beginning of life would contribute to the understanding of the Self. There is presently no developmental psychology that provides a model based on Jung's description of psychological functions that begin in the womb.

Campbell (1973) states the following:

The lapse of super consciousness into the state of unconsciousness is precisely the meaning of the Biblical image of the Fall. The constriction of consciousness, to which we owe the fact that we see not the source of the universal power but only the phenomenal forms reflected from that power, turns super consciousness into unconsciousness and, at the same instant and by the same token, creates the world. Redemption consists in the return to super consciousness and therewith the dissolution of the world. This is the great theme and formula of the cosmogonic cycle, the mythical image of the world's coming to manifestation and subsequent return into the *nonmanifest* condition (emphasis mine, p. 259).

I will return to this important quotation by Campbell throughout this work and in detail in the chapter on the Genesis myth. Here it suffices to state the following: The Genesis model that I propose assumes that a super consciousness (which could also be called Being, Eden or Paradise) in the same sense that Campbell describes and which I equate with the unity of soul, spirit, and body (Self) begins in the womb and is associated with the psychological function of intuition. It also assumes an ego/body consciousness that begins at birth, when the functions of sensation and feeling become conscious in that order, negating intuition to a separate, unconscious (soul) function, while thinking begins on an unconscious (soul) level. I suggest that this is the split of the original unity of the Self and what is often called the split in human consciousness. It is my belief that this is so not only in persons who become sensation types in the course of their psychological development, but also in the so-called intuitive types. In other words, I feel this initial ordering of functions—intuition as the beginning of consciousness in the unconscious, and sensation as the beginning of consciousness in the ego-complex—is universal, just as the myths which illustrate this process are universal in their distribution and in their application regardless of the local type emphases of particular cultures and the individual type preferences of the individuals in those cultures.

I am defining soul consciousness as closely related, but not identical, to the Self archetype or any archetype that represents God. Since the soul archetype contains everything in the beginning, it is seen as a symbolic reflection of the Self, or the first differentiation of the functions that flow out of the Self. When the functions become differentiated, intuition can be seen as the function that represents the soul complex, (at the moment of birth) and any time thereafter when conscious sensation predominates. This is because it then becomes the other side of the sensation function or unconscious sensation, which is a mirror image of conscious intuition. Both are connected to the body, intuition as unconscious body perception and sensation as conscious body sensation. This is why, as Jung described, the two functions do not work at the same time, although it might be more accurate to say that they are working together at all times; the absence of one is essential for the presence of the other. In other words, unconsciousness is a primary necessity for the presence of ego consciousness. The differentiation of the first two functions establishes the ego complex and consciousness and at the same time, the soul complex and unconsciousness. One is a mirror image of the other. It is the pouring out of what appears to be a division of the undifferentiated Self that creates two kinds of consciousness, that of soul and that of ego, leaving the Self unaltered, constant, as the core of being and the source for both modes of consciousness.

The Self is present in the child in the womb, existing as what Jung called the objective psyche, which in mythology is often called Paradise. The Self archetype includes God, mother, father and child, and all things in the universe existing as one. Intuition is seen as the psychological function that contains the four functions in undifferentiated form. Intuition is because the functions of sensation, feeling and thinking are unconscious, undifferentiated, psychic potentials. In other words, intuition is sensation, feeling, and thinking that are unconscious, and these three merged functions are the soul complex, which contains consciousness and unconsciousness in undifferentiated form. This concept appears to be comparable with the idea of the Holy Trinity or any three-in-one symbolism and therefore difficult to grasp in a logical or rational manner. It is possible that any "truth" contained in what appears to be irrational can only be known by experience. Jung (1971/1921) said the following concerning the subject of rationality:

> What is rationally correct is too narrow a concept to grasp life in its totality and give it permanent expression. The divine birth is an event altogether outside the bounds of rationality. Psychologically, it proclaims the fact that a new symbol, a new expression of life at its most intense, is being created. Every Epimethean man, and everything Epimethean in man, prove incapable of comprehending this event (p. 189).

Difficult as a rational explication may appear to be, I do not believe it is entirely impossible. It may be that in the past mythology and religion have been the primary expressions for psychological contents that have always been there. Giving them psychological names, however, does not change the nature of the contents, but may allow us to gain additional insight into human nature. If the psychological process was self-evident and clear from the beginning, what would be the need for mythology or religion to express such things by symbols or by metaphor?

It appears to me that the emergence at birth of the three functions, beginning with sensation, which is the opposite of intuition, then the feeling function, followed by the thinking function, creates ego consciousness. Birth can also be seen as the cause of the so-called split in human consciousness, because at this point consciousness and the unconscious become divided, whereas previously they were undifferentiated and differentiated in the function of intuition.

Intuition is the psychological function that can be seen and compared with the archetype of the Father God in the cosmological myth of Genesis. It can also be seen and compared with a biological level of interpretation, where chaos represents the womb or body of the mother. On the second and psychological level, the Father God can be seen as the psychological function of intuition, which "divides" into the four psychological functions or psychic energy. At this point, these three forms of "chaos" or God can be seen as one and the same; each produces the archetype of "child" which on the fourth level is an archetype of the new Self or consciousness that is not divided from the unconscious, but contains both in equal measure.

Campbell (1979) talks about the biological level and psychic energy in the following way:

> Certain imprints impressed upon *the nervous system* in the plastic period between birth and maturity *are the source of many of the most widely known images of myth. Necessarily the same for all mankind, they have been variously organized in the differing traditions, but everywhere function as potent energy releasers and directors* (emphasis mine, p. 61).

I would add to this statement that these imprints begin in the womb, where experience is not lost, but remembered by the body. In the womb, where the three unconscious functions are merged and exist as one function, intuition, or the soul complex, is dominated by darkness or unconsciousness, yet the opposites are united in a single psychological function. Consciousness is also present and merged with unconsciousness. This image is the theme, so prevalent in mythology and religion, of three that exist as one, or the fourth, which turns into one. This concept, so difficult to put into language, has repeatedly been described by art and images in every culture, because the experience, as Campbell tells us, is necessarily the same for all mankind. It is because this experience is universal that comparisons can be made, identifying seemingly divergent myths with one another as different expressions of the same occurrences. The ability to see similarities in the symbols, rather than differences, was, I think, one of Joseph Campbell's greatest contributions to mythology.

Another image to describe this might be the two principles of Yin and Yang, where nothing exists but Yin or darkness, which, nevertheless, contains a speck of Yang, its opposite. At birth, there is a dramatic change, which occurs as the process of enantiodromia, which Jung (1971/1921) describes as:

> the emergence of the unconscious opposite in the course of time. This characteristic phenomenon practically always occurs when an extreme, one-sided tendency dominates conscious life; in time an equally powerful counter position is built up, which first inhibits the conscious performance and subsequently breaks through the conscious control (p. 426).

Here it is necessary to see Jung's description of enantiodromia in reverse, as psychic energy that is operating from the beginning of life, insuring growth in the womb. It is not that the opposites do not exist, but that they exist in a merged state where there is no ego consciousness to perceive them, and the consciousness that does exist, soul consciousness, has no awareness of the opposites. The image is similar to the Chinese symbol of Yin or darkness that contains a seed or spark of its opposite, which could be described as a small light. A small light, however, is different from total darkness or unconsciousness, and this is an important distinction, because it signifies life, movement, and possible change from one state to the next. Other metaphors in mythology used to describe this state are twilight, moonlight, dusk, dawn, in-between, and middle. Hillman (1991) describes the soul much in the same way:

> We have lost the third, middle position which earlier in our tradition, and in others too, was the place of soul: a world of imagination, passion, fantasy, reflection, that is neither physical and material on the one hand, nor spiritual and abstract on the other, yet bound to them both (p. 121).

This adequately describes the soul complex, which I would associate with the psychological function of intuition. If a way of knowing is present from the beginning of life and gives birth to imagination, passion, and especially fantasy, what psychological function could describe this consciousness better than intuition?

Assuming that intuition is conscious in the womb, while the other three functions are unconscious, it is not difficult to see that the situation is reversed at birth. As the functions of sensation, feeling, and thinking become conscious, intuition becomes, as Jung (1971/1921) says, "the function that mediates perceptions in an unconscious way" (p. 453). Intuition becomes the fourth function, and conscious sensation necessarily delegates intuition to an unconscious position. The intensity of conscious sensation assures that intuition will remain unconscious, because these two functions are opposites and do not work at the same time.

There is some ambiguity in Jung's description of intuition. He names intuition as a primary conscious function, yet he describes it as the function that mediates perceptions in an unconscious way. This confusion can be dispelled if one sees intuition as the function that contains both consciousness and unconsciousness. Intuition is not total unconsciousness and it is not total ego consciousness; it appears to be connected to both. Soul consciousness would better describe the middle position that I am attempting to define. In this sense, the soul draws from the Self, and later, after birth gives to the ego. It is the mediating function, the bridge that unites inner and outer worlds. In this manner, the human child is born into the world of opposites; the function of intuition exists along with the function of sensation, and they are mutually opposed. Jung (1971/1921) says that "For me sensation and intuition represent a pair of opposites, or two mutually compensating functions, like thinking and feeling" (p. 463). This was correct, for the simple reason that intuition is unconscious sense perceptions that stay in the unconscious and exist at the same time that conscious sensations are manifested. Sensation creates the first split of intuition, which, nevertheless, remains the same function that it was before the split in the form of soul consciousness. One function divides into four functions, one of which stays the same, intuition.

Perhaps an analogy with modern physics can be made to clarify some of the above assertions. Shiarella (1992) describes electrons, protons and neutrons in the following way:

> Still another amazing phenomenon comes to light at this level of observation. With disbelief we watch as two supposedly solid material particles collide head-on at high speed, and instead of bouncing off of one another or breaking into smaller pieces, they somehow become transformed into *four* different particles, *none of which is smaller than the two which collided*. As if this were not enough of a puzzlement, we then see two of the newly created particles leap together and merge, causing one of the recently annihilated particles to become reborn. (This is comparable to watching a red crystal ball crash into a blue one, and instead of shattering or rebounding, they both simply vanish, leaving in their places four new crystal balls of the same size, none of which is either red or blue; then, as these "spheres from out of nowhere"

roll away from the scene of the accident, two of them suddenly come together and flow into one another, transforming themselves into the red crystal ball once more!) The inescapable conclusion seems to be that *subatomic particles are both destructible and indestructible at the very same time* (emphasis author's, p. 75).

This description of subatomic particles does not appear to be vastly different from what I am attempting to describe as psychological or psychic energy. The cells contained in the human brain are also matter that is very much in motion. The two particles that collide, or the red and blue crystal balls, can be seen as the soul complex (the merged functions), and the ego complex (the separation of the functions), which also collide and subsequently divide. As they do so, they leave in their wake the four psychological functions, which can be compared with the four different particles.

At birth, the "four" can be seen to return to "two" as the functions of sensation and feeling become conscious, leaving the functions of intuition and thinking in the unconscious and creating the split in human consciousness. The split (which is the beginning of the conscious ego and the beginning of the personal unconscious), is then rectified by a return to the Self, created by the satisfaction of the infant's ego desires, which are met by love. (Fordham, whose work will be discussed in detail in Chapter 2, refers to this as "reintegration"). Shiarella's description sounds like the dance of consciousness, which is in constant flux from the beginning of life. I do not think it would be far-fetched to describe psychic energy that is conscious and unconscious at the same time in the same manner: both destructible and indestructible at the very same time.

In Psychological Types, Jung (1971/1921) describes two kinds of thinking: "Active thinking, accordingly, would correspond to my concept of *directed thinking*. Passive thinking was inadequately described in my previous work as 'fantasy thinking.' Today I would call it *intuitive thinking*" (emphasis Jung's, p. 481).

In Symbols of Transformation (1956/1912), the earlier work that Jung refers to, Jung describes what he calls "two kinds of thinking" in the following way:

> Whereas directed thinking is an altogether conscious phenomenon, the same cannot be said of fantasy-thinking [what he later called *intuitive thinking*]. Much of it belongs to the conscious sphere, but at least as much goes on in the half-shadow, or entirely in the unconscious, and can therefore be inferred only indirectly. Through fantasy-thinking [what he later called *intuitive thinking*] directed thinking is brought into contact with the oldest

layers of the human mind, long buried beneath the threshold of consciousness (p. 29).

In the above quote, Jung describes the intuitive function, which he first called "fantasy" and which he later maintained gave him "so much difficulty" (Evans, 1976, p. 100). He also describes quite well the idea that intuition is half conscious and half unconscious and the function that brings directed thinking into contact with the "oldest layers of the human mind." From all these descriptions, it is not difficult to see that this function, which I am equating with the soul complex, can be imagined to be operating in the human child before and after birth, and it is also not hard to imagine that the function of intuition would develop first in the "oldest layers of the human mind."

In a footnote of Symbols of Transformation (1956/1912, p. 29), Jung states that Schelling regards the preconscious as the creative source, just as Fichte regards the preconscious region as the birthplace of important dreams. They both appear to be using the word "preconscious" in the same way Jung uses the word "fantasy," which he later changed to "intuition." What Jung did not state or appear to apprehend was that what he called two kinds of thinking could also be called two kinds of consciousness, one of which is linked to the ego, that is, active thinking, and the other linked to the soul, that is, passive thinking or what Jung calls intuitive thinking, by which he meant the undirected, irrational function of intuition.

Jung (1971/1921) also makes a distinction between active and passive fantasy:

> Active fantasies are the product of *intuition*, i.e., they are evoked by an *attitude* directed to the perception of unconscious contents, as a result of which the *libido* immediately invests all the elements emerging from the unconscious and, by association with parallel material, brings them into clear focus in visual form (emphasis Jung's, p. 428).

Active fantasy, then, can be seen to be the result of passive thinking or intuition, and if it is a definite sum of libido that cannot appear in consciousness in any other way than in the form of an image (Jung, 1971/1921, p. 433), we might conclude that the image or mental representation starts at birth. If 12-to-21-day old infants can imitate adult facial expressions and gestures, which Meltzoff and Moore (discussed in Jackson and Jackson, 1979) conceive as "made possible by some kind of 'abstract representations' of the adult movements that are no longer going on at the time of imitation" (p. 104), it is conceivable that the infant can innately create images at birth. What Jung describes as taking place in the psyche can just as readily be the infant psyche; it is not likely that the process is radically different from that of the adult.

Again, Jung (1971/1921) describes active fantasy, the product of intuition, in the following way:

> Whereas passive fantasy not infrequently bears a morbid stamp or at least shows some trace of abnormality, active fantasy is one of the highest forms of psychic activity. For here the conscious and the unconscious personality of the subject flow together into a common product in which both are united. Such a fantasy can be the highest expression of the unity of a man's *individuality*, and it may even create that individuality by giving perfect expression to its unity (emphasis Jung's, p. 428).

When both ego and soul consciousness flow together, as Jung describes, the infant, in the same way as the adult, is returned to a state of unity or the Self that was first experienced in the womb and is now experienced in the world. The infant who has had this experience may retain the memory as a fantasy, and when a new ego need arises, hopes or expects the same experience to be repeated. In other words, the unconscious archetype may be "filled in" or given content by the sensations and the feelings of the infant. The image may exist in the personal unconscious of the infant long before it is expressed by language.

If the average child is born with the use of two kinds of consciousness, soul and ego, I would also assume that what is often referred to as the split in human consciousness can be identified by this concept. In other words, no human being, Plato, Descartes or anyone else, created by his philosophy the split in human consciousness. It is a condition of human experience created by the very fact of being born; it is phenomenological experience. The act of birth creates two states of consciousness, one which has been called consciousness and the other unconsciousness. This is the split in what Campbell (1973, p. 259) refers to as "super consciousness." What I am calling consciousness is ego-related, whereas that which is often called unconsciousness is soul-related. Soul unconsciousness, however, also contains a type of consciousness. If we concede that these two states of consciousness begin at birth, an idea that the cosmological myths appear to describe and support, it is not difficult to see that the psychological experience contained within a myth could happen at age 1, 50, or 100. Oedipus is an archetype born when the child is born and every child is born an orphan. He leaves the maternal womb (Paradise), where father, mother, and child exist as one. According to the myth, the child is always killing the father to marry the mother. Whenever there is a return to soul consciousness, ego or the father dies. Ego consciousness is also child consciousness, the child who senses, feels, and thinks he is separate; soul consciousness is child consciousness that perceives itself to be one with the mother and father. Whenever an ego experience predominates, the mother is killed by the child, who demands to be separate. Psychological experience does not depend upon a chronological age.

Samuels (1987) states:
> Jung has identified a split in human nature; one part wants to grow outward and onward and the other wants to return to origins for strengthening. One part seeks to assimilate new experiences "out there," the other searches for a new and regenerative meeting with elemental psychological forces. This split is the essential premise of any concept of Life and Death instincts. Though the Death instinct finds external manifestation in aggression and destructiveness, we have seen that its true object is to reduce the known world to a preconceived state that, from the standpoint of psychology, would be inorganic. This is why man's unconscious seeking for regression is also dangerous (p. 149).

Certainly, the split in human nature can be seen in terms of the life and death instinct, but I would not agree that this would be "inorganic from the standpoint of psychology," for to do so would imply that no psychology at all exists in the womb or in the symbolic return to Paradise. The desire for death is often symbolic for a death of ego consciousness to return to soul consciousness, which may strengthen the conscious attitude. There is no desire for life that does not include a desire for death, for we die even as we live.

If we equate the life instinct with ego consciousness and the death instinct with the unconsciousness, the split that Samuels describes can be seen as the splitting of the opposites out of their original unity and a regression as an attempt to restore that unity. Soul consciousness is the reconciling third consciousness that stands in the middle and is connected to both. Soul consciousness is the life and death instincts that are still undifferentiated and exist as one instinct. Thus, it is identical to the function of intuition, and the reason intuition is the primal instinct. Soul is the archetype, intuition is the instinct.

The "preconceived state" that Samuels suggests is "inorganic from a psychological view" is nothing of the kind, because psychological experience would exist in the primal experience of being in the womb in the form of the intuitive function. If the instinct contains the archetype, the soul would also exist in the infant's psyche and could be called psychological. Thus, the origin of the soul would be at conception, when the basic instinct of intuitive matter responds to matter and life begins. To be inorganic would imply that there is no organizational process in the experience of the soul complex, in or out of the womb.

The return to the mother might be a return to the *participation mystique* of infancy, but not the exact experience of the infant in utero. In this case, the mother's state of psychological being might induce "hell" rather than "heaven," for a state of despair might be shared with the infant. The flow of the ego to soul and back to ego is a natural and essential part of the child's life, not unlike what Fordham describes as integration and deintegration. It is not returning to the soul that creates havoc in the adult or the child, but the inability to arrive there safely and return safely. One way back to soul is through love and another is through fear, which is a perception that "oneness" is missing. In the first reintegration, the mother returns the child to unity by an act of love, by meeting the child's ego demands. If needs are not met on a regular basis, the original unity cannot be experienced in the world, which appears to be essential if relationship is to be a positive experience. The result is a state of limbo for the ego, which fears moving in either direction. This is pathology: Whether in an adult or an infant, the experience is the same. Both long for an experience of the original unity and seek it first in a relationship that will match the inner archetype. Ego is then reinforced by the experience, and consciousness is expanded.

The Irrational Functions of Intuition and Sensation

Here I would like to postulate several concepts that Jung did not explicitly address. One concerns the irrational functions of intuition and sensation. According to Jung (1971/1921), these are opposed, but complementary to one another; intuition and sensation do not work together at the same time. Jung (1971/1921) defines both functions in the following way:

> I regard sensation as conscious, and intuition as unconscious, perception. For me sensation and intuition represent a pair of opposites, or two mutually compensating functions, like thinking and feeling. Thinking and feeling as independent functions are developed, both ontogenetically and phylogenetically, from sensation (and equally, of course from intuition as the necessary counterpart of sensation) (p. 463).

I agree with this statement, but propose that the reason is that intuition and sensation are two sides of the same coin. Jung describes how they are opposite,

The Waking

I wake to sleep, and take my waking slow.
I feel my fate in what I cannot fear.
I learn by going where I have to go.

We think by feeling. What is there to know?
I hear my being dance from ear to ear.
I wake to sleep, and take my waking slow.

Of those so close beside me, which are you?
God bless the Ground! I shall walk softly there,
And learn by going where I have to go.

Light takes the Tree; but who can tell us how?
The lowly worm climbs up a winding stair;
I wake to sleep, and take my waking slow.

Great Nature has another thing to do
To you and me; so take the lively air,
And, lovely, learn by going where to go.

This shaking keeps me steady. I should know.
What falls away is always. And is near.
I wake to sleep, and take my waking slow
I learn by going where I have to go.

(Theodore Roethke, 1975, p. 1133)

but does not describe how they are connected. Nor does he suggest how thinking and feeling might develop, both ontogenetically and phylogenetically, from sensation and intuition.

Intuition is unconscious sensation, and sensation is body sensation that becomes conscious and, in doing so, allows for the first conscious perceptions. In the above statement, Jung suggests the premise that I propose by calling intuition unconscious perception—this is exactly what I mean when I say that intuition is unconscious sensation. It is the body that perceives, whether conscious or unconscious; if intuition is unconscious perception, it is also unconscious body sensation. I do not think that the function of intuition, so long associated with the gods and the spiritual, originates from a source that is outside of the human body, even though it often appears to come from out of the blue like lightning, which "has always been associated with intuition and inspiration" (Fontana, 1994, p. 16). Intuition that occurs in this manner was defined by Jung (1971/1921) as "passive fantasy" (p. 428):

> Active fantasies are the product of *intuition*, i.e., they are evoked by an attitude directed to the perception of unconscious contents, as a result of which the *libido* immediately invest all the elements emerging from the unconscious and, by association with parallel material, brings them into clear focus in visual form. Passive fantasies appear in visual form at the outset, neither preceded nor accompanied by intuitive expectation, the attitude of the subject being wholly passive (emphasis Jung's, p. 428).

Here Jung appears to making a distinction between intuitions that occur spontaneously and those that are gained by a conscious involvement in the process, and this is an important distinction. It is here that some of the confusion concerning his description of conscious and unconscious intuition may be understood. Jung (1971/1921) defines attitude as "a readiness of the psyche to act or react in a certain way" (p. 414). Active fantasy is always connected to a conscious attitude, whereas passive fantasy is mainly an irruption of an unconscious content. This is what Jung means, perhaps, by his definition of intuition as a conscious function, although at the same time he often states that intuition comes "via the unconscious," and is "unconscious perception." He goes on to say:

> Both active and passive fantasy could be described as products of the function of intuition, which Jung did not do here. Instead, he calls passive fantasies "automatisms," making a distinction between what is conscious and what is unconscious (p. 428). He

appears to link consciousness with intuition and unconsciousness with "passive fantasy" that is always without a conscious attitude.

In the following statement Jung (1971/1921) again describes active fantasy, the product of intuition, in a way that makes clear the significance he placed on this function:

> This is an accurate description of the function of intuition and the contents made manifest by that function; the expression of those contents is what I would call art. Jung's description and value of the function of intuition reflects my own position; I am using the word intuition in the exact same way that Jung describes.

It must be remembered that I am attempting to describe the intuitive position as it applies to the infant, in the womb and at birth. I think that it is the first function that becomes the fourth function, which Jung (1954/1946, p. 119) called it, and as the fourth, it is identical with the first.

Jung (1971/1921) describes intuition in the following way:

> Jung was obviously not describing the infant at birth or in the womb here; however, if his description of intuition is applied to the newborn infant and the importance of transmitting images in the beginning of life is seen, as well as the method or function by which this might occur, it appears reasonable to at least question the possibility that the infant may be using the function of intuition and the function of sensation in a complementary way shortly after birth. Furthermore, there is no reason to believe that the method applied would be significantly different in the newborn than the method used by the adult. The way the human infant makes an image is thus far basically unknown or certainly not clarified in developmental psychology, just as the "nature of intuition is very difficult to grasp" (Jung, 1971/1921, p 366). Difficult as it may be, Jung (1954/1946) included the function of intuition as essential for a "return" to the Self when he describes alchemical symbolism:
>
> This fourth stage is the anticipation of the lapis. The imaginative activity of the *fourth* function—*intuition, without which no realization is complete*—is plainly evident in this anticipation of a possibility whose fulfilment could never be the object of empirical experience at all; already in Greek alchemy it was called "the stone that is no stone." *Intuition* gives outlook and insight; it revels in the garden of magical possibilities as if they were real.

> *Nothing is more charged with intuitions than the lapis philosophorum.*
> *This keystone rounds off the work into an experience of the totality of*
> *the individual* (emphasis mine, p. 119).

Jung makes it clear in this statement that the function of intuition is essential for realization of the Self to be complete.

There is no reason to believe that the return would not be through the original function (intuition or the soul archetype) from which it first developed, and every reason, supported by the symbols in mythology, to believe that the "fourth" function, which Jung calls "mainly unconscious" and which I see as becoming unconscious at birth, is also the fourth that becomes the "first."

Jung's description of the repression of the functions of thinking, feeling, and sensation, with sensation being the one most affected, is in exact accord with my understanding of the function of intuition. In applying this idea to the newborn, however, it seems reasonable to assume that there is no need for the infant to repress the function of thinking, since that function is probably already unconscious. The feeling function would necessarily follow the function of intuition or the function of sensation because there would be nothing to judge or value that was not first perceived, either consciously or by the unconscious. If sensation becomes conscious at birth, intuition would necessarily become unconscious, along with thinking, which has never been conscious, and sensation and feeling would be the first two functions of ego consciousness in the normal human child.

In his discussion of the Brahmanic conception of the uniting symbol, Jung (1971/1921) states the following:

> Here Jung describes what is necessary (and used by many other religious systems besides the Brahmanic concept) for what I believe to be the route to the knowledge contained within the intuitive function. Note that he describes the elimination of sense-perception, (the function of sensation, not the elimination of intuition) which he earlier described as the primary "hindrance" to the function of intuition. If sense perception is eliminated and conscious contents are "blotted out" to produce an activation of the contents of the unconscious, the function used must be intuition. This is also what I am describing as the unconsciousness of the three ego functions of sensation, feeling, and thinking. When they are unconscious and merged, the function of intuition occurs. In mythology, this is usually described as a sacrifice or death of the conscious ego.

Moustakas (1990), in describing heuristic research, says the following concerning the tacit dimension:
> What Moustakas and Polanyi are calling the tacit dimension, which would be the silent or unknown dimension, would be what I believe Jung would call the unconscious position. Moustakas (1990) goes on to say:
> From the tacit dimension, a kind of bridge is formed between the implicit knowledge inherent in the tacit and the explicit knowledge which is observable and describable. The bridge between the explicit and the tacit is the realm of the between, or the intuitive. In intuition, from the subsidiary or observable factors one utilizes an internal capacity to make inferences and arrive at a knowledge of underlying structures or dynamics. Intuition makes immediate knowledge possible without the intervening steps of logic and reasoning. While the tacit is pure mystery in its focal nature—ineffable and unspecifiable—in the intuitive process one draws on clues; one senses a pattern or underlying condition that enables one to imagine and then characterize the reality, state of mind, or condition. In intuition we perceive something, observe it, and look and look again from clue to clue until we surmise the truth (p. 23).

This appears to me to be an exceptionally clear description (and there are many more in this excellent book) of what Jung called conscious intuition, and I believe it is comparative with what Jung is attempting to describe (in less clear language) on page 428 of Psychological Types. "Every act of achieving integration, unity, or wholeness of anything requires intuition" (Moustakas, 1990, p. 23). I certainly agree with this statement and think that Jung would also have agreed with Moustakas and said almost the same thing in the quote previously stated concerning a return to wholeness, "the imaginative activity of the fourth function—intuition, without which no realization is complete." (Jung, 1954/1946, p. 119).

Obviously, Jung links active imagination with what he considers to be active fantasy, the product of conscious intuition and this requires a degree of conscious participation in observing the images that are produced by the unconscious. In this way, unity between the conscious and the unconscious would be established, being the "highest expression of a man's *individuality*" (Jung, 1971/1921, p. 428). I am in complete agreement with Jung concerning the function of conscious intuition and believe that without the capacity to use this function or without the capacity to use imagination, nothing new would ever be said or created. It is not enough, except perhaps for the individual, to simply have a vision by the function of intuition; the vision must be expressed if it is to contribute anything new or significant to the world.

It is with Jung's definition of the function of intuition that I return to a discussion of the possibility of applying these concepts to the infant in the womb and the infant at birth, assuming that intuition must be as important in the beginning of life as it is in adult life. If intuition is necessary for a return to wholeness, it must be involved with the leaving of what was originally whole.

There is only one instinct, one golden egg, that contains all four psychological functions. At birth, this instinct splits into two psychological functions, intuition and sensation, which are the two perceiving functions. With the first conscious sensation comes the first perception, and it is negative because it is only half of an opposite and because the infant has not yet experienced the other half, which exists in the function of unconscious sensation, which is intuition. With the first sensation of any kind, the opposite sensation has become unconscious and is registered in the function of intuition. This is essential because it allows for sensations to become differentiated. Then, the feeling function enters and desire is born. With desire comes the first perception of the experience of an opposite that does not contain its other half in consciousness. The infant in the womb has not experienced the splitting of opposites; pleasure and pain have not been consciously experienced, nor have love or hate, knowing or not knowing, or any of the opposites. This idea is justified by the assumption that the infant in the womb is without ego consciousness and without the ability to discriminate. Instead, he or she has lived in a *neutral* place, where all opposites are merged and exist as one, which is, as Jung so often called it, the objective psyche. Campbell (1979) describes this state in much the same way:

> *The state of the child in the womb is one of bliss, actionless bliss, and this state may be compared to the beatitude visualized for paradise. In the womb, the child is unaware of the alternation of night and day, or of any of the images of temporality. It should not be surprising, therefore, if the metaphors used to represent eternity suggest, to those trained in the symbolism of the infantile unconscious, retreat to the womb* (emphasis mine, p. 65).

What an incredible statement! And a statement that appears to be mainly ignored. From, perhaps, the greatest mind of our century concerning symbols, mythology and metaphor. Equaled only by Carl Jung, Joseph Campbell could explore and explain meaning in the best possible way.

Desire, that emotion that can and does fill books and is often the subject of major religions, is a quality that belongs to the feeling function. Desire is not the lack of anything, but the perception of a lack of something, and the perception is adequate in all respects, because the infant has yet to experience the other half of the sensation, the opposite that has become unconscious at birth. In order for the infant to experience that opposite, the perceived body sensation must be attended to: What is experienced as cold must be made warm, light made dark, pain made pleasure. This is accomplished by an "other" in the world (thought to be the mother, but in reality, whoever first satisfies the primary needs of the newborn), who removes the negative sensations by introducing the opposite ones, which are positive.

In other words, conscious sensation introduces the human infant to the experience of opposites, and the feeling function must also become conscious to make a value judgment concerning the positive or negative sensation.

With the experience of having its needs met, the infant has experienced the opposites, merged in the womb, with this difference: They have been experienced in succession or in time and space, and separately in the world. They have been experienced by relationship. Regardie (1970) quotes the alchemists when he says that the "*white space*" is the "Catholic Magnesia and Sperm of the world out of which all natural things are generated" (p. 166). This white space can be compared with relationship between subject and object, which separates and unites conscious and unconscious perceptions. The white space is the Divine male Child. I shall return to this topic with more discussion of the rational functions of thinking and feeling in the following pages, but I would first like to continue with a discussion of the irrational functions, the functions of perception.

What we know of an object through sense perception comes from focused awareness; if we listen intently, for example, we no longer see the object with our eyes, even though our eyes are open. The more focused we are with one of our senses, the more the other sense perceptions recede. They do not, however, disappear, but are recorded as unconscious information. One can experience all five senses and become acutely aware of sense perceptions, in which case, that which does not include the object recedes into the unconscious. Another example would be that when there is a global view, with no focus on a particular object, intuition records this in a diffuse and holistic way. This is a simplification of the process, but what is important is the idea that we are always perceiving on two levels and in two ways, and the first way is limited compared with the second way, which duly reports or perceives what is going on, whether we will it or not. In other words, the body is always in relationship to the surrounding world, as well as the inner world, and those "messages from the gods" depend on our ability to turn down or turn off our conscious perceptions based on sensation, and sometimes feeling and thinking. When feeling, thinking, and sensation shift into neutral, we respond with instincts that are supplied by the intuitive function. One could liken this to a stove with four burners, supplied by a tank of gas that is distributed in four equal ways. If we turn down the flame on the functions of sensation, feeling, and thinking, the flame that is intuition will be using all the fuel and will burn with an oversized flame.

This concept is extremely important to the hypothesis that I am suggesting. It assumes that the process of knowing begins as a biological factor, existing in the cell, the fetus, or the prenatal infant's body on an unconscious level. The cell is living matter that is organized and contains a form of consciousness. Intuition does not come from outside our own bodies and is not something disconnected from the human body. I would suggest that intuitive knowing is the basic instinct that contains all other instincts because it is the first to contain psychological knowledge. The instinct to life is also the instinct to death because these are opposites that are dependent upon one another. When one is in the intuitive function psychologically or what I would call soul consciousness, the ego is absent or partly absent, and this can be described as a state of death. When ego is present, the "I" that knows itself to be alive and separate describes conscious life, but this is a state of death for soul consciousness. Ultimately, these two states of being, which appear as opposites, can be seen from a middle, united position, and maintained in consciousness. This is the purpose, as I understand it, of what Jung called the transcendent function or the union of opposites. The union of soul and ego returns one to the Self, where there is no relationship, because both archetypes exist as one united psyche represented in the myths as the Divine Child. Jung (1958/1952), says that "the self is the whole man, whose symbols are the divine child and its synonyms" (p. 106). Thus, the Divine Child archetype is the prevalent symbol of psychological wholeness and the Self.

The Rational Functions of Feeling and Thinking

The rational functions of feeling and thinking are also two sides of the same coin: Thinking contains unconscious feeling and feeling contains unconscious thinking. There can be no thought that does not having feeling attached to it either consciously or unconsciously. Likewise, there is never a feeling that does not suggest at least a potential thought that can be expressed. In the womb,

In addition to inherent duality of Universe
There is also and always
An inherent threefoldedness and fourfoldedness
Of initial consciousness
And of all experience.
For in addition to (1) action, (2) reaction,
(3) resultant,
There is always (4) the a priori environment,
Within which the event occurs,
i.e., the at-first-nothingness around us
Of the child graduated from the womb,
Within which seeming nothingness (fourthness)
The inherently threefold
Local event took place.

(R. Buckminster Fuller, Intuition, 1972, p. 14)

PSYCHOLOGICAL FUNCTIONS OF THE CHILD IN THE WOMB

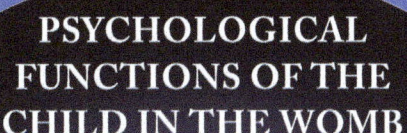

FOURTH FUNCTION (ACTIVE THINKING)

THINKNG (UNCONSCIOUS)

FIRST FUNCTION TO APPEAR (IN THE WOMB) (PASSIVE THINKING)

INTUITION (PRIMAL CONSCIOUSNESS)

OPPOSITES ← Rational Function / Rational Function → Irrational Function / Irrational Function OPPOSITES

EGO SOUL
SELF *(Undifferentiated)*
EGO EGO
Contains Consciousness & Unconsciousness Merged

OPPOSITES   OPPOSITES

FEELING (UNCONSCIOUS)

SENSATION (UNCONSCIOUS)

THIRD FUNCTION | SECOND FUNCTION

Intuition or passive thinking is defined as psychic energy that moves *toward* (extroverted) or *away from* (introverted) the object because of information stored in the genetic structure of the organism. This is in response to information supplied by the genetic structure of the object, i.e., the relationship of matter to matter, or child to mother. Here it can be imagined that the second, third, or fourth functions are still merged, undifferentiated and unconscious. This merging of the three unconscious functions "creates" intuition as a conscious function; in the womb, consciousness and unconsciousness exist as one Superconsciousness. Intuition is the function that contains all four functions in One. Unconsciousness cannot exist without its opposite – consciousness.

both are unconscious; at birth, sensation becomes conscious, along with feeling. Feeling is contiguous with sensation and dependent upon it. The seed or the beginning of thought is (conscious) sensation and with the first (conscious) sensation comes the first feeling (value judgment), which may produce the first symbol in the form of a primordial image, the precursor of thought. Because the feeling function is eminently conscious, the thinking function is equally unconscious and contains the archetype in form only, as Jung so often pointed out, but the form is given content by the experience of body sensations and the feeling function, which gives value to the experience. The feeling function, which is rational and conscious, gives content and meaning and helps to create the image.

For instance, assuming we have never seen light, if we close our eyes and perceive darkness, and then open them and perceive light, light is the object of our conscious perception. We may respond that "it is good" without knowing what the "it" is, thereby making a value judgment. The "it" is the unnamed object, but feeling has made a judgment concerning the "it" before it is named. The "it" can be said to exist in the world and in the psyche in the form of a symbol, which may be simple and abstract, but still a representation of the object. It may also be subject to change, as experience changes. Our feeling—negative, positive, or neutral—helps to create the symbol that connects the visual and outer perception of the object to the inner, or what Jung (1921/1976a p. 445) called the primordial image or archetype. In this manner, the thought, feeling, and sensation would all exist in the original experience. The idea is always contained in the experience. The feeling of good, bad, or indifferent always has an object of reference and a body that first perceives the sensation, either consciously or unconsciously.

What is revealed as thought that does not have an equivalent in the concrete world or is not arrived at through the physical senses is seen as that which is given in the form of intuition or what Jung referred to as "passive thinking." Therefore, unconscious physical sensations (which I am calling intuition) would precede conscious, active, rational thinking. It appears reasonable to think that active thinking is preceded by passive thinking, which does not appear from outside oneself, but is connected to the body. An example of this would be Einstein's flash of intuitive knowledge concerning relativity, which occurred before he could work out the details in a rational manner that could be explained by reason and empirical means. This would be the realm of the archetypes, or archetypal knowledge that Jung claims is not knowable in and of itself, but is the source from which the forms and images are created as archetypes. Every abstract and divine thought could be conceived as occurring in this manner, and what is seen symbolically as soul, which would be the function of intuition, would be connected with the function of thinking, which is often symbolically as the spirit. But nothing would exist, including the most pristine of philosophical or spiritual thought, that was not first connected to the body and the soul.

If the first sensation creates ego consciousness of one of the opposites and is connected to the feeling function, which makes a value judgment concerning a second choice of opposites, such as good or bad, it can be said that these two conscious functions match the image or archetype that is contained in the thinking function, even though the thought may remain in the unconscious. Intuition, which contains the unconscious body sensations, and sensation, which contains the conscious body sensations, would produce the "whole" of the experience, just as the thinking function would contain the image or idea in its completed form. In other words, the instinctual functions would be identical with the rational functions; archetypes and instincts would be identical at this point.

This image would correspond to what Jung (1971/1921) describes as a "primordial image or archetype" (p. 442). Although he appears here to be speaking of this experience as "a fantasy-image" in the psyche of an adult, there is no reason to believe that this idea cannot be applied to a child.

Elsewhere, in discussing the child, Jung (1959/1938) says that "we can only suppose that his behavior results from patterns of functioning, which I have described as images" (p. 78). If it is true that the first conscious sensation produces the first conscious feeling, which in turn produces the first primordial image, this is more than the potential for thought: It is the beginning of thought. What Jung described as "passive thinking" (intuition) would begin in the womb with active thinking unconscious; what Jung described as "active thinking" would begin at birth with passive thinking (intuition) also present and now unconscious, representing the split in human ego consciousness and the unconscious soul. This describes the beginning of human conflict as the functions differentiate.

Jung (1959/1938) describes the instincts in this way:

> Instincts are not vague and indefinite by nature, but are specifically formed motive forces which, long before there is any consciousness, and in spite of any degree of consciousness later on, pursue their inherent goals. Consequently, they form very close analogies to the archetypes, so close, in fact, that there is good reason for supposing that the archetypes are the *unconscious*

images of the instincts themselves, in other words, that they are patterns of instinctual behavior (emphasis mine, p. 43).

The archetype appears to be contained in the instinct and in the original experience of the infant. Sensation and feeling provide the experience, and the archetype remains mostly unconscious in the thinking function. But universal experience, even if it is unconscious, will be activated by the expression of the experience in the form of a myth, such as the creation myth of Genesis, which best describes that experience in archetypal terms. In other words, many people accepted the myth as true (and still do) because it best describes what is unconscious in their own psyche. It matches their own instinctual patterns of behavior, experience, and unconscious knowledge of the event. Neumann (1949/1954) describes the beginning as:

> the symbolic story of the beginning, which speaks to us from the mythology of all ages, is the attempt made by man's childlike, prescientific consciousness to master problems and enigmas which are mostly beyond the grasp of even our developed modern consciousness. If our consciousness, with epistemological resignation, is constrained to regard the question of the beginning as unanswerable and therefore unscientific, it may be right; but the psyche, which can neither be taught nor led astray by the self-criticism of the conscious mind, always poses this question afresh as one that is essential to it (p. 7).

The beginning is equally important for developmental psychology in understanding the fundamentals of infancy.

Aspects of Jung's Four Psychological Functions and their Relationship to One Another before and after Birth

I see psychological experience as dependent upon physiological experience and created by it. In other words, body sensations that are unconscious in the infant supply him or her with the knowledge that becomes the psychological function of intuition. Seen from this perspective, the biological would never be separated from the psychological; indeed, the psychological would be dependent upon the biological, but it would not be in the same way that conscious body sensations give specific or isolated knowledge of the object. Psychological knowledge would be more global and diffuse, just as the function of intuition usually is, with all body sensations participating at the same time. Put another way, sensation that is conscious separates, divides, and gives

PSYCHOLOGICAL FUNCTIONS (INTROVERTED) OF THE
CHILD AT BIRTH

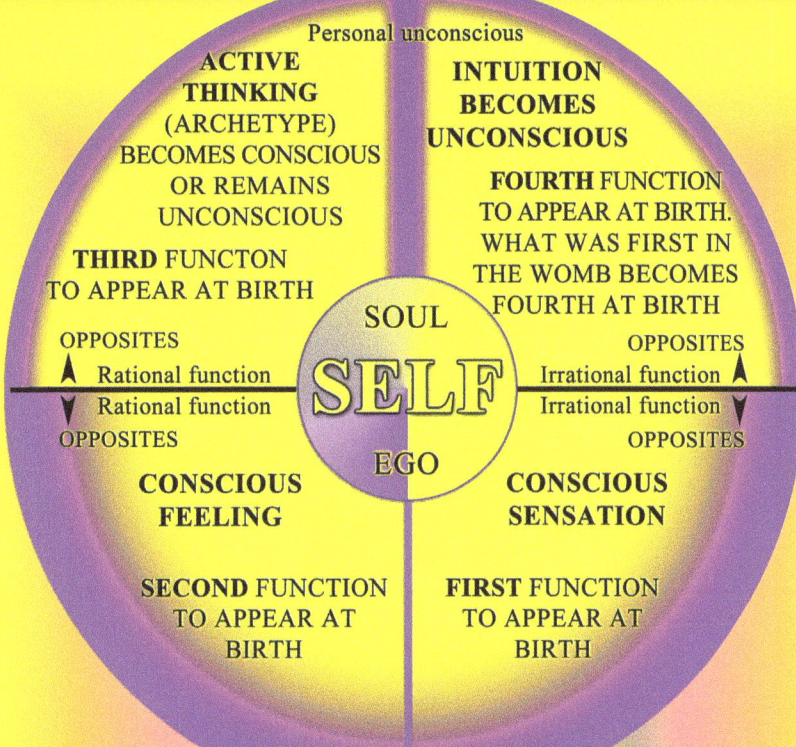

At birth, the sensate function becomes conscious first and is connected shortly thereafter to the feeling function, which also becomes conscious. At this point, intuition, which is the opposite of sensation, returns to the unconscious. Thinking, the function that produces the image or representation of the object becomes partly conscious and remains partly unconscious. Thus, the personal unconscious is born at the same time consciousness appears, and they are opposites.

"Superconsciousness" (intuition) has been divided into the conscious and the unconscious. Active thinking, along with passive thinking or intuition, can be called soul functions, because they exist as one undifferentiated function, spirit and soul as one, before they are differentiated. Sensation and feeling, which are conscious, are the first functions of the ego, with the soul as the unconscious opposite in each function. Two types of consciousness are created at birth. Intuition is first in the womb, and at birth, the second function to appear is sensation. Feeling becomes the third, while thinking becomes the fourth. The fourth is then identical with the first, intuition. At birth, sensation appears first, feeling occurs second, thinking is the third function to appear, while intuition becomes the fourth. Unconscious thinking is identical with intuition, or passive thinking. This is the "Maria axiom" – "one becomes two, two becomes three, and out of the third comes one as the fourth" (Jung, 1979, p. 153).

THE FOUR PSYCHOLOGICAL FUNCTIONS AS PSYCHIC ENERGY

THE OPPOSITES WITHIN EACH FUNCTION

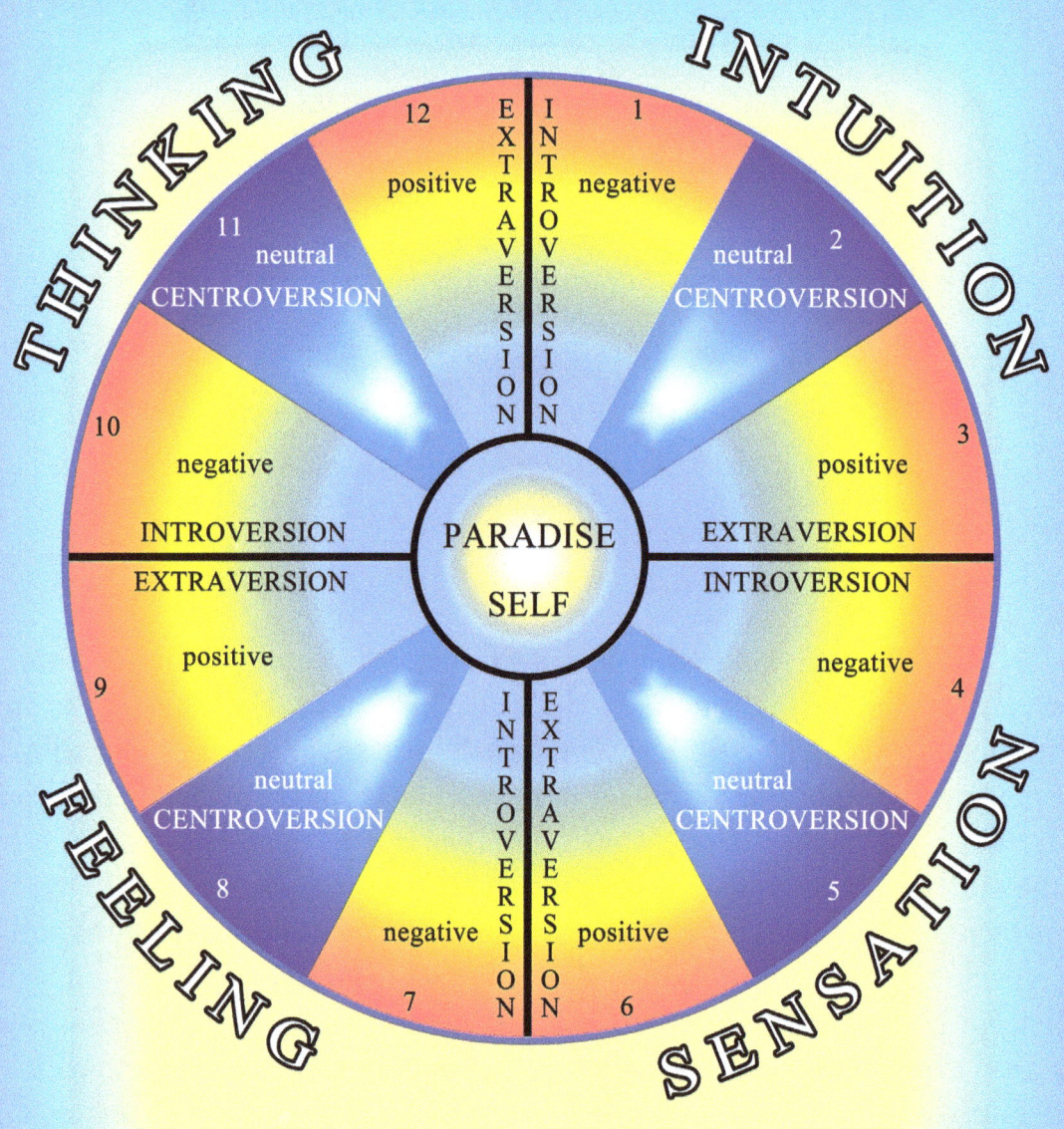

THE TWELVE GATES OF THE NEW JERUSALEM

CENTROVERSION OR NEUTRAL ENERGY - THE FOUR RIVERS FLOWING OUT OF PARADISE

In one creative thought a thousand forgotten nights of love revive, filling it with sublimity and exaltation. And those who come together in the night and are entwined in rocking delight do an earnest work and gather sweetnesses, gather depth and strength for the song of some coming poet, who will arise to speak of ecstasies beyond telling. And they call up the future; and though they err and embrace blindly, the future comes all the same, a new human being rises up, and on the ground of that chance which here seems consummated, awakes the law by which a resistant vigorous seed forces its way through to the egg-cell that moves open toward it. Do not be bewildered by the surfaces; in the depths all becomes law.

(Rainer Maria Rilke, Letters to a young poet, 1962, pp. 37-38) specific information, whereas intuition does just the reverse and gives information as a whole.

Of the four psychological functions, which are methods of knowing, intuition is seen here as the psychological function that develops first. We can reasonably conclude that the other three functions do not appear to be operating on a conscious level in utero, although intuitive knowledge in the form of instinct does appear to be operating. If this is so, is this not the beginning of intelligence when knowledge is supplied or given to the organism by the experience?

Pearce (1980) appears to be asking a similar question: "At what point does intelligence, the interaction between an organism and its environment, begin to function" (p. 46)? Surely, if one takes this definition of intelligence as correct, one would have to consider the possibility that intelligence begins in the womb because the organism is in constant interaction with its environment from the beginning. Pearce (1980) suggests this when he states: "Even two brain cells in proximity begin some preliminary form of interaction. This may not rate as thought in any mature sense, but there is almost surely a form of learning taking place" (p. 47). I would agree. This is not active thinking, but what Jung (1971/1921, p. 453) called "passive thinking," a name he suggested to clarify the function of intuition.

The form of learning taking place is obviously not constructed by the ego, but can be connected to soul or God or whatever archetype is chosen to describe the Other that provides knowledge or information that is not dependent upon "I" or ego. One could say that God, or what Jung called the Self, exists in the human body as instinctual behavior that provides experience, behavior that is determined by body sensations that are not always conscious. I would question Pearce's use of the term "learning," because it cannot be determined that anything has been learned by the fetus. It is rather a "knowing" that has been given, not learned, especially if this is inherent in the genetic make-up of the fetus.

In turning to Jung's description of psychological functions, it is possible to examine them one by one to determine the following:

a. Does an order exist?

b. If so, what is the order?

c. If an order exists, at what point in human development does each function appear?

Jung (1971/1921) describes thinking as "active, concerned with logic, reason and abstractions" (p. 481). Thinking falls into the realm of cognitive development and what is often called the logos. It appears reasonable to assume that the infant in the womb is not involved with active thinking; he or she cannot "name things" and has no language. All thought would exist as potential, and negative and positive thoughts, or the opposites, would be merged in a state of neutrality which would be a description of the opposites contained. This function, by most psychological standards, appears to be the last to develop in the human child.

The feeling function gives value judgments. It tells us if a thing or object is good or bad. It is often related to "Eros" in mythology. An infant in the womb cannot give a conscious value judgment, assuming he or she is without a conscious ego. He or she does not have knowledge of good or bad and cannot differentiate his or her body sensations. The feeling function, then, as Jung describes it, appears to be unconscious in the womb, just as the thinking function is unconscious. Both exist as potential. In creation myths, such as Adam and Eve in Paradise, this would be called innocence. The first couple in Paradise had no knowledge of good or evil. The same thing might exist in a fetus in the womb. The sensation in the body would exist, but a "bad" sensation would not be experienced any differently than a good sensation. Without the ability to make a value judgment and without an ego, all sensations would be experienced as the same. The feeling function would also exist in a state of neutrality, where opposites are merged or undifferentiated.

The third function is sensation. Mothers and scientists, I think, would agree that infants in the womb experience sensation. They obviously react to stimuli and movement. Their experience of sensation is pure experience because they are not conscious of what they are experiencing. They may hear their mother's voice, but there is no conscious awareness that they hear. There is no ego (as we know it), and like the functions of thinking and feeling, sensation is unconscious. Thinking is pure unconscious potential. Feeling is also potential; it is unconscious but experienced, and undifferentiated from sensation. Sensation is also unconscious and undifferentiated, but very much experienced. I would suggest that this unconscious sensation, which is merged with the other functions, is what we call intuition. The functions of thinking, feeling, sensation, and intuition are psychic energy that is merged, undifferentiated, and unconscious. In this state, they are the intuitive function, which has a consciousness of its own. In other words, consciousness and unconsciousness are both present, but not separated. They exist in a state of "oneness." In the womb, the function of sensation, as well as the functions of feeling and thinking, can be seen as being in a neutral state with the opposites merged.

Seeing them in this way suggests a comparison with the myth of Paradise.

The infant in the womb would never experience pain or pleasure as we know these experiences; one would be the same as the other. This would be a neutral state, a state without desire, and a state of being that would embrace the opposites. It could, indeed, be called a state of Paradise or what Campbell called "Bliss."

In speaking of the birth trauma as an archetype of transformation, Campbell (1979) says:

> In the imagery of mythology and religion this birth (or more often rebirth) theme is extremely prominent; in fact, every threshold passage—not only this from the darkness of the womb to the light of the sun, but also those from childhood to adult life and from the light of the world to whatever mystery of darkness may lie beyond the portal of death—*is comparable to a birth and has been ritually represented, practically everywhere, through an imagery of re-entry into the womb. This is one of those mythological universals that surely merit interpretation, rather from a psychological than from an ethnological point of view* (emphasis mine, p. 62).

This "re-entry" into the womb is what I would call a psychological return to the function of intuition, whether it is immediately after birth or in any later experience of transformation. It is a way of returning to the mother while in the world, rather than in the womb, which was the original experience.

Intuition is irrational and instinctual, like sensation. It is knowledge or information that comes to one with no known cause or reason. It is given. Intuition has often been linked to the gods or angels or divine entities in mythological literature. Jung (1971/1921) quotes Spinoza as describing intuition as the "highest form of Knowledge" (p. 453). I would suggest that it is also the lowest form of knowledge (certainly from a scientific view and considered as a basic instinct) and that the lowest and highest are two opposites that are reunited in mythological literature when the hero "returns to Paradise" or, clinically speaking, the client desires or experiences a return to the womb. In this way, intuition can be seen as both the highest and the lowest of all the psychological functions, as well as the first and the last.

Intuition also would contain the opposites, negative and positive merged, and exist in a state of neutrality or undifferentiation on the one hand, and as a differentiated function, on the other.

This function appears to be experienced by the infant in the womb from the beginning. From cell to fetus, there is movement toward (growth) or away from (decay) the environment, which is the womb. Dennett (1991) describes this process, using the word "wired" in the same way I would use the word intuition, in the following quote:

> Even more primitive are the withdrawal and approach responses of the simplest organisms, and they are tied in the most direct imaginable way to the sources of good and ill; they touch them. Then, depending on whether the touched thing is bad or good for them, they either recoil or engulf. They do this by simply being "wired" so that actual contact with the good or bad feature of the world triggers the appropriate squirm (pp. 177-178).

Whether one uses the word "wired" or the word "intuition" makes no difference, to be wired means to have the knowledge built in, and both refer to basic instincts. (And neither word explains who or what does the wiring or provides the information) Science usually describes instincts, human or animal, as "matter at its lowest." Instincts in general are not usually seen as a form of intelligence, even though they obviously contain knowledge.

Pearce (1980) says that "intelligence is the ability to interact with one's matrix" (p. 23). If this is so, the living cell contains intelligence from the beginning, but this knowledge would fall under the realm of intuition if viewed as a psychological experience. No learning, as we know it, is taking place; the cell or the infant learns as Roethke (1975) writes, "by going where I have to go" (p. 1133). It is a given, contained within the experience, which in mythology is always linked to God, the gods, angels, or the unknown. Pearce calls this an act of intention, but that word seems to imply a conscious will, and it is doubtful that this is possible if there is no ego to will. The organism responds intuitively to its environment. It knows what to do without being told, or rather it is told by its own body sensations, which are unconscious, but nevertheless in constant interaction with its environment. It is possible that the subject (fetus) is wired by instinct to respond to the object (womb or environment) in the best possible way, and that the womb (the body of the mother) is also wired to respond to the fetus in the best possible way. A relationship takes place from the beginning, one could almost say a silent relationship, between the mother's body and the unborn body of the child. Instinctual relationship may be considered a lower form of knowledge, but it is still knowledge that must precede, and be the foundation for, all knowledge that follows.

Pearce (1980) describes the first matrix, the infant in utero, as "only a symbiotic extension of the mother" (p. 20). This is certainly different from Fordham (1976), who sees the infant "as separate from his mother from the beginning" (p.11). I would agree with Pearce that the infant is a "symbiotic extension of the mother," excluding the word "only." Because he or she is also "separate," as Fordham describes, from the beginning his or her experience in the womb is not the identical experience of the mother. It would appear more reasonable to argue that both Pearce and Fordham are correct: Mother and child exist as one unit, yet they are also separate from the beginning.

In a rather sardonic vein, Pearce (1980) states: "As everyone 'knows,' this psychologically undifferentiated organism lacks consciousness, perception, sensation, and all other psychological functions" (p. 46). I understand this statement to reflect what Pearce does not believe to be true, and if this is so, I agree. I believe that the newborn infant is conscious, perceiving and experiencing sensation, and that the infant in utero is also conscious, but in a different way. That the experience in utero is different from the experience the infant has after birth appears certain; it is just this *difference* that needs to be explored.

The psychological function of intuition appears to be present in the infant in utero. It is my assumption that this function is conscious, although perhaps in a different and more mysterious way than we usually think of consciousness. I see the function of intuition as identical with the soul complex. From this function, all of the other functions and archetypes follow. Intuition stays the same: It is intuition because the other three functions are merged and unconscious. In other words, it is the one function that contains the other three to make the fourth function, which is a return to "one."

This description is not meant to be mystical although it may appear to be if one uses ordinary logic. Reason and Rowan (1989) discuss "the Hegel level" of understanding when they describe three levels of consciousness, the Primary level, the Social level, and the Realized level:

> At the Primary level, we were at the mercy of symbolic forms, in our unchosen dreams and daydreams: at the Realized level we are now able deliberately to use images and symbols in creative ways for our research purposes. At the Primary level, intuition was an occasional flash of insight, often accurate but quite unbiddable; at the Realized level it is our main way of thinking, enabling us continually to see the wood as well as the trees. And because we now see the world as *our* world, rather than *the* world, we can see clearly through our own eyes. Being rational, we see at this stage, is doing justice to the whole—to all that is out there in the world and to all that is in here, inside ourselves (emphasis authors', p. 116).

Thus, it may be necessary to use the very function which I am attempting to describe to understand the concept of three functions that become one. It is probably for this reason that the image of three-in-one (another example is the Holy Trinity) has been used in symbolic and seemingly mysterious ways that exclude ordinary rational language, but not art, poetry, myth, images, and archetypes. Yet, I believe, difficult as it may appear to be, it is not impossible to describe with language. What is needed is thinking that goes beyond Aristotelian logic (see Reason and Rowan, 1989, p. 114).

Sensation introduces consciousness and the child ego, and is always followed by the feeling function and the thinking function. When sensation and feeling are conscious, the ego complex begins. Thus, two kinds of consciousness can be seen to begin at birth, that of soul and that of ego. The opposition appears obvious and I would suggest, is psychic energy that is always engaged in coming apart (the splitting of the opposites) or coming together (the uniting of the opposites). In mythology, this is often described as the hero (ego) in a quest for something that is missing or lost (soul).

In alchemy, which is not a description of birth in the sense of a creation myth, but a description of rebirth or Paradise regained, ego and soul are referred to as Sol and Luna, sun and moon, gold and silver, brother and sister, male and female. The four functions are the psychological quaternity and can be seen as comparable with that mythology. The two that are to be re-united are ego and soul, represented in the alchemical literature as male and female. The ego functions of thinking, feeling, and sensation are to be married to the soul function of intuition, which contains the same three functions as one, merged in unconsciousness and undifferentiation. This marriage produces the Self.

Jung (1954/1946) says that "the quaternity is one of the most widespread archetypes and has also proved to be one of the most useful schemata for representing the arrangement of the functions by which the conscious mind takes its bearings" (p. 45). Here Jung is referring to the four psychological functions and their relationship to the alchemical myth of squaring the circle or obtaining the philosopher's stone.

Obviously, Jung saw a relationship between the four functions and alchemy. What never occurred to Jung was that he was only a step away from seeing how closely his descriptions of the four functions as psychic energy did exactly fit the process that the alchemists described. I have been unable to find a description in any of Jung's extensive writing, including <u>Psychological Types</u>, that indicates he had conscious knowledge of the three functions of sensation, feeling, and thinking, as being the "three that becomes four, which becomes one." Jung (Evans, 1976, p. 100) said that intuition was a "difficulty" because we do not know ordinarily how it works, indicating that he did not equate the psychic energy of the three functions as being contained in the function of intuition. I have little doubt that he knew this intuitively, but it was never brought to conscious thought, awareness, or expression. I do think that he might have eventually understood the possibility of how the three functions might be seen symbolically as the one function of intuition, because it is the natural outcome of his work on this subject. His fascination with the "axiom of Maria" and the Trinity archetype indicates his interest in the three-in-one phenomenon.

By seeing the three functions of sensation, feeling, and thinking as contained within the function of intuition, one can compare the four psychological functions with the *"axiom of Maria"* which Jung referred to so often in his writing. He (1954/1946) says that "this progression from the number 4 to 3 to 2 to 1 is the 'axiom of Maria,' which runs in various forms through the whole of alchemy like a *leitmotiv*" (p. 45). What is three becomes one, which is also the fourth.

If we look at this "progression" backwards, as we would to see it as a symbol for birth or the beginning of things (creation), we can see that one refers to the undivided Self that exists in the womb, where consciousness and the unconscious are united and undifferentiated. Two represents the division of that Self, which reflects the soul and ego as still one, but separated from the Self. Three refers to the birth of the Divine Child (ego) that becomes the one that is also the fourth.

When the movement is away from the center and consciousness is coming into play, three and four can be seen as the human child who contains the soul and ego in child form, in the functions of sensation and feeling. Sensation and feeling are the shadow side of intuition and thinking. Undifferentiated, they are the child soul and child ego or archetype of the human child, who is a reflection of the Divine Child contained in the center. Four also refers to the fourth function, intuition, which becomes unconscious at birth and the function that, as Jung so often said, is connected to the unconscious or Self. This axiom is another description of the soul archetype and the intuitive function. What is three becomes one, which is also the fourth. The three unconscious functions of thinking, feeling, and sensation are intuition as one function, and that which becomes the fourth function of the quaternity, when seen on a conscious level. The progression is Self or Divine Mother (three-in-one), Soul or Divine Father (also three-in-one), the Divine Child/human child archetype, the third that also contains all three. These three archetypes (three-in-one that becomes the fourth) are the psychic energy that moves away from the Self and becomes conscious; they are a reflection of the Self-made conscious.

Jung (1954/1946 talks about the fourth stage, the anticipation of the lapis in the following way:

> The imaginative activity of the fourth function—intuition, without which no realization is complete—is plainly evident in this anticipation of a possibility whose fulfillment could never be the object of empirical experience at all: already in Greek alchemy it was called "the stone that is no stone." Intuition gives outlook and insight; it revels in the garden of magical possibilities as if they were real (p. 119).

Here Jung describes the intuitive function as necessary for the final realization of the stone or a return to the Self, and states that realization would not be possible without this function. Looked at backwards, the same can be said: Realization is always contained in the function of intuition. Paradise or the soul state of intuitive knowing, which the stone represents, would not be lost if the infant was not born. At birth, he acquires all four psychological functions: sensation, feeling, thinking, and, finally, intuition by a reintegration with the other three functions, a return to soul or the intuitive function, which will be equally divided now. What was one in the beginning shatters into three and finally four or the quaternity and represents, as Jung (1954/1946) says, the pluralistic state of the man who has not yet attained inner unity, hence the state of bondage and disunion, of disintegration, and of being torn in different directions—an agonizing, unredeemed state which longs for union, reconciliation, redemption, healing, and wholeness (p. 46).

Jung calls this the state of the man, but I think one could readily see that it could also describe the human infant, crying and demanding to be loved, or the infant in the human adult, suffering from the same need.

Psychological experience begins in the womb. I think that the first psychological function is intuition; the second is sensation, which becomes conscious at birth; the third is feeling, which also becomes conscious at birth; and the last is thinking, which also becomes activated at birth in the form of the personal unconscious. Most developmental theories completely disregard the function of intuition in infancy, whereas sensation and feeling are fairly obvious in the newborn and are given more consideration, even though they are not considered ego functions. Thinking, on the other hand, is usually thought to begin around the age of 2 or thereafter. It appears reasonable to me, however, to think that active thinking—Jung's thinking function in his later writings—is preceded by the qualitatively different passive thinking, which Jung later called intuition. Active thinking contains the archetype, which had its beginning in passive thinking or intuition, which is the basic instinct.

The four functions are present in the womb and exist as the unconscious ego functions that are the shadow side of the soul, which has a consciousness of its own. At birth, this is reversed. The ego functions of sensation and feeling become conscious, and intuition and thinking are unconscious. The order that I have given previously does exist although the functions are contiguous with one other. This process can be seen as occurring in fractions of time, which to the observer may seem spontaneous. The process is in motion, however, and continuously repeats, which is why it can be seen as circular. In this way, all the functions can be seen to begin at birth, even though they had their genesis in the womb, where the soul complex contained the ego complex in potential and unconscious, undifferentiated form. The Self comes first, then soul, then ego.

The Womb Archetype and the Psychology of the Child in the Womb as Metaphors

Paradise, the womb, and the Divine Child as fruit of the womb all appear to be related archetypes significant to the early stages of developmental psychology. If "the archetypal form or pattern is inherited but the content is variable, subject to environmental and historical changes," (Samuels, 1987, p. 25), I would suggest that the cosmological motifs of mythology that depict creation and those that have the theme of rebirth reflect humanity's attempt to reconstruct its origins, and quite possibly its endings, reflected in myths concerning death. The myths, stories, images, concepts, or ideas are art as the reconstruction of the basic experience of Being or being alive, as well as the experience of death. It is our reconstruction of the existing archetypes, and how we arrange the forms and patterns, that create new archetypes, expanding our vision of human experience and consciousness.

Samuels' (1987) interpretation of Jung concerning the symbolic regression to the mother is that it "is for regeneration or rebirth, perhaps before moving on developmentally" (p. 167). But what is there in that experience that provides regeneration? If regression becomes a psychological experience after birth, could regression be less than psychological during the primary experience? If we substitute the mother archetype for that of the soul archetype or complex and imagine that this takes place as psychological knowledge contained within the intuitive function, it is not difficult to see that a longing for mother might

Life's original event
And the game of life's
Order of play
Are involuntarily
initiated,
And inherently subject to modification
By the a priori mystery,
Within which consciousness first formulates
And from which enveloping and permeating mystery
Consciousness never completely separates,
But which it often ignores
Then forgets altogether
Or deliberately disdains.
And consciousness begins
As an awareness of otherness,
Which otherness-awareness requires time.
And all statements by consciousness
Are in the comparative terms
Of prior observations of consciousness
("It's warmer, it's quicker, it's bigger
Than the other or others").
Minimal consciousness evokes time,
As a nonsimultaneous sequence of
experiences.
Consciousness dawns
With the second experience.
This is why consciousness
Identified the basic increment of time
As being a second.
Not until the second experience
Did time and consciousness
Combine as human life.
Time, relativity and consciousness
Are always and only coexistent functions
Of an a Priori Universe,
Which, beginning with the twoness of secondness,
Is inherently plural.

(R. Buckminster Fuller, Intuition 1972, p. 11, 12)

simply be a desire to return to that middle position where the soul is connected to the Self or unconsciousness and also connected to ego consciousness. Seen in this way, regression would not really apply, because it is possible that this connection was not meant to be destroyed in the first place, and when it is damaged or destroyed, it is that rather than the desire, which causes pathology.

If the experience of being in the womb and the experience of rebirth or a return to the womb is often a central theme in the mythology, literature, and initiation rites of many cultures down through history, perhaps we should ask about its psychological importance. Is there a psychology of the organism or infant in the womb? If so, what is that psychology? Certainly, there is an experience in the womb, and I think that this can be called a psychological experience, based on what we know about the four psychological functions as described by Jung (1971/1921) and by investigating when and in what order each function might appear in the human infant.

Samuels (1987) states that Fordham, a Jungian developmental psychologist, "postulates a primary self, existing in a sense before birth, and containing all psycho-physiological potentials" (p. 155). I agree with this statement with one exception: There is an experience in the womb that does not depend on "potential." It already is! From cell, zygote, organism, embryo, to an 8-or 9-month-old fetus, there is always potential, but there is also always the experience of the moment. Whatever this experience is, and I would assume that it has a significant role to play in human development, the nature and contents should be questioned if they contain an experience that humans often yearn to recreate. Literature appears to contain symbols in abundance that express a desire for the "return to the womb" experience.

Paradise "symbolizes primordial perfection and the Golden Age; the Cosmic Centre, pristine innocence; beatitude; perfect communion between man and God and all living things" (Cooper, 1988, p. 126). This description could easily be interchanged with the symbol of the womb which Cooper (1988) describes as "the feminine principle, the matrix, the Earth Mother . . . the well and all waters and all that encloses or contains, such as walls, caskets and cups, are symbols of the womb" (p. 122). The womb can be seen as a symbol of Paradise, and Paradise can be seen as a symbol representing the womb experience. Womb symbolism is linked in a spiritually positive way, as described by Cooper, or a pathological way, as described by Guntrip (1989), who says that "womb fantasies and/or the passive wish to die represent the extreme schizoid reaction, the ultimate regression, and it is the more common, mild characteristics which show the extraordinary prevalence of schizoid, i.e., detached or withdrawn, states of mind" (p. 58).

In a discussion of schizoid withdrawal and reasons for this action, Guntrip (1989) names one reason for the regression to a symbolic womb in the following way:

> Since this regressed ego is the basis of the most dangerous and undermining psychopathological developments, it is as well to reflect on the fact that it is in itself a necessary, reasonable, and healthy reaction to danger. Something is wrong primarily not with the infant but with the environment (p. 75).

Guntrip sees the fantasy of regression to the womb as a reaction of the infant or adult to its (negative) environment, with dangerous implications, which certainly appears to be one possibility. Guntrip apparently overlooks the possibility that the infant might be attempting to return himself to the womb position when the environment fails to accomplish this for him. This experience might be very different when the return is a defense mechanism, rather than a positive experience provided for by the mother. In a positive experience, the ego might be strengthened, but as a defense mechanism, the ego might not wish to return, becoming stuck in a position that becomes pathological because it does not allow for the flow of ego to soul and soul to ego.

Jung sees the entire experience in a different and more positive light. Jung (1959/1938) gives as an example of the process of transformation, the eighteenth Sura of the Koran, entitled "The Cave," which is a womb symbol:

> Anyone who gets into that cave, that is to say into the cave which everyone has in himself, or into the darkness that lies behind consciousness, will find himself involved in an—at first—unconscious process of transformation (p. 135).

Jung (p. 136) goes on to say, "This may result in a momentous change of personality in the positive or negative sense," indicating that a womb regression may be dangerous, but is also necessary for a process of transformation to occur. If we assume that this "womb regression" takes place immediately after birth, in what Fordham refers to as reintegration, it is possible to see that this experience is natural and what happens in the beginning of life. The infant has by being born lost the original state of oneness experienced in the womb and is returned to that state, transformed, one might say, by the experience of having his body/ego desires met by an "other" in the world.

Eros, Thanatos, and the Desire for Paradise

Psychoanalytic theory, as developed by Freud, is concerned with instincts,

Because the brain's TV prime resource
Consists of images,
We may call the total brain activity
Image-ination.

All we have ever seen
Is and always will be
In the scopes of our brain's TV station.
All that humanity has ever seen
And will ever see
Is his own image-ination;
Some of it is faithfully reported new,
Some of it is invented fiction or make believe;
Some of it is doggedly retained "want to believe."

(R. Buckminster Fuller, Intuition, 1972, p. 122)

mainly the sexual instinct (which Freud attributed to Eros) as a primary source for all physical and psychic development. Libido is sexual energy, and all other instincts flow from this basic force. Miller (1983) says that Freud, "in his final account, described two basic instincts, Eros (sex, self-preservation, love, life forces, striving toward unity) and the destructive instinct (aggression, undoing connections, the death instinct, hate)" (p. 112).

Freud apparently was concerned primarily with the irrational function of sensation as it applied to sex, and considered it the basic instinct. For Freud, everything starts with the body. In a certain sense this may be true, but not in the way that Freud described it, which leaves out the possibility of body instincts that are connected to the soul. Looking at Eros as an archetype of one kind of love or only half of what love is, connected with the ego and the body, and Psyche or the soul as the other half of love, love that is not in need or that does not desire, it is not difficult to see that love also relates to the death instinct, because it always means a death of the ego or a death of desire. Consummated love, whether it be in the psyche of one individual expressed as union between two different states of being or two different people in the world, always cancels the subject and object, two become one. One cannot strive towards life and love without striving towards death. If one sees death symbolically, as it is often intended to be seen in mythological literature, death represents a desire to leave ego consciousness for a return to a non-ego consciousness, which would give the experience of unity to the person rather than that of being separate. This was probably one meaning inherent in the Greek Eleusinian mysteries. The destruction of the ego allowed a non-ego or soul consciousness, which I equate with the function of intuition, to prevail and witness the bliss of unity. Life and death are not separate, but contained in one another in the form of soul, which embraces both in one and expresses the mystery of being and the mystery of nonbeing. Soul looks into the eternal on one side and the finite on the other and knows that this moment contains both. Death cannot exist without life, and life cannot exist without death. This experience takes away the fear of actual, physical death, which would have psychological value in any age or society.

When Jung (1971/1921) introduced the function of intuition as one of the basic four psychological functions, inherent in a healthy or ideal psyche, he assigned an importance to that function that has (especially in psychology) often been overlooked. That the body experiences sensation appears in the literature as a given fact. What, how, where, when, and why are equally significant questions concerning intuition as an important psychological function. Jung called intuition the function closest to the unconscious and considered it necessary for individuation, yet little has been included in developmental psychology literature on this function compared with the other three functions. It would seem that children, who live close to the unconscious, are excluded from the possibility of using this function in a significant way that may contribute to their growth and development in ways yet unknown.

It may seem strange to speak of psychological development in a fetus or in the womb, yet if that experience exists, it is one that all humans share and suggests a universal archetype that exists in the psyche of every adult.

Hall and Lindzey (1978) state that "Freud believed that the most extreme symptom of dependency is the desire to return to the womb" (p. 55). Does this statement imply that the independent ego that no longer desires to return to the womb or, indeed, to "Paradise" is the psychologically healthy ego? To take statements about the desire to return to the womb literally, we might deduce a desire for incest, which is how Freud viewed it, but if it is seen symbolically, it might be interpreted as a desire for a relationship with the mother where two are fused in oneness by the act of mutual love. This could take place in the actual blissful experience of the child with his mother after birth or it could describe the experience in the womb, where ego and soul were not separated. In either case, the desire is for the psychological experience of being "one with" in spirit, soul, mind, and body. If after birth the infant never had that blissful experience with his mother or a mother substitute, he or she might spend a lifetime looking for the experience in the world. If a oneness does exist in the womb, this experience would be universally true for all individuals and would explain why a womb fantasy was imagined more often than a fantasy of being an infant in a mother's arms. What the individual appears to be seeking is the archetypal match that was not provided after birth.

Pearce (1980) stresses the importance of early relationship when he says: "Bonding is a psychological-biological state, a vital physical link that coordinates and unifies the entire biological system. Bonding seals a primary knowing that is the basis for rational thought" (p. 72). The return of the infant to the state that he experienced in the womb or to the experience of being in the soul or intuitive function is what "bonding" is about. I agree with Pearce that this "seals a primary knowing" that allows for and is the foundation of rational thought. It begins, not after a year or two, but at birth. I may be accused of adultomorphism when I state that if reintegration to the soul or intuitive function shortly after birth could be put into language, the infant might say "I know love." This is knowledge experienced by the ego-body of the child. Knowledge of love and love of knowledge are not inseparable; they can exist in the first experience of the newborn's life. When they do, cognitive development or rational thought takes place at the same time as affective development, and they are certainly complementary to one other. Knowledge does not require language any more than love does; what is required is the experience. Feeling, as Jung described, is a way of knowing and one of the rational functions. Few would deny its existence in the newborn, yet the knowledge that it provides appears to be overlooked. That rational thinking proceeds from that of rational feeling is the point that Pearce appears to be making, and I agree with him.

No one is more dependent than the newly born human infant, who seeks a return to bliss through relationship, which gives knowledge that "we are one" and knowledge that "we are not one," opposites that either are united or shattered by the experience with the "other."

The experience of soul consciousness depends on the loss or partial loss of the ego to love the "other," whereas ego love is always a desire to be loved. These two different states of consciousness and two types of love, often conflicting in nature, exist in the psyche of one person or in a complex relationship. If the desire to return to the womb is such a common experience, it is possible that the reasons are more significant than merely dependency needs or, rather, that dependency needs are basic and significant for human relationship. If, indeed, mythology is the expression of psychological experience, many of Freud's interpretations can be seen as limited, for on a depth level, they would represent something very different indeed. The desire for Paradise would not only be considered normal, but perhaps essential, because this metaphor would describe an ultimate human experience designed to produce psychological wholeness. If it begins at birth and is part of a psychological process that all humans engage in to some degree, there would be nothing pathological about it. The metaphor would simply describe humanity's desire to be one with God and the world, and to know it on a conscious level. The transcendent function or the symbol that unites these two types of consciousness, ego and soul, would be the way and the means to achieve that goal. The experience of being separate created by birth and the experience of not being separate created by an assimilation of the womb experience would be two opposites experienced in the world, and the transcendent function would provide the symbol that unites them. I think this takes place in relationship, both within and without, and creates that middle place where both experiences exist and both are equally important. If a transcendent function exists in the human child, it is reasonable to assume that it begins at birth, when opposites as well as the need to reconcile them begin. It is creation that destroys oneness. Without creation, there would be no need for a transcendent function or a symbol that describes the experience of the opposites reunited.

Many people still adhere to the view that we are more than ego and more than body. A psychological concept of how or why humans cling to a spiritual or soul view has not been explored thoroughly, with the possible exception of Jung and analytical psychology. Faith and reason appear forever divided. A psychological concept, however, that attempts to provide a more total picture of early human experience might come closer to objective truth than one that ignores or considers pathological human beliefs that refuse to die. That consciousness of some kind, which I am describing as intuitive or soul consciousness, may exist in the womb does not appear to be the prevalent mainstream world view; however, it appears safe to say that research is being done that supports this view and that makes this possibility increasingly credible.

Our birth is but a sleep and a forgetting;
The star that rises with us, our life's Star,
Hath had elsewhere its setting
And cometh from afar;
Not in entire forgetfulness,
And not in utter nakedness,
But trailing clouds of glory do we come
From God, who is our home:
Heaven lies about us in our infancy!
Shades of the prison-house begin to close
Upon the growing Boy,
But he beholds the light, and whence it flows,
He sees it in his joy;
The Youth, who daily farther from the east
Must travel, still is Nature's Priest,
And by the vision splendid
Is on his way attended;
At length the Man perceives it die away,
And fade into the light of common day.

(From William Wordsworth, "Intimations of Immortality," 1888, p. 355)

Chapter 2
Michael Fordham

Michael Fordham and Jungian Developmental Psychology

Michael Fordham is considered a pioneer in Jungian developmental psychology, not only because he extended Jung's concept of individuation to include children, but because many of his concepts are based on actual clinical experience with children.

Both the primary question that I have asked (whether an order to Jung's psychological functions can be determined) and my answer that a circular order (and other descriptions of order) does exist with the psychological function of intuition being first, are more compatible with the work of Fordham than with the work of most other theorists. They are also more easily linked to Fordham's concepts of the child as an individual from the beginning, although Fordham exaggerated the possibility that the infant is totally separate from the mother from the beginning. Fordham does not give a structural concept of the experience of the fetus in the womb, except in his description of the primary Self, but he does often refer to the inherent possibilities; furthermore, he proved that Jung's concepts can be used to expand upon knowledge pertaining to child analysis, not only the archetype of the child, but the actual child. For these reasons, I have included his psychology here at length.

The ideas offered here presupposes many of Fordham's ideas concerning integration and deintegration. Also, by starting at the beginning, it completes a theory of developmental processes using basic Jungian concepts of psychological functions, as well as integrating many of the ideas of Michael Fordham.

Fordham had an excellent grasp of Jung's theory of individuation, and he was familiar with Jung's book on Psychological Types, which he helped to edit, but he apparently did not always make the link between all four functions as they pertain to individuation. Fordham begins with a construct of the Self that includes the ego and a description of the ego flowing out of the Self; what appears missing in his construct is the soul archetype, which necessarily needs to be differentiated from the Self or the ego and which is, I think, directly concerned with the psychological function of intuition. Intuition is the basic instinct; the Self, the soul and the ego are the archetypes that are contained in the basic instinct. My assertion can be supported by a depth interpretation of the cosmological mythology, about which Fordham says very little.

There is also, not surprisingly, very little in Fordham's writing concerning the psychological function of intuition or its importance in the psyche of the child.

Fordham on the Child in the Womb

Fordham asked many questions concerning the child in utero and after parturition because many of his theories rested on the concept that a child was an individual from the beginning and not just an extension of the mother. Just where to place the emerging ego is also a question related to the child in utero, and Fordham fluctuated in his opinion concerning this difficult but important aspect of his theoretical construct. In 1970, he says:

> Since the time that the self concept was originated, much more has been discovered about ego fragments and there can be no doubt that quite a firmly established ego structure is in being by two years of age; therefore the concept of the self may not be so necessary or central. The new data have indeed suggested an alternative theory of the ego, just because its organisation begins much earlier than was believed (p. 100).

By 1976, Fordham appears to have accepted the idea that the ego is present much earlier than he had previously conceived. In 1951, Freud, Jung, and other psychologists thought the ego to "be in place by the age of 5 or 6," which Fordham began to doubt. By 1970, Fordham thinks the ego is firmly established by the age of 2 years, but by 1976, Fordham accepts that the ego or parts of it are present at birth and that the importance of when the ego begins is crucial to child psychology:

> The time at which the ego is formed is important for the study of child psychology. The discovery of its early appearance has compelled a substantial revision in much of our thinking and understanding of infants; it has had repercussions on our orientation toward the structure and organization of the infantile psyche; it has compelled a revision of views about the possibilities of infant and child management and therapy. But, in spite of all this, the necessary modifications are congruent with the main body of Jung's thesis, which was so much ahead of its time (p. 37).

By placing the ego as emerging at birth with the soul complex also present at birth, many of Jung's descriptions of the soul archetype can be seen to apply to early childhood. The intuitive function, which is often placed willy-nilly, or worse yet, totally ignored as an important psychological function, can be seen to commence and work in relationship with the other three functions from the beginning, which is in the womb.

Concerning the child in the womb, Fordham (1976) says, "recently there have been serious attempts to investigate this difficult topic and, while there is not yet a psychology of intrauterine life, there is now a growing consensus that there are organized perceptual ego-functions at birth" (p. 46).

Here Fordham accepts the view that the ego or at least some organized perceptual ego-functions are present at birth, an idea that slightly alters some of his original ideas concerning the infant. Fordham's views on consciousness and when the ego begins vary considerably and obviously changed over the years. In 1970, he states:

> Just when consciousness of any kind begins can only be inferred, because the study of intra-uterine life is manifestly difficult, but enough is now known about the foetus to state confidently that he experiences some kind of rudimentary consciousness. Rapid as development may be after birth, in the first weeks of life there is every reason to suppose that perception is vague and transitory. Consequently the ego can play only a small part in the infant's existence, which is best understood in terms of patterned archetypal drives. Soon, however, ego fragments can be noted; they are closely related from the beginning to the drives and their unconscious fantasy representations (p. 93).

Here I suggest that what Fordham is calling "vague and transitory perception" is what Jung would have called "unconscious perception" or intuition (Jung, 1971/1921, p. 463); the unconscious fantasy representations are created by the intuitive function, which sees into the Self and returns with a symbol that not only expresses the ego, but strengthens and reinforces the ego complex. By this method, Self, soul, and ego archetypes can be seen to be organized and working together from the beginning, and the soul archetype, which I equate with the intuitive function, can be seen to be the mediator, as Jung described, not only in later life, but from the beginning.

Fordham never seems to expand upon his statement that a rudimentary consciousness might exist in the womb or what kind of consciousness it might be; from this statement, however, he obviously did not believe it to be ego consciousness, which he says only plays a small part in the infant's existence. A "rudimentary consciousness," however, implies several things; either the ego is present in the fetus or another kind of consciousness is present. I would suggest that this consciousness is not ego, as many of the writers who consider some kind of consciousness present think, but comes from the absence of the ego and is the soul complex or intuitive consciousness. Other adjectives that could be used to describe this consciousness are: basic, elementary, fundamental, initial, original, and primary. What is present in the womb is passive thinking (intuition) rather than active thinking, and Jung makes the necessary distinction in his description of the two functions. It seems almost obvious that passive thinking would precede active thinking and be the foundation upon which all future active thinking rests. What Jung called passive thinking or intuition, however, consists of more than unconscious thinking; it also contains unconscious feeling and unconscious sensation. In other words, these three major psychological functions exist as one undifferentiated function, which is intuition.

By 1976, Fordham is even more empathetic with the idea that an infant has conscious (ego) experiences and that the fetus may have "perceptual experience," even if it is vague. He states:

> It would, I think, be very daring to assume that an infant is not capable of any conscious experience and there is some indirect evidence in favour of there being ego-consciousness in very early situations. Right from the start, i.e., after birth, and indeed while still in utero, the infant (or foetus) reacts to stimuli. That the responses involve reflexes and neural discharges of an organized kind is certain and it would be much more logical, since reflexes involve afferent stimuli, to assume that at least some of them are accompanied by perceptual experience, however vague (pp. 45-46).

Again, Fordham uses the word "vague," which is closely related to words chosen by other writers to describe this state, such as dim, faint, or blurred, but he does not attribute these vague perceptual experiences either to the ego complex or to the soul complex; indeed, he does not comment on the nature of what he is describing as consciousness in the womb. I think that what he describes quite well can be seen as intuitive consciousness or soul consciousness, which exists simply because there is no ego consciousness present.

Fordham (1976) calls instinctual behavior a release-manifestation that is laid down within the organism before birth by the innate release-mechanism. He compares this to the baby gull who first feeds because of the red color, which is a sign-stimulus. The behavior of the infant is considered to be caused by the same sign-stimulus. Fordham states:

> When a baby starts to feed at the breast it is likely that there is a

sign-stimulus that starts him feeding. It would not be a breast, or a nipple as such. I emphasize this because it would seem that the sort of consciousness that an infant has is most unlike anything we know of, but it is not necessarily hazy but remarkably precise (p. 173).

If the sign-stimulus is not the breast, nipple, or the body of the mother, the human infant appears to be somewhat different from the baby gull, who is stimulated by a red color on its mother's beak. Fordham does not specify what this stimulus might be in the human infant, but he does attribute this activity to consciousness that is remarkably precise and different from anything we know. Here I would conclude that the infant "knows" by the consciousness of soul, that is, by the psychological function of intuition, which informs the ego that it is in a state of need or a state of desire, which is manifested in the body by the sucking behavior of the infant. Thus, the infant draws on the Self from the soul position and expresses what is needed through the ego; unconsciousness and consciousness are connected by the soul position. Jung (1971/1921) describes this process in the following way:

> The soul never loses its intermediate position. It must therefore be regarded as a function of relation between the subject and the inaccessible depths of the unconscious. The determining force (God) operating from these depths is reflected by the soul, that is, it creates symbols and images, and is itself only an image. By means of these images the soul conveys the forces of the unconscious to consciousness; it is both receiver and transmitter, an organ for perceiving unconscious contents. What it perceives are symbols. But symbols are shaped energies, determining ideas whose affective power is just as great as their spiritual value (pp. 250-251).

Here Jung was not necessarily commenting on the soul as an aspect of infancy, but his description can be seen as one that describes that period just as adequately as any other age in life, especially if we assume that the infant starts life with two kinds of consciousness, one of soul and one of ego. Life appears to be the journey towards reconnecting these opposites in the most possible conscious way, not only year to year, but also moment to moment.

Fordham (1976, pp. 42-43) gives his views on the previously accepted concept of the infant as "psychically part of his mother." Here, he disagrees with the mainstream view and suggests that the baby influences the mother just as much as she influences the baby. He goes on to state:

> The idea that the infant is psychically part of his mother is

> implicitly combined with another one: the infant is said to be unconscious. In current usage the term unconscious is ambiguous: it refers on the one hand to a negative state in which perceptual functions are not giving rise to conscious awareness and on the other to a more or less organized and partly inherited system of structures referred to as unconscious archetypes (p. 45).

Here Fordham has identified a part of the problem due to terminology; whether in the womb or after birth, the term "unconscious" is ambiguous; if the more or less organized and partly inherited system of structures referred to as unconscious archetypes are active and functioning in the fetus or the infant, they could better be described as part-conscious and part-unconscious; this would be a middle position and one that I would call soul consciousness or intuitive consciousness. The infant could be said to have an unconscious, in which the primary Self exists; and a soul consciousness that contains the major archetypes, including both consciousness and unconsciousness; and ego consciousness, which is always connected to the body in the beginning. Here it is not difficult to see the soul position as that which can be compared to a twilight state; it is not all dark or all light, but contains both to produce a different state of consciousness, which describes the intuitive function quite well. "Through a glass darkly" could be said to be describing the function of intuition as the way we first see.

Jung (1971/1921) describes the soul complex in this way:
> Looked at historically, the soul, that many-faceted and much-interpreted concept, refers to a psychological content that must possess a certain measure of autonomy within the limits of consciousness… It must be a content in which spontaneity is inherent, and hence also partial unconsciousness, as with every autonomous complex (p. 247).

This is a good description of the child in the womb, and the child at birth, who has his original state of unity shattered by birth into two types of consciousness that appear split or divided; one is soul consciousness and one is ego consciousness. In the womb, these two existed as the Self archetype and the soul archetype that reflects the Self.

It is possible that Fordham carried his idea of the child, especially the unborn child, being separate from the mother to the extreme, possibly to refute Neumann's insistence that they exist as a symbiotic pair in utero and a year after birth and possibly to allow him to formulate ideas that were not conceivable by using the concepts that Neumann proposed.

Fordham's arguments concerning the infant in the womb are sometimes hazy and often rather ineffective. He maintains (1976) that an infant has boundaries in the womb that "may very well be thought of as present at conception" (p. 11). Before this, he claims that we can ask how these boundaries are formed, but it is not possible to answer that question. He then goes on to say:

> There is a common fantasy that, during pregnancy, a mother and her baby live in a special state of intimate fusion disrupted at birth. The true state of affairs is different for, although a mother provides a stable aquatic environment and feeds her baby through the umbilical cord, the growth of a foetus is determined in all other respects by its genetic constitution (p. 11).

Fordham is wrong concerning "all other respects," because the baby responds to other conditions in the womb besides the very important one of nourishment. The womb is the baby's environment, and he or she constantly responds by being in relationship with its surroundings. What about the possible effects of the mother's emotional life on the fetus? In addition, the baby has inherited the genes of both parents. A particular baby has the genetic make-up of specific parents and does not acquire a random genetic system. The parents, genetically speaking, live in the child. Pregnancy can be seen as a "special state of intimate fusion," and it is certainly disrupted at birth; there is nothing fantastic about this assessment. The infant's body is connected to the mother's body via the umbilical cord; it is also contained within her body surrounded by the womb. It is difficult to conceive of a more intimate relationship. Furthermore, the physical as well as the mental condition of the mother may affect the fetus; a mother who uses crack cocaine or various drugs may produce an addicted, lethargic, or psychically damaged child; a mother who has the HIV virus may give birth to a child with AIDS. These conditions have nothing to do with the genetic constitution of the child, but they certainly have an influence upon his or her body and ability to respond had they not been present.

Kay (1984) cites research that was concerned extensively with stress, depression, and the effect of the mother's negative or positive emotions on the unborn child, and concludes with the statement: "What seemed to matter most of all was what the mother felt about her unborn child" (p. 326). If the mother wanted and loved her unborn child, the child appeared to be protected by a "shield of protection against adversity" (p. 326).

Fordham's statements concerning the separate state of the infant in the womb appear simplistic because they don't consider many aspects of the child in the womb that might be affected by the mother. A more reasonable view might be that the infant in utero has a separate Self and separate soul that is always acting and reacting to the mother or the mother's womb, which is its environment. They are separate bodies, but always connected by the umbilical cord, which is a connection that cannot be ignored; without that connection the infant would not survive. The state of unity or fusion that the fetus experiences may be because of the three psychological functions of thinking, feeling and sensation being unconscious and merged in the function of intuition, which allows the fetus to respond to stimuli from within or without in the best possible way. The genetic inheritance would be present in the intuitive function, making the child an individual from the start, but he or she would always be an individual in relationship to his or her surroundings, practice, one might say, for life after birth, which is the same, with the exception that the ego comes into play and ego consciousness usually takes the lead, whereas soul consciousness becomes or is called "unconscious." For these reasons, I would consider both Neumann and Fordham to be correct if taken together; the unborn child is separate, but also lives in what Neumann called "primal unity." In the womb, these opposites are united.

Fordham on Cosmogonic Myths and the Womb as Paradise

Fordham did not comment on the cosmogonic myth of Genesis, although he does correctly state that the closest parallel to the deintegration concept lies in cosmic creation myths. I would add that perhaps the most important cosmogonic myth in our Western culture is the creation of Adam and Eve, who lived initially with God in the garden of Paradise. Paradise and the enclosed garden are symbols that are equivalent to the cosmic egg described by the Greeks, and both can be seen as symbols of the womb.

Fordham (1957) describes the Greek myth of Eros who sprang from the cosmic egg:

> The most probable source of parallels to the deintegration concept lies in cosmic creation myths, and indeed they are to be found amongst our Western cosmogonic myths, the Greek ones showing the essential features most clearly. In the Orphic cult we find the cosmic egg as "the symbol of what gives birth to all things and in itself contains all things" and the Clementine Homilies say: "Orpheus likened Chaos to an egg in which was the commingling of the primeval elements." From the cosmic egg springs Eros, he

> "revealed and brought to light everything that had previously lain hidden in the golden egg" (p. 118).

Indeed, if we take Eros to represent the first deintegration or the first "coming apart" of the Self, it is not difficult to see that he can be compared with the emergence of ego and the first body sensations or the psychological function of conscious sensation and the psychological function of feeling, because the sensation produces the first desire, and the image created is the desired object, which is a product of the thinking function, conscious or unconscious. Eros, which means "demanding love," (Jung and Kerenyi, 1949, p. 53) can be seen as the ego of the newborn child who demands to be loved. At this point he represents only half of the feeling function or half of love, the desiring half. The other half remains in the unconscious. Freud called this primary narcissism, which has pejorative connotations similar to those placed upon Eve, who was cast from Eden when she first experienced desire. A more positive view would be one that called this primary love, which is the body ego or child ego, and its demand for survival, which appears to be a reasonable attitude for the infant to possess. Feeling is, as Jung pointed out, a rational function.

Eros does contain the contents of the cosmic egg; the cosmic egg can be seen as a symbol of the Self that contains all four, undifferentiated, unconscious psychological functions. The cosmic egg contains everything, including soul and soul love, and when it bursts (when the child is born), Eros comes forth and all the functions that were merged begin as conscious functions connected to the ego and unconscious functions connected to the soul. Love is the double-edged sword that severs and unites and can be seen as the Divine Child and the human child. (Most Divine Children in mythology are portrayed as having a double nature, for example, Hermes.)

The integration of the ego takes place when its demands are met with soul love from the mother or other and it returns to that psychological place where there is nothing to want or desire. The experience of the other half of feeling or love that was left in the unconscious replaces the ego needs of the infant and he has experienced the opposites in time. This is a return to the womb experience that allows the infant to match inner world with the outward world, ensuring a sense of wholeness. Metaphorically speaking, the child is returned to the cosmic egg or the Self by a process of assimilation. This process is continuous in the beginning of life and essential for the child-body-ego to develop adequately. The early mother and child relationship can be seen as one of soul (mother) to ego (child); the return to the mother at any age is a desire to return to soul consciousness, which has been damaged or blocked for whatever reason.

Kaplan (1978) expresses much the same thing: "all later human love and dialogue is a striving to reconcile our longings to restore the lost bliss of oneness with our equally intense need for separateness and individual selfhood" (p. 27). In early infancy, this is a natural process; Eros or the ego must be expressed, satisfied and, by satisfaction, be lost, in order to be returned to soul, which strengthens the ego that next expresses itself in consciousness. It appears as a peculiar quirk of fate that the old ego consciousness must die before a new ego consciousness can be expressed—or put another way, consciousness is only enlarged by the loss of consciousness. This is true in adult life, but it is no less true in infancy, where the process first began. Two kinds of consciousness that appear split or divided must be reconciled in the human psyche, which is what so many of the myths appear to describe. Jung (1959/1938) describes this when he says:

> The conflict between the two dimensions of consciousness is simply an expression of the polaristic structure of the psyche, which like any other energetic system is dependent on the tension of opposites. That is also why there are no general psychological propositions which could not just as well be reversed; indeed, their reversibility proves their validity (p. 269).

Fordham apparently did not agree with Jung on the interpretation of the myths describing a desire to return to the mother, and although he saw the Eros myth of the cosmic egg as a parallel to describe the deintegration process, he does not appear to equate Eros with ego (even though Eros is always portrayed as a child, youth, or young god), which is necessary to link his concepts with what the myth is describing. The Self deintegrates or comes apart to create the soul complex and the ego complex but the Self remains the same. Put another way, the Self is the soul and ego merged. When it splits or divides, it becomes soul and ego that have become differentiated and conscious.

Gayley (1939) describes the Orpheus version of the Greek cosmological myth as, "assuming the form of a huge world egg, [which] flew, by reason of its rapid rotation, into halves. Of these, one was Heaven, the other Earth. From the center of the egg proceeded Eros (Love) and other wondrous beings" (p. 3). Heaven and earth can be seen as another form of the Divine Syzygy or opposites that become soul (Mother) and ego (Father). Eros, as the Divine Child, proceeds from the center. Here he represents the adult ego and soul merged, or the functions of intuition and thinking merged. In the coming apart of Heaven and Earth or the Self, he represents the beginning of consciousness in the functions of sensation and feeling in the human child. These are the "child" functions;

sensation is the child soul and feeling is the child ego. As a symbol of the Self, Eros contains them all, and they flow out of him (deintegrate) or back to him (reintegrate).

Ryce-Menuhin (1988) describes Fordham's hypothesis:
> Fordham's deintegration hypothesis proposes a spontaneous division of the self. Indirect evidence may be gathered from various sources. Jung believed that a new concept has certainly been reflected in ancient myths, and this can amplify the concept of deintegration. The cosmic creation myths may be a source of ideas parallel to the deintegration theory. In the Orphic cult in Greece we find the cosmic egg as "the symbol of what gives birth to all things and in itself contains all things." (Plutarch, quoted in Harrison, 1908). (p. 57)

It is not the Self that spontaneously divides to become Self and ego, as Fordham apparently thinks and Ryce-Menuhin suggests, but the Self that divides to become the soul complex and the ego complex. If the Self is what Jung described as God or totality, it would not be subject to division; indeed, it would be the core aspect of life impervious to division or change of any kind. Jung (1971/1921) described the soul as "the organ of perception, the soul, apprehends the contents of the unconscious, and, as the creative function, gives birth to its dynamis in the form of a symbol" (p. 251). What would the organ of perception be if it is not one or both of the irrational functions of sensation or intuition, which Jung referred to as the perceiving functions? If it is the soul that perceives, it appears to me that the psychological function that it perceives with must be intuition. (It is the body that perceives by the function of sensation.) If this is so, it would be the irrational functions of sensation and intuition undifferentiated (the soul complex and the ego complex combined) that would create the symbol. It could also be seen as conscious and unconscious perception working together in the psyche. Conscious sensation would be the ego function and unconscious intuition would be the soul function. If all opposites meet in the middle and I think that they do, sensation and intuition probably work together (ideally speaking) in the human psyche in a way that has yet to be explored. And if they are, as I later suggest in more detail, mirror images of one another, it would be both instinctual and irrational functions that create the archetypes or fill in the empty forms. The irrational functions would both contain each of the other three functions in unconscious form or, put another way, each irrational function would contain the other three functions in unconscious form. This would also be a description of the instinct that contains the archetype and will later become the archetype. Intuition and sensation appear to be the psychological functions that are personified in mythology as the twin Serpents (Sumerian) or the twin fishes Lucifer and Christ (Christian) which will be discussed in detail in Chapter's 3 and 4 of this work.

It is the leap from the Self archetype to the ego archetype, leaving out the soul archetype that caused Fordham difficulty with his hypothesis; it is probably the soul that is the organ of conscious perception and the cosmic egg is a symbol for the Self that contains the ego and the soul within itself. One could say that it contains the contents of the Self as a reflection of the soul and ego merged; the soul, ego, or the reflection comes apart or deintegrates, but the Self does not. The cosmic egg symbolizes the four functions in undifferentiated form. Intuition is the first function out of the cosmic egg (symbolized as mother or earth or soul) and still contains all the other functions within itself. These are the ego functions of sensation, feeling and thinking. The soul is a reflection of the Self and identical with the Self, but has also become something separate (the spontaneous division that is also a state of transition) and can be identified as the soul archetype which is identical with the instinct of intuition. Her child is the function of sensation or the child soul that has not yet become fully conscious. At birth and the experience of the opposites, sensation (soul) and feeling (ego) become conscious ego functions and intuition (soul) goes into the personal unconscious. The thinking function or what Jung called active thinking is either not yet conscious or possibly contains the thought as an unconscious image that was experienced in the rational function of feeling and experienced before that in the irrational function of sensation.

As Ryce-Menuhin and Fordham attest, the cosmic creation myths are an excellent source for parallel ideas of the deintegration theory; what is missing in some of Fordham's concepts is a better description of what happens before birth, a more precise definition of the beginning ego and the role the soul archetype plays in the process of individuation in childhood, based on Jung's excellent description of that archetype as a mediator between the Self and the ego.

Fordham (1982) did not comment specifically on the cosmological myth of Genesis, but he did have definite ideas concerning the womb experience as one related to or describing a state of Paradise. He states:

> Take the idea of Paradise being in the womb, well, if you study what goes on in the womb and quite a lots been done—it's not particularly Paradisical, it's, what it is, or if it is, Paradise is a very noisy place, indeed. The beating of the aorta in the mother is a constant sort, like an old fashion steam train going on all the time.

> Then you [presumably the child] get cramps, can't get sorted out—have to kick—turn yourself upside down by peculiar spiral movements. External noises can be quite intrusive, too. You can't say you would like to call that Paradise, a place like that; it's not likely anyone will (recorded lecture).

In this unlikely research, I am making exactly that proposal; I am looking at the myth of Paradise as a metaphor that describes the womb experience and the experience of the child at birth. This is not a new idea; Heinberg (1989) gives the following example:

> The idea of interpreting the Paradise myth as an analogy for the mother-infant relationship did not originate with Feud or Jung, however. Indeed, its roots go at least as far back as the Gnostics of the first century. Simon Magus, whose views are preserved (no doubt in distorted form) in Saint Hippolytus's Refutation of All Heresies, taught that the Garden of Eden was not a geographical place, but a metaphor for the womb; "If God forms man in his mother's womb—that is, in Paradise—then let the womb be Paradise and the after-birth Eden, a river flowing forth from Eden, for the purpose of irrigating Paradise. This river is the navel" (p. 194).

The world navel is a symbol for Paradise, as Eliade (1991) tells us. "Paradise, where Adam was created from clay, is, of course, situated at the center of the cosmos. Paradise was the navel of the earth and according to a Syrian tradition, was established on a mountain higher than all other" (p. 16). In biological terms it is not difficult to see this mountain as the pregnant body of the mother and her navel as the center of the world, the connection between Heaven and Earth. It is also not difficult to see the umbilical cord as the container for the river (water of life) that flows into Paradise or the womb, thereby nourishing it. Biologically, one can also compare the act of physical love and female orgasm (water of life) to the river flowing out of Paradise, leaving behind the egg that will generate new life at conception.

Fordham did not make a connection with the myth of Genesis as a metaphor for the experience of being in the womb or birth. His rejection for the experience of the unborn child being in a Paradisical state, however, appears to me to be extremely subjective and therefore not a very convincing one. The beating of the mother's heart or noise in the womb means very little; it implies that the infant prefers silence, indeed, that the infant has a preference, which is probably not the case at all.

If there is no ego (as we know it) present in the womb and no knowledge of the opposites, the infant is not able to make a value judgment concerning his or her own body sensations, such as the one Fordham is making. (Fordham appears to be identifying with the conscious sensate and conscious feeling and conscious thinking experience of the infant in the womb, from an adult, conscious, ego position, which certainly does not sound like Paradise. But what would an intuitive description sound like?) The infant may act and react to stimuli, but does not appear to be using the functions of active, conscious thinking, conscious feeling or conscious sensation, as defined by Jung. The one psychological function that appears to be possibly present and possibly conscious is intuition; the infant moves toward and away from the object or stimulus by what appears to be an in-born instinct, and intuition appears to fit the description more than any other psychological function, especially if we consider the possibility that it contains some form of consciousness. The infant appears to know what to do and when to do it, in most cases, intuitively. (The infant in the womb is alive and it is my assumption that the state of being alive contains some form of consciousness, even if we have not yet been able to define what it is.) If there is no ego present, the experience of the body sensations of the infant might be such that what is pain is experienced no differently than what is pleasurable. The experience of differentiating opposites would not be present. If this is the case, one might readily define such a state as Paradisical.

Birth, which can be seen as the beginning of the ego, represented in the Genesis myth as the "Fall," would create the second kind of consciousness, ego, which would exist as a conflict with soul consciousness from the beginning. The soul contains all the psychological functions merged; the ego separates all the functions as consciousness comes into being. Thus, the opposites are born and in conflict, represented in the myths as the hero and his search for Paradise or what was lost by consciousness. An interpretation of the myth of Genesis will be discussed later in this research in detail, where I suggest that the four major archetypes of the myth, God, (intuition) the snake, (sensation) Eve (feeling) and Adam, (thinking) all represent psychological functions and psychic energy that can be seen as a description of the infant in the womb and the experience of birth and a description of psychological processes that can occur at any age. The creation myth of Eros can be seen as comparable to the creation myth of Genesis; in both myths Chaos comes first, then Heaven and Earth in the Genesis myth, and Earth and Heaven in the Greek myth. Chaos is the Self, Earth is the soul, and Heaven is the Ego. But the child ego is the shadow of Heaven and Earth or the unconscious side of the "Divine" functions of intuition and thinking. Paradise is identical with Eros or Love, and both are symbols that unite the opposites.

Because I think the functions of unconscious thinking, unconscious feeling, and unconscious sensation are merged and, by the merger, create the function of intuition, I consider this to be the first conscious psychological function present in the human psyche and the psychological experience that is desired by the symbolism of a "return to Paradise" motif in mythology. One cannot return literally to the womb, but one can return to the psychological experience that one had in the womb and do so on a conscious level, which the idea of rebirth symbolizes. This is the message of the myths, especially the religious myths that promise a "new Heaven and new Earth" or a "New Jerusalem." This experience, I would suggest, also takes place in the beginning of life, if the infant is fortunate, every time the child is returned to an assimilation of the original state of what I would call soul consciousness. After birth, Paradise is to be found and recreated in relationship, by loving and being loved.

Fordham (1982) concludes: "All this longing for the mother, which Jung talks about—I'm afraid it's not so" (recorded lecture). Jung (1959/1938) is more convincing on this point:

> Symbols of the mother in a figurative sense appear in things representing the goal of our longing for redemption, such as Paradise, the Kingdom of God, the Heavenly Jerusalem. The archetype is often associated with things and places standing for fertility and fruitfulness; the cornucopia, a ploughed field, a garden. It can be attached to a rock, a cave, a tree, a spring, a deep well, or to various vessels such as the baptismal font, or to vessel-shaped flowers like the rose or the lotus. Because of the protection it implies, the magic circle or mandala can be a form of mother archetype. Hollow objects such as ovens and cooking vessels are associated with the mother archetype, and, of course, the uterus, yoni, and anything of a like shape (p. 81).

The longing for the mother can be seen as a desire to return to the original experience of unity and wholeness or a desire to return to the psychological state of soul consciousness, which observes the Self and the ego simultaneously.

Even though Fordham (1976) rejected the idea of the womb experience being symbolized by the myth of Paradise, he gives an excellent description of a state of complete integration in the beginning:

> A symmetrical theory of the relation between the first and the second half of life can be envisaged: assuming that complete

integration, based on realization of the self, is the final aim of individuation, it becomes possible that there is also a state of complete integration in the beginning. It is not realized, nor realizable, at all because there is no ego distinct from the self to perceive it. When the original integrate exists must be left open; it may, however, be conveniently located before birth, which disrupts it—hence the persistent idea of birth as the earliest source of anxiety (p. 16).

Here Fordham apparently contradicts himself when he says that the original integrate must be left open because he goes on to say that it may be conveniently located before birth, which disrupts it. I do not think that the original integrate must be left open, but does exist before birth, which is in the womb. Birth would certainly be a disruption of that original state of unity and the first deintegration. Fordham says that there is no ego distinct from the Self to perceive that state of harmony, and it is therefore not realizable or realized, yet one has to question the purpose of such a state; if it is not realizable in any way, how can we imagine that it ever existed? I would agree that there is no ego (as we know it) present to perceive, but ego consciousness is not the only kind of consciousness possible. The experience of the Self is perceived by soul consciousness, which also contains memory, and depends on the absence of the conscious ego. If the Self, indeed, is the archetype that contains everything within itself, that would have to include some form of consciousness. It would also have to include a psychological function, which is the human means to knowledge, and that function would necessarily be the function of intuition.

The absence of the ego as a means of obtaining spiritual knowledge or transformation is documented in numerous accounts of religious or mystical literature. Jung (1971/1921) describes this process as:

> The yogi seeks to induce this concentration or accumulation of libido by systematically withdrawing attention (libido) both from external objects and from interior psychic states, in a word, from the opposites. *The elimination of sense-perception and the blotting out of conscious contents* enforce a lowering of consciousness (as in hypnosis) and an activation of the contents of the unconscious, i.e., the primordial images, which, because of their universality and immense antiquity, possess a cosmic and suprahuman character (emphasis mine, p. 202).

The infant in the womb, however, does not need to eliminate conscious sense impressions; he already exists in the state that the yogi is attempting to return;

he exists in a psychological state of being where opposites are united, thus the many references to returning to the state of infancy for union with God.

Fordham states that his theory of integrates and deintegrates can best be compared with the cosmic creation myths, but he only mentions the myth of Eros and the cosmic egg; it is regrettable that he did not link his theory with the myth of Genesis or the idea of Paradise in the womb, because by doing so his theory could be seen from the beginning of life and connected to the very important Western cosmic myth of Genesis. In addition, the link or comparison between the Greek cosmological myth of Eros and the Jewish and Christian myth of Genesis can be more readily seen. Fordham was correct when he said that cosmic myths could be compared with deintegration, but he failed to see a connection between integration and the Paradise myth of Genesis. If, as Piaget previously stated, every Genesis has its roots in a previous Genesis, integration can readily be seen as a Paradisical state of being that begins in the womb, and can only be recaptured after birth by a reintegration to the previous condition.

Archetypes, the Unconscious, and Mandalas

Concerning the unconscious, Fordham (1957) states:
> It will be assumed that the unconscious, whose organs are the archetypes, is formed before birth. Since the archetypes are bound up with the functioning of the central nervous system it must presumably be there by the time the brain is formed (p. 105).

This concept can be extended to assume that consciousness and unconsciousness both exist, as living potential, in the body or in the cell from the beginning or even before the brain is formed. If the brain did not exist as potential in the beginning organism, how could it come into being? The point I believe Fordham to be making is that the archetypes exist in the unconscious before birth and exist in a state of unity. Fordham (1957) continues:
> In 1951 I put forward some tentative formulations starting from the assumption that the self is the original archetype of infancy and further that the emergence of the ego was closely related to it. I based this upon the observation that children produced pictures of mandalas, and further that when they did so a process of integration occurred in which the ego was clearly strengthened. I went on to show that very small children, even those of one year old, connected the circle with the word I or me and that here also their behavior showed an integration comparable to that

observed in older children. From this I concluded that the circle represented the self in union with the ego. These observations ran counter to what I thought was an established concept: that the ego was not formed till much later (pp. 112-113).

Fordham (1957) goes on to say that he compared his observations with the work of A. Gessel (The First Five Years of Life), who found that children of 18 months used the word "I" with some regularity, inferring that it must have appeared for the first time even earlier still (p. 113).

Fordham (1957) compares his views with those of Winnicott, who postulates a primary unintegrated state in infancy (p. 114), which would be in direct opposition to Fordham's description of a primary integrated state out of which the ego emerges. In discussing Winnicott's concept of a "continuity of being," Fordham (1957) says, "the notion of a 'continuity of being' in a single psyche-soma implies a condition of wholeness, but where Winnicott speaks of the psyche-soma and environment then the self has already been divided up even if the fit be perfect" (pp. 114-115).

This is an excellent observation by Fordham; if the ego flows out of the original Self, yet the Self remains intact, obviously there are two states of being at this point: one of non-ego or what I would call the soul and one of ego. Why would it not be possible to assume that each "bit of consciousness" can coexist with what is unconscious or preconscious or undifferentiated by the infant? This would imply a continuity of being in which the infant would acquire consciousness, but it would still flow out of the unconscious.

My research supports that of Winnicott; at birth the self of the infant is divided; two kinds of consciousness come into being, one of soul and one of ego. Fordham is also correct if he means that the infant is, right after birth, in a state of primary wholeness or a state that could be called the Self because it includes both states of consciousness. If he means the infant is born with a Self that is not in conflict and in a state of unity, however, he is only half right. Fordham defines the primal Self as an integrate, a steady state, that must deintegrate, and one that contains opposites within itself; when the self deintegrates it will divide into opposites that are psycho-physiological in nature (1976, p. 12). It is unclear in Fordham's many descriptions, as well as in other explications of his work, whether Fordham's primal Self, described as a steady state or integrate, is the state of the infant at birth and shortly thereafter or if it is a condition present only in the womb. It would appear that he thought the Self existed in the womb and was also present at birth and shortly thereafter.

Fordham (1979) says:

The unity of the infant expresses his individuality and it is attractive to think that it could provide the motivation for individuation as follows, just because the primary wholeness can never be achieved again once individuation has taken place, there is a drive to regain what is impossible. It can, however, be approximated to in sleep, in blissful experience; later on it can be represented in omnipotent, wishful, ideal and holistic imagery. But in all these the original condition can only be sought and when self representations are developed as a creative imaginative act, individuation is facilitated (p. 27).

This kind of unity can only be described as that which occurs in the womb, and it is not difficult to see that it is symbolically represented as Paradise or the Golden Age in mythology. In the myth of Genesis, the gates of Paradise are guarded by cherubim with flaming swords, meaning that one cannot reenter by that route; one cannot go back into the womb, but must find a new Paradise, one that will be obtained through relationship, love, and (usually) the mother. The "drive to regain what is impossible" can be seen as the infant's desire to return to that blissful state that can, according to Fordham, never be re-gained, only approximated in sleep or in blissful experience. Elsewhere, the investigator (Lenhart, 1990a) has described something very similar to Fordham's description of returning to the original unity through relationship with the mother:

The relationship with mother or primary caretaker, will consist of two different, but related aspects thereafter, nonego (or soul) to nonego, and ego to ego. The mother, in her acts of care-taking, loving and full-filling the child's basic needs, which are also ego demands, will assimilate the original experience of unity, primal unity that existed in the womb and was shattered by the act of birth. When the ego, or "I" that is separate has these basic needs given on a regular basis, he experiences an assimilation of the unity in the womb, which is now in the world, with another person (mother) and it is the experience that he is having as subject and object that allows him to know himself as both subject and object. His subjective ego demands are fulfilled by the object (mother). *This assimilation is of the greatest importance, because each time mother and child re-enact a state of "unity" the ego or "I that am separate," I that demand: food, warmth, comfort, love, relinquishes itself in the process of accepting those needs. Ego that is satisfied returns to a nonego state, the state of unity,* at least temporarily, until a new need arises (emphasis author's, p. 7).

This description is very much in keeping with Fordham's idea of the infant attempting to return to a state of primary wholeness; I have called it an assimilation of the original experience, for the same reasons Fordham gives.

More on Mandala Symbolism

The mandala played an important role in the formations of Fordham's early hypothesis of childhood individuation. His reference is often to Jung's description of mandalas and the significant role they can play in the process of individuation. Fordham (1957) states:

> The contents of a fully developed mandala are variable but in every case they are arranged about a centre. The space between the centre and the circumference is divided up in various ways. The most frequent and stable number of the divisions is four, or a multiple of four, and Jung has put forward the view, elaborated in many of his works but above all in Psychological Types, that these represent the fourfold structure of the psyche (p. 132).

If the mandala represents the fourfold structure of the psyche, all the psychological functions would be present, but in the child many aspects of the functions would still be unconscious. Those images put in the mandala might represent aspects that have been seen by the soul complex and made conscious, which is described by the pictures that the child draws and puts into the circle.

Fordham (1957) gives a description of a 1-year-old child who scribbles on the wall of the nursery and began to make circles. After doing this for some time, the child says the word, "I," and the circles stop. Fordham continues:

> Far from contradicting our interpretation, Jung's observations that the circle represents an archetypal nonego confirm it, even though his researches are on individuation in which the separation is essential and this research is based upon the concept that the separation has not yet occurred. This inversion is a logical consequence, as we have seen, from Jung's theories (p. 134).

Fordham is right in saying that the mandala represents the Self or totality of the child. If separation had not yet occurred, however, why would the child make mandalas as protective devices in the first place? Jung (1959/1955) said of mandalas, "their object is the self in contra-distinction to the ego, which is only the point of reference for consciousness, whereas the self comprises the totality of the psyche altogether, i.e., conscious and unconscious" (emphasis author's, p. 5). If this is the case, the mandala would represent an already present ego that expresses its connection to the Self. Fordham (1957, p. 135) quotes Jung, who states that the circle is a protection against the "perils of the soul," but it is conceivable that this is a natural occurrence in infancy and early childhood, and is necessary for the filling out of the ego rather than from an always inherent danger. It is possible that the archetype of the circle may be present at birth or shortly thereafter and represents the soul position, where the four psychological functions existed as one in the form of intuition in the womb and later or after birth when the infant has experienced a return to that state via the mother, by having needs met. A return to the soul position would allow a view of the Self, which would be expressed by the ego. If the soul is the archetype that the adult returns to, as Jung describes, to return to the Self, then the reverse would be true in childhood: The soul would flow firstly out of the Self. It would be a reflection of the Self, but not the Self in its totality, which would not be needed. The progression would be away from the Self, via the soul, towards ego consciousness. The ego would regress in that case for two different reasons; when it is threatened (fear, which is ego love), and when it is loved by "other." In both cases, the purpose would be the same—the strengthening and protection of the ego.

Fordham here (1957) gives a case of a 2-1/2-year-old girl who he invited to sit on his lap and draw. He describes her first scribbles as "aggressive" and concludes that:

> her apparent acquiescence had been under secret protest; it was only when the circle appeared, however, that her ego could express itself in action. It seemed to represent the statement that my power had become neutralized and that there was now a magical boundary between herself and me which made her position safe; no aggression from me was now possible (p. 135).

He continues:

> Jung states that the circle is a protection against the "perils of the soul" thereby relating it to psychical functions rather than to real persons. This contradiction is, however, more apparent than real, for the child must have seen me as a danger—I would not have pressed her to scribble had she not acquiesced. The danger was due to a projection of the "soul," in this case the father imago. If I had been more active the projection would not have been withdrawn, therefore in cases where the environment is dangerous or hostile the projection becomes indissoluble because it is "true" and strong indissoluble defenses are set up against it (1957, p. 135).

Fordham concludes:
> These observations and reflections point to the circle as representing a delimiting or protective magic used to ward off real or imagined dangers from without or from within, or a danger inherent in the condition itself, a condition which provides the circumstances out of which the ego can come into being (1957, p. 137).

I would suggest that Fordham's description is accurate. By making the circle, the little girl returned to an earlier state where the father imago was contained in the primal unity of the soul complex: father, mother, and child as one. I do not think, however, that the making of the mandala is necessarily always a protective or defensive device by the child, but can be seen as an attempt to communicate and express psychic experience in the form of symbols and images, which probably are formed long before the formation of language. Jung (1959/1938) describes something like this when he says:
> Wholeness is never comprised within the compass of the conscious mind—it includes the indefinite and indefinable extent of the unconscious as well. Wholeness, empirically speaking, is therefore of immeasurable extent, older and younger than consciousness and enfolding it in time and space. This is no speculation, but an immediate psychic experience. Not only is the conscious process continually accompanied, it is often guided, helped, or interrupted, by unconscious happenings. The child had a psychic life before it had consciousness (p. 178).

Therefore, I would conclude that early attempts to make mandalas, such as those by the 1-year-old girl or the 2-year-old child that Fordham describes, are or can be protective devices, but they can also be more than that. They are possibly an early attempt by the child to express the psychic life that is becoming conscious. Ego, which I consider to be present at birth, is certainly present at the age of 1 or 2 years. The making of the mandala is the ego complex that returns to the soul complex and draws from the Self, then returns to give expression to that experience via the ego. Jung (1959/1955) had this to say concerning the mandala:
> The "squaring of the circle" is one of the many archetypal motifs which form the basic patterns of our dreams and fantasies. But it is distinguished by the fact that it is one of the most important of them from the functional point of view. Indeed, it could even be called the archetype of wholeness (p. 4).

The young child, however, does not appear to be attempting to "square the circle" as the adult might be doing, but instead trying to give expression to the circle itself and its contents, which would denote a developmental difference in the making of mandalas and suggest that the early attempts to make mandalas have a different purpose than those made by the adult. The squaring of the circle may well be the incorporation and consciousness of all four psychological functions, which would be the work of a lifetime and what Jung called individuation. The individuation of children would necessarily be different and the reverse of adults. Children would have first to empty, so to speak, the contents of the circle, which I would take to represent the soul or Self, and make thinking, feeling, sensation, and intuition, conscious and differentiated, before they could begin to "square the circle." But they would be individual from the start, because that circle or that soul would contain all the contents of their own unconscious psychological functions. Most of childhood would, in fact, be devoted to this task, which is probably why Jung thought that this was a time for ego development rather than soul.

Fordham's work on the mandalas of children is important because it helped to establish his idea that individuation, although different, begins in childhood.

Primary Narcissism or Primary Love?

Fordham (1979) states that he derived his ideas on primary unity and individuation from Freud's "ingenious derivation of the ego ideal from primary narcissism:"

> The idea that I found especially interesting was that since the earlier state of primary narcissism could not be regained—but continues to be desirable—it leads to the construction of an ideal which refers to but does not repeat the original condition. Individuation, though conceived as a process, is also thought of as an ideal state that can never be reached (p. 27).

I would have to take "primary narcissism" to be the original state of the infant at birth, which is what I would call primary or ego love. This is the first state of desire experienced by the child. But the child does not long to get back to a state of ego love, indeed, it is just the opposite: What he desires is to return to a state of soul, where ego is still connected to the Self. But the experience of unity does not necessitate a narcissistic state, only at birth is this possible, when the desire to return to that state becomes apparent. The infant or even the adult, who desires to experience this state of unity, does not wish at this point to be individual; he or she wishes to be reunited with "other"; he perceives that "other" in the world (the mother), will return him to that state of unity. I see primary narcissism as the ego's demand via the body to be returned to that original state of unity, and when this has been accomplished by the unconditional love of the mother, the infant is returned to that experience.

Balint (1992) describes this in a similar way when he says, "the aim of all human striving is to establish—or, probably, re-establish—an all-embracing harmony with one's environment, to be able to love in peace" (p. 65). The striving of the adult to return to that state of unity could be seen as a desire to return to the moments in infancy when the child had that experience (which is how Jung described this desire), but it could also be seen as a striving to return to the original experience, especially in those cases where the child lacked the necessary reassimilation of the primal experience.

Fordham (1979) goes on to ask this question:

> But is there a persistent period in the life of an infant that can be called primary narcissism? The idea that states of satisfaction, of unity, fusion or bliss have their root in a natural "stage" in the early life of an infant is very persistent. The idea that there is a stage in infancy when there is no conflict because there is no ego and the mother's provision is so good that there is no conflict and the infant is always satisfied, is elaborated by Neumann as the "primal relationship." (p. 27).

I do not believe there is such a stage either, except for the infant in utero; after birth, there is a recreation of the womb experience, which comes and goes for the most part, and appears necessary for the development of the ego. The experience of the ego being returned to soul and back to ego appears to be a cycle necessary in infancy, childhood, and possibly throughout adult life. A stage is reached that embraces both positions and the opposites are united, which is possibly the method nature intended for healthy psychological functioning; when it does not occur, neurosis and pathology become apparent. If the soul is the archetype that connects the conscious to the unconscious, the "system" does not come into being at random, but probably is fully in place from the beginning of life. The psychological function that the soul archetype represents is intuition. The idea of a primary state of unity persists, as Fordham states, because it is a universal experience that all humans share. The only possible explanation for this experience is the unity of the infant in the womb, and very small children who have not had this assimilated often enough in infancy can be seen as attempting to get back there, that is, to recreate the experience, any way possible.

Neumann (1973/1976) considered this primal relationship as one before birth as well as after birth. I think it is better described as the infant in the womb; after birth, the infant is brought back to that blissful experience by being loved and by having his needs met by the mother or primary caretaker. It is just this experience that reinforces the ego and leads it to believe that one can be separate, but still united, through the act of love.

Fordham (1957) continues:
> It is held that the development of the conscious in the child violates the original condition of wholeness to which more mature persons attempt to return when confronted with insurmountable difficulties. Thus the retrospective tendency met with in analysis is considered as an attempt to re-establish the primal condition of wholeness termed the original self (115).

The return to wholeness, however, would mean first a return to soul consciousness. If the soul is the bridge or the guide that leads to the Self, then it follows that the archetype of the soul would first flow out of the Self, and that this would precede ego consciousness and be necessary as a link between the Self and the ego. But Fordham appears to see the ego flowing out of the Self with no thought to the soul archetype, even though he later speaks of a progression of archetypal images where the Self is followed by the mana personalities.

The point I am trying to make is that the infant would need to return first to the soul archetype before the Self is reached, and it is just this archetype that gives a sense of unity as it was originally experienced. It is from the soul position that the Self is seen. The experience cannot always be described. It is, as Jung states, unknowable in its entirety because it depends on the uniqueness of each individual soul's experience. But it is just this experience that finds expression in art, especially for children, and later language and every form of creative expression that human beings are capable of achieving, whether in the arts, science, mythology, or religion. The soul observes the Self and returns to give form and content to that experience via art, science, and literature from the position of the ego. (This is a description of the adult; the infant creates symbols that assist him in making sense of his experience; a concept probably contains thousands of perceptions, conscious and unconscious, that are arranged and rearranged in the psyche to form a picture that becomes archetypal.) Thus, the soul looks both ways. It sees into the depths of the Self or the collective unconscious, and it returns to record what it has seen by means that are always ego-related. This is the middle position, the "bridge," that connects Self to ego and the archetype that Fordham appears to skip over in his description of the Self. Jung (1959/1938) described this bridge as: The unity of our psychic nature lies in the middle, just as the living unity of the waterfall appears in the dynamic connection between above and below" (p. 269).

Fordham (1976) states some of the views of Balint, a psychoanalyst, on primary narcissism. "In the place of primary narcissism, he substitutes primary love" (p. 52). Object-cathexis, Balint maintains, is very intense, but there are no definable objects, only a vague or nebulous experience of them which slowly comes to clear definition. (This is an excellent description of the intuitive function.) Fordham suggests that Balint supports the idea that object-cathexis before birth is possible:

> It does not, however, seem plausible to suppose that there is anything like the global object-cathexis before birth that Balint proposes. After birth there is good evidence for object-cathexis during waking periods, but only reactions to noise, thumb-sucking, swallowing amniotic fluid, etc., suggest anything like cathexis of the environment during embryonic existence (p. 52).

Balint's description of an intense object-cathexis that has no definable objects describes the essence of experience that is intuitive. Balint (1992) describes this as a "harmonious interpenetrating mix-up" (p. 66).

Piontelli (1992) also might support Balint. She saw many variations of fetus activity in the womb. If one assumes that the global (it is interesting that Balint uses the word global because this word is often used to describe the function of intuition) object-cathexis is unconscious, that is, the feeling function is unconscious because there is no ego to perceive the feeling, one can also assume that the feeling or the object-cathexis is known intuitively. If intuition is conscious in the womb, and is the only conscious function, Balint and Piontelli are right—with this difference, that what is conscious is not the adult ego, as they are inclined to believe, but the soul complex represented in the psychological function of intuition.

Balint's (1992) views, which are not discussed at length, support the work of more recent psychoanalysts, such as Piontelli (1992) who questions the possibility of mental life, ego functioning, and awareness in the fetus, and David Kay (1984), a Jungian analyst, who writes of foetal psychology and the possibility of a "rudimentary form of consciousness in utero." Using the model that I propose, one can see that these functions all exist in the form of what is usually called unconsciousness. Thinking, feeling, and sensation are merged, and from the merger, the psychological function of intuition is in operation. It is just this function that is conscious. I would question whether this state of consciousness is as faint or dim as some writers describe. It might be that this description is our view looking in from the outside and to be in the actual experience of the intuitive function, is less than "dim"; it is a "knowing" that often contains certainty beyond doubt and what Jung called "numinosity."

Balint (1992) describes this effectively as "primary love," rather than primary narcissism. After rejecting Balint's idea of a global object-cathexis before birth, Fordham (1976), states:

> Nevertheless the idea of the infant's first cathexis being active "loving" and seeking satisfactions, rather than his having to be seduced out of his primary narcissism, is in line with conclusions arrived at from infant observation and experimental data on early modes of perception (p. 52).

Both Balint and Fordham recognize that the first cathexis (at birth) is love, and active is a just description. Balint (1992, p. 69) gives an example of what he calls primary love. The Japanese have a very simple, everyday word, amaeru, which means "to wish or to expect to be loved." Balint claims that we have no equivalent simple word like this in the West, only long psychological phrases that describe something similar.

I believe that we do have such a word, although the significance has been largely ignored, and a simple one, the word Eros. What Balint is calling primary love is described in the myth of Eros. The name Eros means "demanding love," and from birth the human child demands to be loved by having its needs met. Eros and the Japanese word amaeru appear to have very close meanings. It is possible that unconditional love is the goal behind every object that the infant seeks and demands. When the "I want" has been obtained, such as food, warmth, or comfort, the infant experiences the state of "I have"; in other words, desire has been met and the infant is returned, if only momentarily, to a state of "oneness." If one sees the infant as being in a state of Eros, but defining this state as the ego that is in need, it is not difficult to say that the human child is "born loving," even if this loving is ego centered.

If love is the second or indeed, the real, object of all desire and has been supplied, Eros can be said to be closely related to death. For when the object is no longer desired, the ego or Eros has "died." Thus, the striving toward life and love would also be the striving toward "death," and the dual instincts of love and death could be seen to coexist from the beginning. But death of the ego that puts the infant back in the state of original oneness can simply mean that he or she is satisfied, he no longer desires, and this can be seen as a state of the soul or the soul complex. What is usually referred to as the death complex can be seen as the soul complex, for they have the same meaning symbolically. The child does not have to "fall back asleep" as Fordham suggests to be in this state; indeed, it is the infant who has been fed, cleaned, or cared for, and who does not want anything, but is awake, who is capable of play. Ego and soul are merged in one psyche, and joy is the natural outcome.

The child who seldom has his or her needs satisfactorily met is continuously in Eros or ego love; he or she is always hungry with a hunger that is seldom satisfied, for there might have been food provided without the real object yearned for by the infant, that of love. If the ego is injured, the soul is also injured and both are separated, just as Psyche and Eros were separated, as the myth describes. It is their reconciliation and unity that symbolizes the birth of a girl-child named Joy, and she is born in heaven as an immortal, because these two "opposites" or two kinds of consciousness, or two kinds of love, Eros or ego love, or Psyche or soul love, are united and give birth to Joy. Psychologically speaking, Eros or ego love is the conscious function of sensation, feeling, and thinking; Psyche or soul love is equivalent to the function of intuition, which Jung (quoted in Evans, 1976, p. 100) refers to as "perception by ways or means of the unconscious." Shortly thereafter, Jung says, "you cannot tell why or how, but we have a lot of subliminal perceptions, sense perceptions, and from these we probably draw a great many of our intuitions" (my emphasis, p. 102). This sentence indicates to me that Jung saw a connection between body sensations and the function of intuition. In many myths, these two states of being are often described as opposites at war: the hero and the dragon, the two brothers at war, and good and evil.

The soul can be seen as one who does not desire and love that does not want because there is nothing it does not have. It exists in the original state of oneness where thinking, feeling, and sensation are merged and unconscious, described in mythology as Paradise. This is a description of the two types of consciousness or two types of love that appear to be opposites in the human psyche. This topic will be discussed later in this research in more depth, in the interpretation of the Greek myth of Eros and Psyche, which is a myth that describes a psychological process that I would contend begins at birth and continues throughout life.

The Self, Ego and Individuation

When Fordham deviated from the idea that the infant was primarily a part of his mother, which was the attitude of Neumann and other analytical psychologists before him, he postulated the possibility of what he was to call the primary child self. Fordham (1988) states:

> While the nature of the self, according to Jung, was not all that clear, its action was usually thought of as essentially integrative. The mandala, for instance, tended to appear when the psyche was disorganised in one way or another. Thus the self seemed to introduce an organising process that centralised the personality. It could be defined as a totality, a system that combined in itself both the conscious and unconscious structures and processes. It followed that descriptions of the self involving the idea of its being an archetype are inappropriate, and I found it better to think of the self as beyond archetypes and the ego. In its original state the self was thus before consciousness, in the way analytical psychologists conceive it, and so before the psyche becomes structured into conscious and unconscious elements (pp. 24-25).

Here Fordham again appears to be describing two different archetypes, that of the Self and that of soul, without differentiating between the two. He appears to disagree with himself in the same paragraph, for at first, he says that the Self contains conscious and unconscious elements, then he states that the Self exists before consciousness. But before consciousness there was unconsciousness, which still does not define what the Self is. It seems more appropriate to stay with the description of the Self as that which contains everything or that which contains all the opposites including the soul and the ego. The soul can better be described as that archetype that contains three other archetypes merged into one, and one that does contain both consciousness and unconsciousness because intuitive consciousness is born out of the other three unconscious functions.

From these conclusions Fordham (1979) began to formulate the idea that an infant is separate from his mother, not only after birth, but also while in utero, and is an individual from the beginning:

> Applying the idea of integration means that an infant began from a state of unity—a primary unity of the self. This conception leads on to seeing a number of quite obvious facts in a way that had not been possible before because an infant was conceived, among Jungians, to be in all essential respects a part of his mother. The hypothesis of a primary self leads in quite a different direction: the foetus can be seen as essentially separate from his mother and so also can the new-born child. This being so, then coming into

relation with his mother becomes an achievement worked out gradually as maturation progresses. It begins with behaviour which involves deintegration out of his primary integrated state (p. 2).

This primary unity, however, is a psychological unity, where the four functions exist in a state of oneness, but this state is also a state of oneness with the environment, which is the mother's womb and her body, as well as the world. One cannot say that the infant is in a state of oneness that excludes the mother or the world, which is apparently what Fordham is attempting to do. To be "one with" must include the inner world, that is, the psyche of the infant in utero, as well as the outer world, which is the mother. Fordham apparently had difficulty with seeing these two opposites as united in the womb, which they must certainly be, if a primary unity is to be described in any way. His description appears to only describe the infant in a state of unity with itself.

Fordham writes extensively of the relationship of the Self and the ego and their relationship in the process of individuation, but there is little mention of the soul archetype or the soul complex, even though Jung (1964, p. 185) describes the soul as the mediator that returns the ego to the Self. In "Individuation and Ego Development," Fordham (1958) states that various analytical psychologists "all agree, following Jung, that in individuation the ego gives way to the self, which becomes a 'new centre of the personality'" (p. 59). Fordham then goes on to ask:

> But what of infants and children, who must inevitably be given some status on the thesis that the process is innate? In their case the ego develops away from the self, for the wholeness of the self is dangerous to them for reasons the exact inverse of those found in adults (p. 59).

The point that Fordham appears to be making is that the reverse is true in infancy; the ego flows out of the primary Self, a reasonable view except for one point, the archetype of soul, the mediator between the Self and the ego is not included in this premise, yet Fordham does include the possibility of this archetype being included. If we reverse this situation, which seems necessary, it can be said that infants and children innately complete the process by having the soul flow out of the Self and the ego flow out of the soul. The Self is not dangerous to the child, unless he or she never manages to leave it by the soul, but this is not possible if one sees that the child in utero is contained in soul, which is a reflection of the Self. What is dangerous for the infant is the possibility that he or she will not be returned to the soul complex after birth when the ego has come into being. The ego does not, as Fordham state, develop away from the Self; it returns to soul, where it can see the Self and then return to its ego position. The progression is circular and experienced in the moment-to-moment life of the infant, as well as day to day and year to year. To be stuck in any archetype and not having the flow of psychic movement is dangerous, not only for the child, but also for the adult.

In speaking of the archetypes in childhood Fordham, (1957) states:
> There is an obvious conclusion to be drawn from the regular progression of archetypal images in individuation: in childhood one would expect them to appear in the reverse order to that found in individuation, i.e., instead of the progression, shadow, animus, or anima, mana personalities, self, we should find the self first followed by the mana personalities, animus or anima and lastly the shadow. Search for such a progression in children is beginning to bear fruit, but the problem is difficult in infancy because the lack of ego makes the recording of images impossible and we have to rely on behaviour alone to confirm or disprove our hypothesis (p. 117).

Here I assume that the example Fordham gives of a 1-year-old child who scribbles a picture and says "I" is a progression that bears fruit, for it appears to be empirical evidence that the ego is formed at a much earlier age than what was previously accepted by psychologists.

The difficulties that Fordham mentions do not appear to be insurmountable, however, and a hypothetical model can be construed that gives information on the process. In the model that I propose, the archetypes do appear in reverse order, if one begins in the womb instead of at birth. The Self is the center, containing all, and by all, I mean unity, oneness, and the usual metaphorical definition of that word; in addition, I would state that this all contains the four psychological functions, merged and undifferentiated. Out of the Self comes God or the "mana personalities" as Fordham refers to them, animus and anima (or soul and spirit) and finally the shadow or that which is still unconscious or the child/animal archetype. These three exist as one, and in the Genesis myth are symbolized by the Golden Age of Paradise. From a psychological view, they can be seen as the functions of thinking, feeling, and sensation, which are unconscious and therefore merged and existing as one function, intuition. Thus, the first psychological function that flows out of the Self (intuition) is knowledge that we are one with God, in other words, in Paradise. This is the state, or at least it appears to be what the myth is telling us, of the child in the womb;

active thinking, feeling, and sensation, all exist in the unconscious and merged, producing that often-called "dim" state of perception called intuition. I am aware of the difficulty in proving such an abstract concept as being a possibility in the womb, but would suggest that this idea can be supported by numerous myths, not just the Judaic or Christian myth, but mythologies from around the world. Campbell (1988c) said, "When your eyes are closed to distracting phenomena, you're in your intuition, and you may come in touch with the morphology, the basic form of things" (p. 202).

Intuition can be seen as the first psychological function that contains consciousness, or one might call this state "pre-conscious," to distinguish it from what is unconscious or what is conscious. I dislike the term preconscious because it implies before consciousness; however, I would argue that it is a type of consciousness that must be distinguished from ego consciousness. Non-ego or soul consciousness is a better description. Fordham (1957) says, "In using the term preconscious Jung means to designate a state of consciousness in which the ego is very weak and the images representing unconscious vitality are highly charged with libido, i.e., are numinous" (emphasis Fordham's, pp. 107-108). This would fit my description; sometimes the ego is weak, sometimes the ego is absent altogether. The contents would certainly, as Jung described them, be numinous. The important point is to recognize that it is a state that contains knowing and a knowing that great religious leaders, mystics, and philosophers often consider the highest way of knowing. Thus, what appears to be lowest could also be seen as highest; what we had in the beginning and did not know we had (Paradise, innocence) would be the state (Paradise) to which we desire to return, symbolized by the myths of rebirth, and a second birth. This state, however, would necessarily be different, for it would contain ego consciousness (knowledge) of our original innocence, which was a knowing or a consciousness that existed without the ego. In the first state, we would know without knowing that we know; in the second state, we would know that we know. There would be no tension of the opposites because they would be united if a return to Paradise or what I would call a return to the intuitive function or soul consciousness has been achieved.

Ryce-Menuhin (1988) appears to be describing something very similar to the idea of intuition as a way of knowing when he writes:

> In my view there is a fourth knowing, or a consciousness in which knowing is not known or transformed to cognitive knowing. If behaviour does not become an object of another behaviour by the same actor it is less than conscious or unconscious, but one can

none the less speak of it as a knowing, or at least as a ground of knowing. This fourth level, a ground of knowing or being, is not a higher level of cognitive judgment but may relate to a ground of self-experience that intuitively includes unconscious and conscious self-integrates in its psychological resonance. Both Jung and Fordham have clinically elaborated a possible psychotic core of experiential influence of the self, thought of not only empirically but experientially as "beyond experience," that is, in the totality-of-self. My theory of a fourth level of knowing that is not dual or cognitive clarifies the sense that every experience is a partial experience of mind's total nature and activity, or totality-of-self (p. 169).

This is an excellent description of the function of intuition; it is not dual or cognitive, but contains the other three modes of knowing within itself in unconsciousness that is also conscious in the form of intuitive knowing. In other words, as Ryce-Menuhin states, it contains both consciousness and unconsciousness. What Ryce-Menuhin, a Jungian analyst in developmental psychology, describes as "my theory of a fourth level of knowing" is not, however, something new that he has suddenly discovered; Jung gave the function of intuition an equal billing when he included it in the four basic psychological functions, a fact that Ryce-Menuhin and Fordham before him tend to overlook. Part of the problem is understanding the function of intuition, about which Jung (quoted in Evans, 1976) said, "and intuition—there is a difficulty because you don't know ordinarily how intuition works" (p. 100). It works automatically when the ego withdraws, in whole or part, from conscious sensation, feeling or thinking. It works in small, everyday ways like knowing in advance who is calling when the phone rings; it works in larger ways, like Einstein's theory of relativity, which he first saw in an "intuitive flash," or in the way that Bucke (1948) described when he referred to cosmic consciousness:

> The philosophy of the birth of cosmic consciousness in the individual is very similar to that of the birth of self consciousness. The mind becomes overcrowded (as it were) with concepts and these are constantly becoming larger, more numerous and more and more complex; someday (the conditions being all favorable) the fusion, or what might be called the chemical union, of several of them and of certain moral elements takes place; *the result is an intuition and the establishment of the intuitional mind, or, in other words, cosmic consciousness* (emphasis mine, p. 18).

The self consciousness that Bucke refers to is what we would call ego consciousness. He saw a similarity in their "birth" although he did not entertain the idea that they might originate simultaneously (or appear to do so) and operate in rhythm from the beginning, mainly because he saw intuition as an acquired function that evolved in the race in the same way that he thought simple consciousness and self consciousness evolved. Simple consciousness can be equated with the ego function of sensation and self consciousness can be equated with the ego function of thinking. The feeling function or what Bucke referred to as the moral nature was the most important function for the development of cosmic consciousness. Bucke is correct in believing that it is feeling that returns the infant to the soul or intuitive consciousness. This is probably also often true in the case of an adult. If the feeling is conscious and intense, the thought exists equally powerful in the unconscious. In that case, both functions would be working at the same time, one conscious and one unconscious. The reverse would be equally true. If the thought is conscious and the feeling intense but unconscious, the result would be the same. In other words, either function might return an adult to an intuitive state in the way that Bucke describes. But in the infant, it is the feeling function because active thinking is unconscious in the very beginning.

There is little doubt that Bucke saw cosmic consciousness as the result of the intuitive function. Throughout his work he attempts to show what it is and how it is acquired. Bucke describes Walt Whitman, his idol and close friend as referring to cosmic consciousness as "my soul." Yet, it does not seem likely that one's soul would be the product of evolution; what would appear more likely is the possibility that the evolution would be in consciousness itself. This would imply soul consciousness, the archetype that represents the instinct of intuition, which is in the psyche from the beginning. Cosmic consciousness is another name for the Self archetype. Yet another name is Being, which describes Being one with God.

Fordham, Jung, and the Genesis Hypothesis

At this point, I would like to briefly recapitulate my hypothesis, which is based on Jung's four psychological functions and show how I think these concepts can be linked to Fordham's theory of deintegrates, mainly concerning the unborn child.

My hypothesis assumes that from the beginning of life at conception and during the approximately 9 months in the womb, the unborn human child

Everything that the human race has done and thought is concerned with the satisfaction of deeply felt needs and the assuagement of pain. One has to keep this constantly in mind if one wishes to understand spiritual movements and their development. Feeling and desire are the motive forces behind all human endeavor and human creation, in however exalted a guise the latter may present itself to us.

(Albert Einstein, The World as I see it, 1979, p. 24)

contains within itself the potential for all the psychological functions which are present and individual from the beginning. Since thinking, feeling, and sensation all appear to be unconscious and undifferentiated, I am also making the assumption that they exist as one psychological function, intuition, which is necessarily conscious in the womb and can be called the soul complex. At birth, there is a major change and by the process of enantiodromia (Jung, 1971/1921, p. 426) the extreme position of intuitive or soul consciousness, which prevailed in the womb, is changed to one of consciousness, where the ego, especially the ego that is connected and related to the body, begins to function and uses from the beginning the functions of sensing, feeling, and thinking. The soul complex or intuitive function recedes and has much the same position that the other three functions had in the womb. It is usually called unconscious, although it also contains consciousness. The soul is the middle position and the complex to which the ego, which has just begun, returns, and from that position is connected to the undifferentiated Self and the conscious ego. The newborn child now lives in a state where consciousness and unconsciousness are present, and at the moment of birth they are equally present and begin to function together. With ego and body consciousness present in the form of conscious sensation and conscious feeling, the functions of intuition and thinking form the personal unconscious. Intuition becomes the fourth function to appear at birth, which makes it identical with the first function that appeared in the womb. The intuitive function or soul complex is not entirely unconscious, but different, as Hillman previously stated, from ego consciousness.

Ryce-Menuhin (1988) states the following: "Fordham argues that the development of consciousness in the child violates an original condition of wholeness and postulates, theoretically, a primary integrated state at birth" (p. 55). Fordham never states for certain when he thought consciousness actually started and his views appear to fluctuate and change over the years. How could the child be integrated at birth, if it is consciousness or the ego that disrupts the integrated state? If it is not ego that disrupts the Self and creates consciousness, what is it? Sometimes Fordham attributes ego consciousness to the infant at birth and sometimes he does not, but the point he appeared to be defending was that the child is separate and an individual from the beginning. He starts his theory with this assumption and states that the infant is in an integrated state at birth.

Fordham (1976) states:
> The primal self can be conceived as an integrate, a steady state,
> but if the dynamic systems that we observe later on are to come

into existence, it must deintegrate. According to current theory of analytical psychology the self combines opposites within itself; therefore we may assume that when the self deintegrates it will divide into opposites that are psycho-physiological in nature. We may assume, following Jung's theory of psychic energy, that the energy bound in the primary self is neutral and divides into creative and later loving activities on the one hand, destructive and aggressive ones on the other. Each drive follows a partly predetermined pattern and is directed towards objects (p. 12).

Certainly, the energy bound in the Self appears to be neutral, as Fordham claims, and divides into opposites that are psychophysiological in nature, but the division is not one of loving activities on the one hand and destructive and aggressive ones on the other hand, as Fordham describes. This description is too simplistic in giving a value judgment of good or bad to what has been created by the division of the Self. The word "division" is subject to question, because the Self really does not stay divided, it creates the soul and the ego complexes, both of which contain new opposites within each complex. The soul complex can be seen as the psychological part of the psychophysiological duo, whereas the ego complex can be seen as the physiological part of this combination. In his description of the deintegration of the Self, Fordham leaves out the soul archetype, a crucial omission, because the instinctual psychic energy that it represents is the intuitive function that Jung so rightly described as essential to the individuating process.

Fordham earlier says that the primary Self is disrupted by birth, which I would take to mean that in the womb the Self is whole or unified and separate from the mother, and it is birth that disrupts this steady state. This is identical to my theory that the child in the womb lives in a state of wholeness that I am equating with the psychological function of intuition or the soul complex, because the soul is a reflection of the Self. What Fordham calls "prototypic anxiety" (desire) would be the first deintegrative. He places it right after birth, which supports my idea that ego or ego consciousness creates the loss of soul consciousness. With the first experience of the opposites, the soul complex becomes temporarily unconscious.

Fordham calls this the "psyche-soma," which is identical to what I would call the soul (intuition) and body (ego) consciousness that begins with body sensation that is conscious and conscious feeling that makes value judgments). When the "psyche-soma" deintegrates, the infant can be seen to be aware (consciously) of body sensations and how he or she feels about them; functions that were contained in the state of soul or intuitive consciousness have become conscious or deintegrated. When these disturbances have been rectified or the needs of the child satisfied, he or she returns to an integrated state of unity, as Fordham describes, only there will be this difference: The unity then experienced will be in the world, not in the womb, as it was in the beginning of life. The child is satisfied and probably returns to sleep, which Fordham compares with the original state of the Self, but I believe that he equates that state too much with sleep, which is not always the case, and he suggests that the state of unity is also disturbed in the uterus when the fetus is awake and responding to stimuli from within or without. But if the unity is disturbed in the uterus, how could a steady state of integration in the womb be possible?

Fordham (1970) gives a description of the child in utero:

> Whilst in utero, there is minimal exteroceptive sensory stimulation. Increase in knowledge of intra-uterine behaviour reveals, however, that some of the activities in which the foetus engages are responses to stimuli such as noise reaching it from outside its mother's body. There are also signs of muscular activity, besides arm and leg movements; thumb-sucking, swallowing amniotic fluid and breathing "exercises" that take place during intra-uterine life. All these show that disturbances in the unitary state occur whether they be stimulated by sensory stimuli or by spontaneous discharges from within the nervous system. But in spite of all these the predominant state of the embryo and foetus is quiescence and something very much like sleep. If we take the infant's intra-uterine life as sleeping and his emergence into the world as the prototype of waking, the cycle repeats throughout life (p. 111).

Fordham hints here that deintegration takes place in the womb, but he does not elaborate on this interesting thought. Obviously, he thought of integration as occurring primarily in sleep, which is possibly true in early infancy, but not entirely, for if that were so, the infant or the adult would have to go to sleep to be in soul consciousness. This is certainly not the case, although one may be closer to that state of consciousness in one's dreams than in waking life. Dreams, however, can become conscious and their content known and expressed. There comes a time when the infant does not experience bodily needs and is wide awake, and this could be in the first few hours of life. If the infant has been returned to what I have previously called an assimilation of the original experience, which Fordham calls reintegration, often enough, his or her ego would be made stronger, but ego and soul could be seen to be working together. What Fordham calls reintegration, I would call returning to soul or intuitive consciousness. What he attributes to deintegration, I would call related, in the same way he describes, to ego consciousness. But the ego cannot come apart without creating its shadow side, which is the soul.

I am not distinguishing between bits of ego consciousness, although that is certainly legitimate; but I think it becomes easier to see the whole by assuming that ego begins at birth in the form of body sensations, and there are many theorists in psychology who share this view, although it continues to be debated.

The first archetype to become conscious after birth would be the ego archetype, which is related to the psychological functions of conscious sensation, feeling, and thinking. When the ego is born, so also is the shadow, because what was previously conscious in the soul complex disappears into shadow or becomes unconscious; when the infant is in the soul complex, it is the ego that is in shadow or unconscious. The second archetype to become conscious after birth, and there is consciousness even in sleep, is the soul archetype, which returns the infant to the psychological function of intuition, which Jung often referred to as the function that was closest to the unconscious. It is from the soul archetype that the Self is seen and expressed by the ego. This archetype, as Jung describes, is attached to consciousness and to the unconscious. It stands in the middle, looking both ways.

Fordham (1976) states:
> At one time I suggested that the order in which they (archetypes) appeared in maturation was the reverse of that in adults, especially those in later life. Since nothing more has developed from this idea, I do not think it can be decided whether it be true or false (p. 29).

I have previously quoted Fordham's earlier statement concerning the possibility that the archetypes might appear in reverse order (1957, p. 117). I think that he was correct in his assessment, although he didn't appear to realize that he was also describing the soul archetype when he talked of integrates or integration. He did not always believe the ego began at birth and so did not always equate deintegration with the emerging ego at birth, although he does, of course, assume that the ego eventually deintegrates from the Self.

Looked at more broadly, I believe Fordham describes two archetypes, ego and soul, without realizing it. Jung describes the progression of the archetypes in adulthood one should first approach before reaching the Self: First, the ego, then the shadow, then the soul, and finally the Self. The reverse would be true in infancy: first, the Self, then the soul, then the shadow, then the ego. The Self and the soul archetypes would be present in the womb; at birth, the soul and the ego would be present alternately with the shadow because the shadow represents whichever archetype is not in consciousness. A multitude of other archetypes could come under these headings, such as anima (soul) and animus (spirit) or numerous other opposites like the "Divine Syzygy," but the point is that they can be seen, as Fordham described, in reverse order. Out of the Self flows the soul, followed by the shadow and the ego, archetypes that probably appear in quick succession. One could also say that two shadows exist, one dark and one white. When the ego is in a state of desire or deintegrating, as Fordham would say, what has been unconscious becomes conscious, but what remains in the unconscious is what was loss. When opposites come into play, they always have a shadow side.

Fordham (1988, p. 26) undervalued the concept of fusion with the mother and the symbolism inherent in mythology that there is an ideal state equal to Paradise. It is the mother or mother substitute, who helps the baby to reintegrate and return to an experience that simulates the original experience of unity. To that extent, she could certainly be seen as *the soul of the infant*, who has been manifested in the world, and the vehicle that will carry the infant back to a place where she exists as one with him in his psyche as he existed as one with her in her body. If the primal child Self that Fordham described is identical with the Self that Jung described, it is a Self united with God and the world, which certainly could be seen metaphorically as Paradise, a concept that Fordham was never able to accept. Yet, he gives no clear definition of his concept of a child-self that is unified. One has to speculate on what kind of unity Fordham's definition of Self described; to say that it is not knowable is justified, but unity is a symbol that can be imagined and described. The child can be seen as an individual from the beginning without destroying the idea of its being also part of the mother, because it is always in relationship to the mother from conception to birth as well as after birth. Indeed, the personal mother will help to create the archetypal experience of the infant, both positive and negative. The first deintegration may evoke the negative mother (witch) archetype very early in the child's life. Neumann (1973/1976) understood that:

> the primal relationship is the foundation of all subsequent dependencies, relatedness and relationships. Whereas dual union is guaranteed by nature in the uterine embryonic phase, *it emerges after birth as the first need of the mammal and especially of the human child* (emphasis mine, p. 17).

Neumann is saying that there must be an "other" in the world to hold and contain the human child and who, by loving the child, leads him or her to a place of oneness that subsequently allows the child to be separate. The experience of fusion that Fordham (1988, p. 29) says is an idealized fantasy which cannot be maintained over long periods, is simply a state of being loved, and the experience does not need to be maintained forever: If it is only known and believed, the effect will last forever. If fusion is a fantasy, then the idea that "I love" and "I am loved" must also be a fantasy, which I doubt. Love always ends in fusion because subject and object cancel each other by loving; fusion is just another word for one.

The first experience of the infant and mother at birth can also be seen and understood by Jung's definitions of introversion and extraversion or psychic energy that moves toward or away from the object. Although Fordham discusses transference in older children, there is no mention of it in early infancy. It is not likely that transference begins at random.

Many of Fordham's interpretations of mythology, which he mostly only briefly mentions, seem misguided, especially concerning the myth of Paradise. His concepts of integration and deintegration, however, are valuable contributions to psychology, especially if one assumes that the first integration is in the womb and the first deintegration is at birth. He had difficulty making the leap from the child in utero to the child at birth, and his uncertainty was often related to not placing the ego at birth. Even so, his contribution to Jungian psychology is invaluable because he surmised that children are capable of individuation and analysis, and in a pragmatic, intelligent manner, showed how this was possible. He cared about the archetype of child, but more than that, he cared about the experience of the actual, living child.

I have attempted in the previous pages to show how the hypothesis offered in this research, based on Jung's concepts of psychological functions, can be linked with the concepts of Michael Fordham, and I would like to end this chapter with my original question: Does an order of Jung's psychological functions exist? I believe that an order does exist and that the first psychological function is intuition, which begins in the womb and can also be described as the soul complex, which contains the other three functions in unconscious and undifferentiated form. By looking at Jung's description of the functions in this manner, it is possible to see aspects of mythology, religion, developmental psychology, and Jungian psychology in general in a way that connects them and allows one to see that art or the archetype is always a reflection of living, psychic experience that is not separate from the body, but dependent upon the substance of which we are composed. Body, soul, and spirit exist as one in every human individual and the knowing is psychological wholeness; the knowing is going home—a return to Paradise.

Returning briefly to Jung (1959/1955, p. 4) and his description of the mandala as an archetype of wholeness and the importance of the "quaternity of the One," I would like to show how the idea of intuition as the first psychological function relates to Jung's description of what he considered *the most important archetype*. He states:

> *Because of this significance, the "quaternity of the One" is the schema for all images of God, as depicted in the visions of Ezekiel, Daniel, and Enoch, and as the representation of Horus with his four sons also shows.* The latter suggests an interesting differentiation, inasmuch as there are occasionally representations in which three of the sons have animals' heads and only one a human head, in keeping with the Old Testament visions as well as with the emblems of the seraphim which were transferred to the evangelists, and—last but not least—with the nature of the Gospels themselves: three of which are synoptic and one "Gnostic." Here I must add that, ever since the opening of Plato's Timaeus ("One, two, three . . . but where, my dear Socrates, is the fourth?") and right up to the Cabiri scene in *Faust, the motif of four as three and one was the ever-recurring preoccupation of alchemy.* (emphasis mine, p. 4).

What Jung so adequately described as being the most important archetype of wholeness, the motif of four as three and one or, the Maria Axiom, is exactly what I am describing in this research when I say that intuition is the function that contains the other three functions plus itself to equal four which is one. This idea can be seen as the key to my interpretation of psychic energy personified by the archetypes and other symbols of mythology and religion, not only of Christianity, but many other divergent cultures. I believe that an interpretation of the cosmological mythology will support the theoretical hypothesis I have given concerning the infant in the womb and the infant at birth.

Jung described the mandala as the most important archetype of wholeness. This is probably because it describes the first living experiences of the human child from the Paradisical unity in the womb to the first experience of a negative opposite in the form of desire, to the experience of a positive opposite of no-desire that occurs when ego demands are met and back to a recapitulation of the original womb experience. The opposites have been lived and experienced in the world and time, whereas in the womb, they were merged and experienced as Paradisical and eternal. Time and eternity are expressed in the simple, abstract circle or mandala. Its multiple variations express that primary, universal, and important experience.

All the images that Jung describes above in mythology and religion can be seen as psychic and instinctual energy that is expressed by archetypal form. The four psychological functions enable us to see first, the separation of this energy; second, the relationship between the energy patterns; and third, the synthesis of the energy patterns and functions to produce psychological wholeness.

I will attempt in the subsequent chapters to support these ideas by interpretations of Sumerian cosmology and symbols, the archetype of the Fallen Angel, the Divine Child archetype, the Divine Mother archetype, the Divine Father archetype and the Hero archetype. I will also interpret the mythology of the four Archangels: Michael, Uriel, Raphael, and Gabriel, the first and second (lost Paradise) creation mythology of Genesis, American Indian symbolism, and other related mythological references.

The mythologies contain the archetypes, the living expressions of all human experiences that began as basic instincts derived from a single source, the ineffable mystery of the Self.

Chapter 3

First Prelude to Genesis:

Antecedent Archetypes That Describe Basic Psychic Energy and the Four Functions

In Chapter 3, I will briefly identify, compare, and interpret cosmological, archetypal images concerning the mythology of ancient Sumer. The first image discussed is the fourfold structured myth of the creation gods of ancient Sumer: Enki, Enlil, Ki, and An, who can be compared with the Father God, the Serpent, Eve, and Adam in Genesis. Both cosmologies can be seen as personifications of the four psychological functions of intuition, sensation, feeling, and thinking, in their conscious, introverted form. Nammu, the Sumerian mother goddess who precedes the four creating gods (actually three gods and one goddess) can be equated with the Void or Chaos (feminine) archetype, which also antecedes the creation in Genesis. Nammu, called the Primal Sea, and the Void archetypes can both be compared with the archetype of the Self in analytical psychology. I suggest that these five significant cosmological archetypes, in each mythology, are a metaphorical description of the four psychological functions as they differentiate out of the Self, and describe the universal, phenomenological experience of the individual child, as consciousness and unconsciousness begin.

Another related Sumerian cosmological archetype worthy of note is the art image of the Serpent Lord (see Campbell, 1964, p. 10). The Serpent Lord image, which contains two twin images, that of twin serpents and twin lion-birds, is seen as a variation of the Sumerian cosmogony and describes the same process of individuation. The two sets of twins can be seen as the two sets of primal parents in the Sumerian cosmological material, both describing the birth of the hero archetype, the sensate ego. The Sumerian archetypes are comparable with similar personifications in Genesis, which also contain two sets of primal parents: first, as the Divine Void and the Divine Father God, and second, as Eve and Adam, our "human" parents. The tragic Hero archetype in Genesis is the Serpent, the bringer of light or consciousness and the bringer of darkness or unconsciousness. The dual Parents in all three images can be seen as personifications of the Self (Void) and Soul function of intuition (Father God) archetypes (the Primal Parents) as they give "birth" to the ego archetype, in the function of conscious, introverted sensation (tragic hero). The second set of parents (Eve and Adam) are the rational functions of conscious introverted feeling and thinking.

I will also discuss Lucifer, the Fallen Angel archetype, as Hebrew mythology that preceded and is related to the myth of Genesis. I suggest that the myth of Lucifer is describing a biological and psychological experience that is similar to the Sumerian cosmology that preceded it and that the later Genesis symbolism continues the myth. The Fallen Angel archetype can be seen in what I have described as level three, the biological level and creation of the human child. Simultaneously it describes the psychological process of the soul and ego complexes as the functions of intuition and sensation differentiate (fall) from the Self.

The Divine Child archetype, the surface layer of the story, can be seen in what I have described as level one. Moses, as author of Genesis, and representative of the Divine/human Child and Hero archetype, will also be briefly discussed.

Sumerian Archetypes and Symbols as Personifications of Archetypal Energy Patterns

Campbell (1976) states the following:
> In the iconography of the earliest centers of civilization, the Sumerian cities of riverine Mesopotamia, which flourished c. 3500-2000 B. C. and brought into being the symbolic order of the hieratic city state, is to be seen the common source of both the Oriental and the Occidental mythological visions of the universe (p. 242).

The roots of the Genesis cosmology appear to be intertwined with the ancient Sumerian vision of the universe and had their beginning in the same soil. Elsewhere, Campbell (1964, pp. 16-17) describes numerous images and archetypes of Sumerian origin, antecedent to the archetypes in Genesis by at least several thousand years. Campbell suggests that the Creation/Paradise myths in Genesis utilize the same archetypes, and many were borrowed from earlier Sumerian mythology.

"The Hebrew story of creation parallels the Sumerian account of "The Huluppu-Tree" in many ways" (Wolkstein and Kramer, 1983, p. 144). The twin trees in Paradise and the Sumerian Huluppu-tree symbol appear to be describing the same psychic experience in a slightly modified form. "For both cultures the tree represents the first living thing on earth" (Wolkstein and Kramer, 1983, p. 145). I suggest that the tree, in both cultures, symbolizes the human spinal column, which forms early in the living fetus and can be seen as "the first living thing on earth." Wolkstein and Kramer (1983) state the following:

> The tree also provides for both cultures a configuration of the forces of life and death and consciousness and lack of knowledge. It may be that the powers of the biblical trees in the center of the Garden of Eden, the Tree of Life and the Tree of Knowledge of Good and Evil, are based on the joined powers of the Sumerian Huluppu-tree (p. 145).

Both mythologies, I would add, attempt to describe how conscious and unconscious sense perceptions, that is, intuition and sensation, work as separate functions that have a common source.

"One of the great puzzles of biology is the question of how each cell knows what it is to become" (Nilsson, 1993, p. 77). I suggest that this "knowledge" has often been attributed to God in the mythological literature, symbolizing the instinctual function of intuition. Since it is still a great puzzle in modern biology, one can understand the difficulty of cultures existing thousands of years ago, attempting to answer the same question. Their answer appears contained in the metaphorical descriptions of human origin, awaiting a biological interpretation. Although this sort of interpretation does not appear as part of the collective consciousness of modern society, it does appear in descriptions such as the following by Jordan Peterson:

> Tree and serpent, coupled and singly, have an extensive, pervasive, and detailed history as symbolic agents. They serve similar functions in a multitude of myths describing the loss of paradise, and must therefore serve as apt representatives of some process or structure playing a central part in that loss. It appears that this structure is the nervous system, as it manifests itself in intrapsychic representation (1995, p. 12).

The "tree" grows in the human mind and body and is necessarily part of the nervous system. The process that it represents symbolically is birth and two forms of consciousness, ego and soul, which ends the Paradise of the womb experience.

One important distinction that many of the stories appear to have in common is a descent or fall-from-grace theme. I interpret this important theme as an attempt of the authors to describe the transition from the womb, symbolized by Paradise, to the experience of the opposites, as consciousness and unconsciousness are differentiated from the Self. The myths appear to be describing a circular process that takes place in the human psyche and body, the eternal return of psychic energy that is also biological, human experience.

Campbell (1976) describes the Sumerian goddess, Nammu:

> Dr. Samuel Kramer has shown through comparative studies of innumerable Sumerian tablets in the libraries of Europe, the Near East, and America, that the goddess Nammu, whose name is written with the pictograph for "primeval sea," was the ultimate "mother," who gave birth to Heaven and Earth, and that these two were pictured in the single form of a cosmic mountain, the base of which, hovering above the watery abyss, was the bottom of the earth, while its summit was heaven's zenith. The lower portion, Earth (Ki), was female, and the upper, Heaven (An), a male; so that their nature was again that of the dual primordial being we already know (p. 108).

Nammu is the Sumerian Serpent Queen archetype, an older version of the tail-eating uroboros, but appears to represent the same energy of the undivided Self. She divides (while staying herself) into Twin Serpents, who become Enki, her Serpent lover and Enlil, her Serpent child. Neumann (1949/1954) describes the same division when he says: "The uroboros as a ring-snake, for instance the Babylonian Tiamat and Chaos Serpent, or the Leviathan who, as the ocean, "twines his girdle of waves about the lands, later divides, or is divided, into two" (p. 49). Psychologically speaking, the two that Nammu, as a Self representation, becomes the functions of intuition, her Serpent Lord Enki, and sensation, or Enlil, her Serpent Child. Thus, there are three psychological archetypes here, Nammu as the Self, Enki as the soul, and Enlil as the nascent ego.

Neumann (1949/1954) goes on to describe the C archetype: "when the Great Mother assumes human form, the masculine part of the uroboros—the snake-like phallus-demon—appears beside her as the residuum of the originally bisexual nature of the uroboros" (p. 49). And this is exactly what happens in the Sumerian cosmology; after taking the form of Enlil, Nammu takes the form of Ki, the Earth goddess, equivalent to Eve in Genesis. Nammu also becomes An, the Sky god and mate to Ki. Before Nammu becomes Ki, however, she mates with her spouse Enki, the god of the Waters, and together they give birth to Enlil, the god of Air. Nammu's Serpent child is the god of Air, Enlil, a Serpent Lord, equivalent to the Serpent in Paradise.

Thus, Enlil has two sets of primal parents, the first set being Nammu and Enki (both symbols of the primal water and birth) and the second set being Ki and An or Heaven and Earth. The description of dual parents gives Enlil a special importance as a Divine male Child/Hero archetype. Enlil, or the function of conscious sensation, is the male child/hero who separates the World Parents.

The undifferentiated Self, personified as Nammu in Sumerian mythology and the Void in Genesis, and the soul, personified as Enki, the Father God of Sumer and the Father God of Genesis, are the first primal parents who give birth to the ego, personified as Enlil. The second set of parents to Enlil are An and Ki, Heaven and Earth, and they are considered the creating gods in Sumerian mythology, while their equivalent in Genesis are the fallen Adam and Eve, our first human parents. An and Ki, Adam and Eve, are personifications of the conscious, rational, introverted functions of thinking and feeling.

Consciousness does not rise up like an island from the sea of unconsciousness, dividing into the island and the sea or only two that are no longer one. Consciousness and unconsciousness arise simultaneously out of the primal sea of undifferentiation, which might better be described as twins born from the same mother. The Self is the Mother, one twin is (soul) consciousness and the other twin is (ego) consciousness. Or, before the soul becomes undifferentiated further, they are seen as the son/lover, in the Sumerian mythology and other myths with that symbolism. The Self, or Great Mother archetype, remains undifferentiated energy.

Nammu, the Self, who was in a state of total undifferentiation, reflects Enki, the Father God, who symbolizes nascent consciousness (intuition), showing the equilibrium of undifferentiation has been changed or moved. Enki represents the ego in its primal form—soul consciousness—which is passive thinking, or the function of conscious intuition. Conscious intuition is the function out of which all conscious sense perceptions flow and as such, can be identified as unconscious body sensations of the human child. In the myths, conscious body sensations are seen as the Serpent Lord Enlil, or the Serpent of Genesis. In Genesis, conscious sensation is the Serpent, who has as his unconscious and dark side, the Father God, who has been "lost" at birth.

Enki is represented as Father/Son god, who still contains the all as one in the one differentiated function of intuition. This is an important distinction and the same energy that is described in the Genesis myth. Out of the primal sea, the void archetype in Genesis, comes consciousness and unconsciousness, the god and the goddess, still merged but distinguished from Nammu, the void or the Self. The Father God of both religions now becomes the container rather than the contained. Self and Soul are mirror images of one another.

Enki is the Serpent King, mate to Nammu, the Serpent Queen. The snake symbolism represents the world of primal instinct. Jung (1956/1912) calls the snake "representative of the world of instinct, especially of those vital processes which are psychologically the least accessible of all" (p. 396). That is probably why the Sumerians and numerous other people repeatedly use the snake as an archetype for cosmological material, and why it personifies the Self, the soul or the ego in their primal form. As a primal creature that renews itself by shedding its skin, which symbolizes rebirth, it is an excellent symbol of transformation. It can also be seen as an important archetype that represents the process of individuation as the instinctual life energy and the beginning of the four functions. As the initial instinct of super consciousness, we can understand how intuition is represented in the mythology as the creating Father God, with sensation as the Child God or deceiving serpent, depending on the myth.

The Earth Mother Goddess Ki and Earth Mother of all the living, Eve, represent the function of feeling, which, "allies itself with every sensation" (Jung, 1971/1921, p. 434). In this case, sensation would be the Serpent, either Enlil or the Serpent of Eden. On a psychological level, the numerous representations of the woman and the snake can be seen as representations of the functions of feeling and sensation in their conscious and introverted form. The appearance of Ki or Eve can be seen as the further differentiation of the functions as they separate from Nammu, the Void or the Self and become conscious. Eve becomes conscious before Adam in the myth of Genesis and the Serpent is already conscious (knowing) when he offers Eve the infamous apple. Eve, Ki, or the feminine principle (not any living woman) represent feeling as the first conscious, introverted rational function (in the human child) that is closely associated with the irrational function (in the human child) of conscious, introverted sensation or the snake.

Nammu, super consciousness or the Self, mates with the Father God, Enki (intuition), who is her spouse and son. Enki represents the first instinctual movement of life and the first form of consciousness, previously contained in the primal sea of undifferentiation (Self), which is not the same as total unconsciousness. In the human child, this would be the irrational and instinctual function of intuition that contains primal consciousness.

Nammu and Enki, both archetypes of the primal waters, can be seen as personifications of the same primal energy that is described in Genesis as the separation of the primal waters. Nammu is the receptive water of the feminine and Enki is the creative water of the masculine, the human sperm that is symbolized by the serpent. The serpent who is "water," who connects with the living water, is in the water of the womb. Both describe psychologically the first differentiation of the functions as intuition separates from the Self. And both describe the biological conception and separation of the human child. It is necessary to understand my interpretation of the mythology, to see the human cell and body as containing an awareness of its own. "Our bodies are composed of energy and information" (Chopra, 1993, p. 14).

Enki is the Father god, god of the Water, the god of Earth, and the god of Heaven, where he was one with Nammu. He is the Nammu's Serpent Lord and the god of Wisdom. Enki, after being awakened by Nammu and at her instruction, creates humanity out of clay (Campbell, 1976, p. 108). This is comparable with the symbolism of the Father God of Genesis, who creates Adam from the slime of the earth.

Wolkstein and Kramer (1983) describe Sumerian deities:
> The leading deities of this pantheon were the four creating gods controlling the four major components of the universe: the Sky God An; the Earth Goddess Ki, whose name was changed in the course of time to Ninhursag, Queen of the Mountain; the Air God Enlil, who gradually became the leader of the pantheon; and the Water God Enki, who also came to be designated the God of Wisdom (p. 123).

Out of Nammu or the Self, the four creating gods of Sumer are born: Enki, Enlil, Ki and An, which is the same fourfold pattern of Genesis and the archetypes of Father God, the Serpent, Eve, and Adam. "In practically all cultures, the division of the world into four, and the opposition of day and night, play an extremely important part" (Neumann, 1993, p. 108). This is what happens in the Sumerian mythology, as the four creating gods, what I consider to be the four functions in a state of conscious introversion, evoke the opposite positions that are unconscious. Light has been born and with it the unconscious or darkness, is also "born." In psychological terms, this darkness is the unconscious, extraverted side of the four functions.

Of the four creating deities and as the spouse of Nammu, Enki appears to be the most important creating Sumerian male god and can be equated with the creating Father God in Genesis. Both archetypes can be seen to personify the psychic energy of the function of intuition and subjective or introverted intuition as the first movement of creation. Like Nammu, as the primal sea, Enki is the god of water, symbolizing the undifferentiated functions that exist as one in a primal state. Enki can be seen as the soul mate of Nammu, who represents the Self. Like a twin, the image used by the Sumerians when they describe the Serpent twins, he is a mirror image, the same yet different and this difference defines the beginning of the differentiation of the functions as they flow out of the Self.

Heaven and Earth are the second set of parents to Enlil. In the Sumerian cosmology, they are Ki, the Earth goddess, and An, the god of Heaven. These two gods represent the further differentiation of the Self as the rational functions of feeling and thinking begin. Conscious thinking (Heaven) has unconscious feeling (Earth) as its mate. In other words, when thinking is conscious, feeling is unconscious, and when feeling is conscious, thinking is unconscious. Each reflects the other and both personify the conscious and the unconscious that has been divided, what Neumann (1949/1954) calls the "World Parents" (p. 103). In the Genesis myth, this energy is personified by Adam (thinking) and Eve (feeling), the first parents of humanity.

Nammu and Enki and Ki and An are the dual parents. The Divine Child that they all give birth to is unmistakably Enlil, the god of air, who separates both sets of parents, causing the ego and consciousness, as well as the soul and unconsciousness, to begin. This would describe the function of conscious sensation (Enlil) as it awakens in the human child. This is represented as Enlil, who is asleep (unconscious) when Nammu awakens him. He is Enlil while asleep, still contained in the primal parents, and Enki when he awakens (becomes conscious), thus the Serpent Lord or mate of Nammu when awake and her child/son or Enlil when asleep. Enki, as intuition, is Nammu's spouse and Enlil or sensation is Nammu's child. Finally, Enki becomes Enlil, the son that separates the first parents (the Self). This is the function of conscious, introverted sensation. Neumann (1949/1954) describes the separation of the World Parents using Egyptian mythology; the meaning appears the same:

> Space only came into being when, as the Egyptian myth puts it, the god of the air, Shu, parted the sky from the earth by stepping between them. Only then, as a result of his light-creating and space-creating intervention, was there heaven above and earth below, back and front, left and right-in other words, only then was space organized with reference to an ego (p. 108).

Shu appears to be the same archetypal energy that Enlil represents, and both gods of air can be compared with the Serpent in Genesis, who appears to have been sleeping or absent until Eve's scene at the tree.

Campbell (1976) compares Enlil with the Greek Kronos archetype: "An begot the air-god Enlil, who separated Earth and Heaven, tore them apart just as, in the well-known Classical myth of Hesiod, Gaia (Earth) and Uranos (Heaven) were separated by their son Kronos (Saturn)" (p. 108). A numerous pantheon was born in the Greek myth, just as the Sumerian pantheon comes into being with Enlil. The pantheon can be seen as symbolizing the numerous and powerful conscious sense perceptions of the human child. Enlil or Kronos (conscious sensation) will lead the group.

An inversion can be seen at this point. In the Sumerian religion, Enlil is seen as a beneficial, divine creating son/child/god. He is twin Serpent to Enki, the Father God, the same but different, which describes the process of differentiation and the transformation that takes place as one function becomes two functions. In the Hebrew religion that followed, the same energy is seen as opprobrious, as the Serpent in the Garden who deceives humanity and causes the loss of Paradise. The inversion of the Hebrew mythology, however, occurs again in Christianity, where Enlil has his counterpart in the Christ archetype. Like Enlil, who is twin Serpent to the Father God and the spouse/lover of Nammu, Christ announces that he is the Son and one with the Father God. The Virgin Mary is Mother to the Son and Mother to the Father God, since they are one, in the same way that Nammu is Mother to Enki and at the same time Mother to Enlil.

Neumann (1949/1954) describes the transition of Mother and Child as twin Serpents who later become the Madonna and the Christ Child, as something that develops over time. He states:

> The fully human end-figure, the human Madonna with the human child, has her forerunner in figures of the human mother with her companion snake in the form of a child or a phallus, as well as in figures of the human child with the big snake (p. 49).

What appears to have changed, from the Sumerians, to the Hebrews, to the Christians, was the perception of psychic energy or the function of conscious, introverted sensation as positive or negative. Genesis describes the loss of oneness with God, life as now separate from God, while Sumerian and Christian mythology describe the creative potential of energy that is like God or a Child of God or equal as a creating God. This is a description of the differentiation of energy from two perspectives, two opposite views that can be seen as having a common source on a depth level.

The symbolism of the feminine principle, energy that flows out of Nammu, becomes the Earth goddess Ki, Queen of the Mountain. As an Earth Mother archetype, Ki can be compared with Eve and both represent the differentiated function of feeling, specifically introverted feeling (desire) that has become conscious, leaving its opposite of "no desire" in the unconscious. This is the creative energy of the introverted (subjective) feeling function.

The sky god An is also a Father archetype and can be compared with Adam in Genesis. Both represent the function of introverted, conscious thinking. An and Enki are the two "father" archetypes in Sumer; Adam and The Father God of Genesis are the two "fathers" in Genesis. Adam is the first human father; God is the Heavenly Father. Rational, conscious, introverted thinking is the first function to give birth or create; irrational, introverted, conscious intuition is the first function to stir in the body of the human child as primal instinct. God is the instinct that creates the archetype (Adam) in His image.

With the birth of consciousness in each of the rational functions, unconsciousness is also born, separating Heaven and Earth or creating the functions of feeling and thinking. These two opposites are portrayed in the Sumerian myth as the Lion-birds. Thinking and feeling and their alternating rhythms of consciousness and unconsciousness are one twin Lion-bird. The functions of feeling and thinking are opposites that in this symbol are joined as one powerful animal. In the Sumerian mythology, they are An and Ki or Heaven and Earth, separate archetypes when apart and mates when joined, which describes consciousness and unconsciousness in the thinking and feeling functions in the same way.

Sensation and intuition, with the same oscillating rhythm, are the irrational functions that compose the other twin Lion-bird. Enki and Enlil, or intuition and sensation, like the Father God and the Serpent in Genesis, have been separated but are still joined in the image of one robust animal who contains both consciousness and unconsciousness and the power of both. The Lion-birds are personified as puissant, fabulous creatures whose primary task appears to be guarding and protecting the twin serpents and the open doors that lead back to Paradise or the Self. The guard/protector symbolism may describe the necessity of maintaining both the irrational and the rational functions in a balanced state. At the same time, they depict the process of differentiation out of the Self.

The Serpent Twin image describes what I believe to be the same archetypal pattern contained in the cosmological image of the four creating gods of Sumer. Campbell (1964) describes the ancient image of the Serpent Lord:

> There is in the Louvre a carved green steatite vase, inscribed c. 2025 B.C. by King Gudea of Lagash, dedicated to a late Sumerian manifestation of this consort of the goddess, under his title Ningizzida, "Lord of the Tree of Truth." Two copulating vipers, entwined along a staff in the manner of the caduceus of the Greek god of mystic knowledge and rebirth, Hermes, are displayed through a pair of opening doors, drawn back by two winged dragons of a type known as the lion-bird (p. 9).

The winged dragons or lion-birds, which are equivalent to cherubs or angels (see Campbell, 1964, p. 12), link this image to the much later archetype of Lucifer, the favorite angel of God, who is transformed into the rejected child or angel and is seen as a serpent. Both images of serpent and angel appear in the later Paradise myth, the Serpent as the deceiver of Adam and Eve and the Lion-birds as the angels or cherubim who guard the entrance to Paradise with flaming swords. The same sword symbolism is present in the Sumerian image and possibly has a similar meaning. The open doors are the entrance back to Self, Void or Nammu. The copulating vipers are Nammu and her Serpent Lord, Enki or what Jung called the Divine Syzygy. Symbolized by an act of sexual love, they return to the original oneness, or if seen as coming out of the Self, which would be the case at birth, they are the first splitting of the Serpent Lord or primal energy into two, namely, the king and his queen or the ego and soul.

The Queen Serpent Nammu, represents the undifferentiated Self, who contains the Serpent Lord and their child as one. The King Serpent represents the psychological function of conscious intuition, a reflection of the Self as an image of the soul. Thus, the Twin Serpents can be seen as the Self and the soul, followed by the soul and the ego or the two irrational functions of intuition and sensation, who now become the Serpent Twins. While in a state of unconscious sensation, Nammu's son/lover is Enlil. When unconscious sensation becomes conscious, it becomes Enki, the spouse of Nammu. The Self, the Void in Genesis, or the goddess Nammu, is always in contact with either the spouse, Enki or intuition or the child/son, Enlil or sensation. In this way, Nammu or the Self is spouse and mother simultaneously, which is often depicted in this mythology. Ego and soul have not yet been differentiated until Enlil is born, which represents the separation of the soul (intuition) and the ego (sensation) and the beginning of two separate functions in the human child.

The bird/angel, the winged aspect of the lion-birds, represents the divine or that aspect of the creature closest to the Serpent King, God, Heaven, Spirit or the masculine principle. The body of the lion represents one of the most powerful animals on earth, often described as monarch of the jungle. The lion appears to represent the instinctual but royal nature of humanity, symbolized by being associated with the sun and the color gold, both symbols of the divine or the spiritual. The lion half of the Lion-bird archetype represents the feminine principle, being associated with Earth rather than Sky, just as the bird/angel is associated with Heaven. The dragon, lion, or serpent that has wings similar to the Greek caduceus appears to be describing the divinity of consciousness and unconsciousness that are differentiated but united in a new form as a powerful creature.

The twin serpents of intuition and sensation stand alone as separate functions, as Jung described, and appear as opposites of one another. All extreme opposites necessarily depend on one another and are connected to one another; the psychological functions of sensation and intuition, as well as feeling and thinking, are no exception. Each of the irrational functions has a three-in-one motif that is the exact opposite of the other. I have previously described this as the unconsciousness of the functions of sensation, feeling, and thinking, while intuition is conscious. Sensation is the reverse, with feeling, thinking, and intuition unconscious.

As the first function of consciousness after birth, according to my hypothesis, sensation can be seen to stand alone. Intuition is unconscious like the two rational functions of feeling and thinking. I have previously stated the rationale for this description: From birth, feeling is the second function to become conscious because there is nothing to judge before body sensations are experienced. Thinking is the third function to become conscious, and intuition is the fourth function to become conscious after birth, which suggests a return to the first function of intuition, experienced in the womb. This is the theme of Maria's axiom, which states that one becomes two, two becomes three, three becomes four, and the fourth is a return to the first.

In the newborn, but not necessarily later, conscious feeling would necessarily have thinking and intuition as unconscious, but sensation would be conscious and the object of all value judgment. Chopra (1993) appears to be describing the same thing: "Because there are no absolute qualities in the material world, it is false to say that there even is an independent world 'out there.' The world is a reflection of the sensory apparatus that registers it" (p. 11).

Even though conscious feeling later "extends to every content of consciousness" (Jung, 1971/1921, p. 434), in the first round of consciousness in the ego functions, feeling would have no object of consciousness except for its own conscious, perceived body sensations. Conscious feeling would be contiguous with conscious sensation, and it might be said that conscious feeling thereafter could be defined as always containing conscious sensation even when it is seen as an independent function. Feeling is, as Jung (1971/1921) described, "allied with every sensation" (p. 434). Thus, the human infant would have one conscious rational function (feeling) and one conscious irrational function (sensation), whereas one rational function (thinking) and one irrational function (intuition) would remain unconscious. (I am describing the unfolding of the functions in the first moments of life, as I believe the myth does.)

Jung (1971/1921), described the Syzygy archetype:

> It is a psychological fact that as soon as we touch on these identifications we enter the realm of the syzygies, the paired opposites, where the One is never separated from the Other, its antithesis. It is a field of personal experience which leads directly to the experience of individuation, the attainment of the self. A vast number of symbols for this process could be mustered from the medieval literature of the West and even more from the storehouses of Oriental wisdom, but in this matter words and ideas count for little. Indeed, they may become dangerous bypaths and false trails. In this still very obscure field of in full force psychological experience, where we are in direct contact, so to speak, with the archetype, its psychic power is felt in full force. This realm is so entirely one of immediate experience that it cannot be captured by any formula, but can only be hinted at to one who already knows (p. 106).

Thus, the Divine Syzygy archetype of the Serpent Lord image can be seen as a moment frozen in time, either the Syzygy that is born out of the Self or the Syzygy before a return to the Self. The latter is what Jung describes as leading directly to the experience of individualization and the attainment of the Self.

Sensation can be seen as negative and described as the Fallen Angel or Devil Serpent, or positive and described as the Divine Child, depending on the interpretation of the experience. In the old Sumerian myths when the consort of the goddess dies, the death describes a fall from grace and a transformation, birth as the death of oneness followed by a rebirth. If sensation is seen as positive, the myth describes the goddess and her Divine Child or the Virgin and Christ archetypes, which represent a return to Paradise motif by the reintegration of the infant back to its original state of oneness or the psychological function of intuition. Thus, the Divine Child, the psychological child and the biological child can be seen as identical experiences that occur simultaneously.

It is the conscious thought, for example, the god or the old thought that stands alone without its opposite, that dies, and this is necessary for a new thought to be born or created. When this sacrifice is made (often with pain and suffering as well as with unconditional love and joy), the goddess or the divine child or the Father God, for they are all one and the same in intuition, gives a new thought or a new image. It is given or experienced as given by the function of conscious intuition because no effort is required after the sacrifice of the ego has been made.

I suggest that the numerous mythologies and religions that attempt to

FOUR CREATING GODS OF THE SUMERIAN PANTHEON: SKY GOD AN;
THE EARTH GODDESS KI; THE AIR GOD ENLIL; THE WATER GOD ENKI, WISDOM.

*ARCHETYPAL PATTERN OF THE FOUR PSYCHOLOGICAL FUNCTIONS AS
THEY DIFFERENTIATE: INTROVERTED*
INTUITION, SENSATION, FEELING and THINKING.

King Lion-bird

An & KI second World Parents

NAMMU & Enki: Primal Parents

(FATHER GOD OF WATER & EARTH)
CREATOR OF HUMANKIND

SKY GOD AN
(Heaven)

THINKING

LORD TO NAMMU

WATER GOD ENOKI THE GOD OF WISDOM

INTUITION

FATHER ARCHETYPE
(Compare with Adam archetype in Genesis)

Twin Serpent Twin Serpent

SUMERIAN COSMOLOGY
THE MOTHER GODDESS, NAMMU PRIMEVAL SEA FIRST CAUSE
SELF
THE VOID IN GENESIS

WATER SYMBOLIZES UNDIFFERENTIATED FUNCTIONS
(Compare with the Father God of Genesis)

Queen Lion-bird

EARTH GODDESS KI (NINHURSAG) QUEEN OF THE MOUNTAIN

FEELING

MOTHER ARCHETYPE
(Comapare with Eve archetype in Genesis)

Twin Serpent Twin Serpent

Hero (Child) Archetype with two sets of Parents

AIR GOD ENLIL (EARTH) SON OF KI & AN SON OF NAMMU & ENKI

GRADUALLY BECAME LEADER OF THE PANTHEON, WHICH HE CREATED BY SEPARATING HEAVEN & EARTH

SENSATION

CHILD ARCHETYPE
(Compare with Fallen Angel archetype or Serpent in Genesis)

SUMERIAN COSMOLOGY: CREATION OCCURRED WHEN THE CREATING GOD ENKI SPOKE THE "WORD."

THE SEPARATION OF THE PRIMAL WATER BY ENLIL CREATED HEAVEN AND EARTH.

THE FOUR *CREATING* DEITIES ARE PERSONIFICATIONS OF PRIMAL PSYCHIC ENERGY (INTROVERTED) IN THE PSYCHE OF THE HUMAN CHILD. SENSATION IS THE "CHILD" GOD THAT CAUSES THE SPLIT OF THE PRIMAL PARENTS, NAMMU AND ENKI FIRST OR THE SELF AND THE SOUL AND SECOND, THE PARENTS OF KI AND AN, OR THE FUNCTIONS OF FEELING AND THINKING.

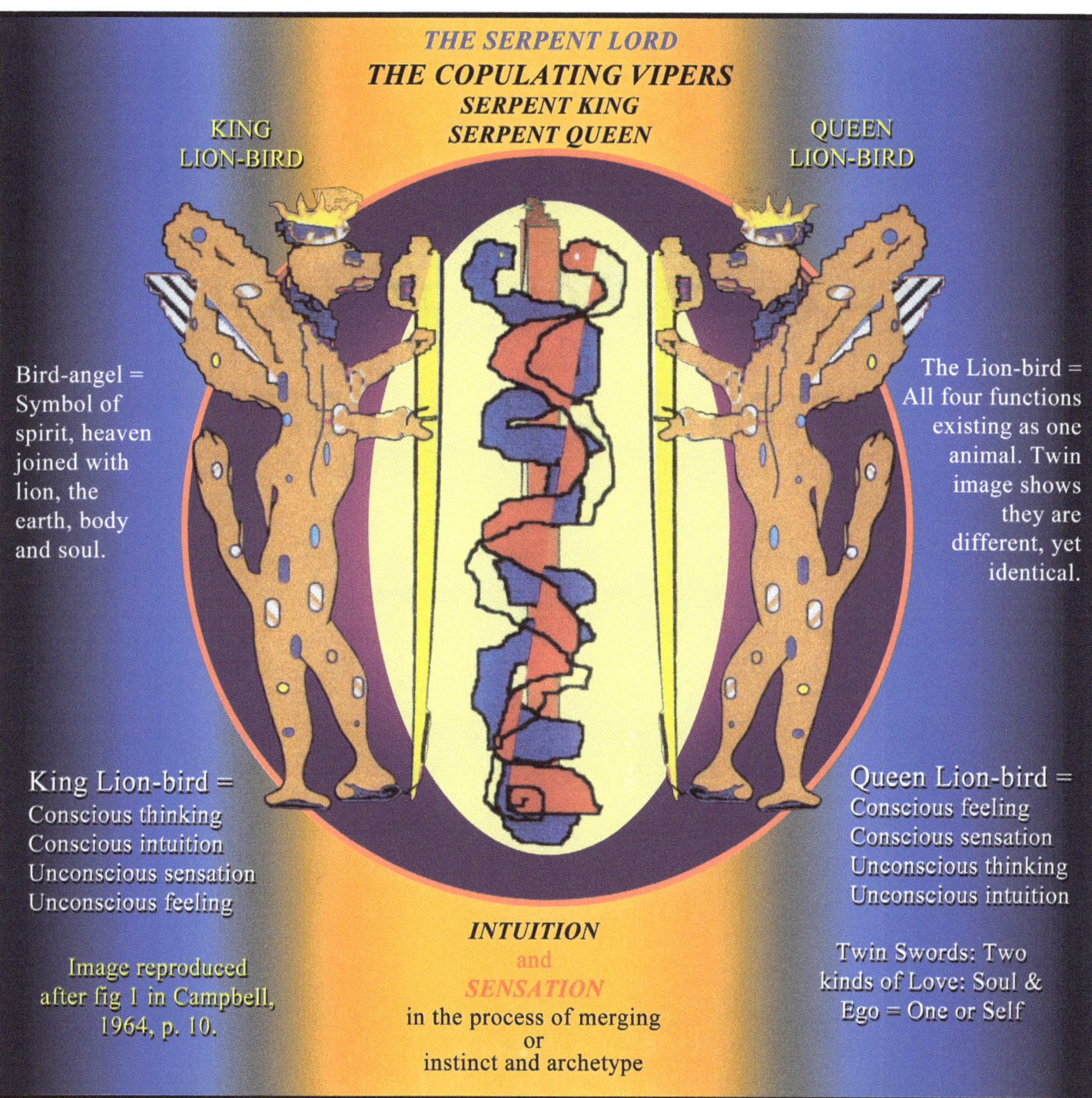

The Serpent Lord = the three unconscious functions of sensation, feeling, and thinking contained within the goddess of conscious intuition where they exist as One. This is the basic instinct which divides and becomes the Serpent Lord of conscious sensation and the Serpent Queen of unconscious intuition. Each Serpent or function can be seen to stand alone and a mirror reflection of the other. A further differentiation of the functions creates the twin lion-birds. The Queen lion-bird is conscious feeling coupled with conscious sensation or one conscious rational function and one conscious irrational function. The Queen has intuition and thinking as her unconscious functions. King Serpent or King lion-bird is just the reverse: He has sensation and feeling as the unconscious, while intuition and thinking are conscious. They are also mirror images of one another. The lion-birds can be seen as the instinct and the archetype and the twin Serpents can also be seen as the instinct and the archetype. The King lion-bird contains the "queen" and her male child or feeling and sensation in the unconscious. The Queen contains the king and his "child" in the unconscious in the same, reverse manner. The twin Serpents can be compared with the winged Greek god Hermes. The twin lion-birds can be compared with the Cherubim or lion-birds who guard the entrance back to Paradise or the Garden of Eden. This would be the archangels of Gabriel and Michael, who contain feeling and sensation as unconscious functions.

describe this process by symbolic images and simple stories were describing, among other things, the making of an image and the process of imagination in the human psyche, as Jung was in his description of active fantasy as the product of the function of conscious intuition. That function so often referred to as the fourth is also the first, the alpha and omega of psychic energy.

Radhakrishnan (1988) describes intuition beautifully:

> When the rational mind is silenced, the intuitive mode produces an extraordinary awareness; the environment is experienced in a direct way without the filter of conceptual thinking. In the words of Chuang Tzu, "The still mind of the sage is a mirror of heaven and earth — the glass of all things." The experience of oneness with the surrounding environment is the main characteristic of this meditative state. It is a state of consciousness where every form of fragmentation has ceased, fading away into undifferentiated unity (p. 40).

Creativity is often described as the ability to see as a child. There is every reason to believe that the human body and brain of the child are working much earlier and, in most cases, in a more structured and organized manner than previously described in psychology. I believe that the process begins when life begins and is the same for an infant as it is for an adult, were we able to observe it directly. How and why a new symbol is given remains a mystery and a question to be asked. It may be that the new message given, like the message of an angel, comes from the depths of the Self, like a divine child waiting to be born. It may even be that this is the information stored in the genetic structure and human instincts of the body of the human child. If intuition is unconscious body sensation, which I believe it to be, the body would help construct the first image given to the human mind, and it would not be separate from the soul.

The motif of the twin vipers or the Serpent's Bride that Campbell says originated in 2025 B.C. is an ancient image (see Campbell, 1964, pp. 9-10, Figure 1) that appears to be related to the much later image of an angel falling out of Heaven into Hell or the fall of Adam and Eve from Paradise to the earthly realm of human struggle. Lucifer will be discussed next, as another image of conscious, introverted sensation that falls out of Heaven.

The Fall of the Divine Child/Angel, Lucifer: The Serpent Archetype and the Four Psychological Functions

The monotheistic religions of Judaism, Zoroastrianism, Christianity, and

Islam share a common belief in angels and demons. Most of the information concerning this archetype comes, as Godwin (1990) describes, "from outside the orthodox scriptures and canons of the four religions that believe in the existence of angels" (p. 9). Godwin (1990) says that "the term angel derives from a Greek translation of the original Hebrew Mal'akh, which originally meant the shadow side of God, but later came to mean messenger (p. 7). Both terms, Thompson (1991) also tells us, "refer to a function or status rather than an essence" (p.148).

The four psychological functions can be seen in the same way, as messengers or angels of the human psyche or brain. The premise that I have previously presented, namely, that intuition is the first function to develop and begins in the womb as the undifferentiation of all four functions, can be applied to the myth of the Fallen Angel. This is comparable to the archaic Sumerian myths that came before, as well as the Genesis myth, which came later.

Schneiderman (1988), discussing Augustine's views concerning angels, states:

> As soon as God gave up speaking directly to mortals and intervening in his person, it was necessary to have a company of angels to pass between him and his creatures. According to Augustine, among others, God never spoke directly to the patriarchs of the Old Testament; so whenever it is said that God spoke this means that angels spoke. He adds that in the New Testament it is not the angels who speak, but the Lord himself through his Word (pp. 31-32).

The Serpent and Angel archetypes are both significant symbols in the Judaic-Christian religions; most of the important messages in the Old Testament come from God through the voice of an angel. Although Augustine thought it was the Lord himself speaking in the New Testament, angels are never far away on important occasions and appear to be the consequential method of communication between God and humanity.

The myth of Lucifer and the Paradise myth in Genesis both appear to be variations of the same theme; both describe the transition of one state of being (Heaven in the first, Paradise in the second) to another state (loss of Heaven and loss of Paradise) by the symbol of a Fall (which represents a physical and psychological birth) from grace that separates first Lucifer, then Adam, Eve and the Serpent from God. Psychologically, both myths also appear to be describing the transition from the psychological function of intuition (Heaven, Paradise or being in the womb) to that of the function of sensation and ego consciousness (birth). Thus, they describe the biological or physical birth of the child and the psychological birth of the child simultaneously. This is in addition to the first level of the myth, in which the Lucifer as Divine Child myth is simply the loss of oneness with God after birth, while the Genesis myth, with Adam and Eve as the divine children, says the same thing but takes the story further.

If the functions of intuition and sensation are mirror images or the reverse of one another (as are the functions of feeling and thinking), they would not function at the same time, although the transition from one to the other could occur expeditiously by human standards of time. To differentiate or become separate, it would be necessary for one function to become unconscious while the opposite function occurs in consciousness. This would be the beginning of not only consciousness, but also unconsciousness.

The human child can be seen as being one in his or her individuality, while possessing two forms of consciousness, that of ego consciousness or the ability of the four functions to operate (apparently) independently of one another and that of soul consciousness or the ability of the four functions to operate as one undifferentiated function. This translates psychologically as consciousness and unconsciousness in Jungian terminology. The marriage of these two forms of consciousness can be seen as giving birth to what Campbell (1973, p. 259) describes as super consciousness, a third position that would represent a return to one or the Self (Being). The human child would thus be more than androgynous in nature, he or she would be tripartite or three-in-one: biological (body), psychological (soul), and spiritual (spirit). He or she could be said to possess consciousness, unconsciousness, and super consciousness, (Being) the third being the result (child symbol) of the first two that are joined.

In Judaic lore, Lucifer was the Bringer of Light (light being a primary symbol for consciousness), and he was also the Serpent of Darkness, symbolizing the unconscious. Peterson (1995) describes Lucifer:

> Lucifer, literally "bringer of light"—a higher deity, in the Gnostic tradition, than the unconscious creative demi-urge—tempts man towards knowledge, and produces a traumatic but potentially redemptive expansion of conscious power. The serpent, for the medieval alchemists, was the arcane substance that transformed itself inside the tree, and which therefore served as its life. The snake is regulator of conscious intensity, in Kundalina Yoga, a creature of the spine, a storehouse of intrapsychic energy, whose activation leads to ecstasy and enlightenment. The snake is the most archaic and transpersonal centers of the central nervous

system—phylogenetically ancient as the reptile—in whose recesses lurk tremendous excitatory power. The deep structures of the brainstem perform activities upon which maintenance of consciousness absolutely depends (p. 15).

Lucifer can be seen as a personification of the human nervous system, which brings not only light, but darkness as well. He can also be seen as the bringer of consciousness, comparable with the Serpent in the Garden of Eden, with whom he is later associated. If, however, consciousness is seen as the loss of super consciousness, light without darkness would be an opposite that lacked its other half, thus, consciousness can be seen in the pejorative way that Genesis describes. Light or consciousness and darkness or unconsciousness that has become divided would destroy Paradise.

As the favorite angel, the Divine Child, Lucifer was one with God and lived in that middle place where consciousness and unconsciousness are not separated, but exist as one. For this reason, I equate Lucifer in his Divine Child aspect with the psychological function of intuition, which I understand to be all the functions existing as one undifferentiated function. When he falls from Heaven, Lucifer becomes the fallen angel turned Serpent, or the function of conscious sensation. The archetype or image representing this function is always subject to change, but it will always be an archetype representing the Divine Father, the Divine Mother, or the Divine Child, either as a person, animal, plant or stone, such as the philosopher's stone.

The image of the Serpent as a deity is prevalent in cultures and religions throughout the ancient world, as is the association of the serpent with the body. Neumann (1949/1954) describes the body scheme in the following way:

> The body scheme, as the archetype of the original man in whose image the world was created, is the basic symbol in all systems where parts of the world are co-ordinated with regions of the body. Not God alone, but the whole world is created in man's image. The relation of the world and the gods to the body scheme is the earliest concretistic form of the "anthropocentric world picture," with man standing in the middle or "at the heart" of the world. *It derives from one's own body sensations*, which are charged with mana and are commonly misunderstood as narcissistic (emphasis mine, p. 25).

Mythology often appears to be describing body sensations when it speaks of serpents, as well as describing the human spine, which can be symbolized as the tree or twin trees or the serpent or twin serpents. The serpent image connected with the spine has its best-known representation in the Indian Kundalini mythology. Chetwynd (1982) describes body symbolism that is related to the serpent as "connected with the spinal column, which joins the physical nature (the genitals) to the spiritual nature (the head)" (p. 65).

Because the Serpent archetype has been symbolized repeatedly in multiple and diverse religions as a god that creates humanity, or a devil who deceives humanity, I believe it can be seen as a symbol for either of the irrational functions. It is with the perceiving functions, followed by the rational functions, that the human child creates and sometimes destroys the world. If, as Freeman (1995) describes, "all knowledge originates within brains of individuals" (p. 2), the only thing known is what we ourselves create.

The human spine delivers the message of sensation, whether conscious or unconscious. Those that come to consciousness can be seen as Lucifer after the fall, while those that remain unconscious can be seen as the Divine Child archetype, that is, unconscious sensation or intuition, still contained in God.

It was Lucifer, angel turned serpent (or our human, animal nature, that is, the instinctual function of conscious introverted sensation), who offered the apple (consciousness) to Eve, which psychologically speaking, would mean that the function of sensation offers or introduces consciousness to the function of feeling, personified as the innocent Eve, who is still contained in God as undifferentiated energy.

It is the subjective body experience of the human child that provides an object (of self-reference if the emphasis is placed on the subject (introversion) rather than the external object (extraversion), which would mean that the subject and object are not yet separated—the object is also the subject) on which a judgment of good or bad can be made. Eve does not use her feeling function; she is the archetype that represents feeling in the human child. In the very first experiences of the human newborn, which is the topic explored here and what I believe to be an underlying theme of the cosmological material, sensation could not possibly follow feeling. Feeling that is undifferentiated is feeling that is still, like Eve, in a state of innocence. There must be an object of reference before a value judgment can be made and the only object present in the beginning is the body of the infant as it experiences body sensations stimulated by his or her experience of opposites in the world. After the first experience, and with many repetitions of sensuous or feeling experiences in the child or adult, feeling could follow sensation. How the mythology might appear to be describing that experience is another topic. The objective of this research, however, is the beginning experience of the infant (before and immediately after birth). I am not concerned with inferior or superior functions in any way. I do not believe that consciousness is superior to unconsciousness or the reverse. If anything is superior it would be the state of super consciousness, which would describe a balanced Self.

Western mythology usually assigns the masculine principle to consciousness and the feminine principle to unconsciousness. The subjective value judgment that states that consciousness is superior to unconsciousness has often been erroneously used and applied to living women, rather than the archetype and used against them in the most derogatory way. Not being able to see the archetypes as possible representations of psychic energy inherent in most human psyches, male and female, leads to a concrete, literal, and fundamental interpretation of the myth that has been used (especially in the Judaic-Christian religion) to subjugate and control women. That is not the fault of the myth but the shortcoming of those who interpret any literature in a rigid, simplistic, and concrete way, ignoring the implications of metaphor.

It appears logical to me to assume that a pure phenomenological experience of the body can and does exist that is free of a value judgment, but the reverse does not appear to be logically true. No value judgment can be made that does not refer to an object of some kind. In addition, if sensation is an irrational and instinctual function, it would necessarily precede feeling as a rational function, and as Jung (1971/1921) stated, be "the matrix out of which thinking and feeling develop as rational functions" (p. 454).

Conscious sensation seeks to divide and separate, giving specific knowledge of the object as perceived by the subject. It appears reasonable to me to assume that a function that gives a picture of the whole would precede a function that gives specific isolated information and that sensation would be the function that flows out of intuition, and not the other way around.

Intuition may provide what is perceived as catastrophic and evil information; the function itself, however, has always been identified with a Divine God or Goddess or a variation of the Divine Child archetype, such as the angel. Because intuition appears to me to be the function that contains all the other functions, the Father God archetype in the Judaic-Christian religion appears to be the closest description of this energy. One function contains them all, just as one Father God contains everyone in Paradise. This, from my perspective, supports the premise that Paradise is in the womb, where all functions are contained in potential form, including the ego, which is first represented by the sleeping or absent Serpent.

The function of sensation, unlike intuition, has not been associated with the divine, but just the reverse. Body knowledge, carnal knowledge has its best representative in the idea of sin and separation from God. This is my rationale for defining the Father God as an archetype for the function of conscious, introverted intuition and the Serpent as an archetype for the function of conscious introverted sensation. It is also my rationale for seeing the first function present in the fetus as the intuitive one and the second function present as that of sensation, which begins at birth and like Lucifer, brings consciousness, and at the same time, darkness or unconsciousness. He then becomes the angel or Prince of darkness. From my reading of the myth, this describes the split, which is not in consciousness, really, but in the super consciousness or Self that preceded it. We can know little or nothing without a return to that state, which may necessitate first a return to the function of intuition. If it is the first function to flow out of the Self, the ego complex merged with what I am calling the soul complex, would precede the ego and ordinary ego consciousness. It would be the splitting of the merged ego/soul that creates them as separate functions and separate complexes, the soul being attached to the function of intuition and the unconscious, and the ego being attached to the function of sensation and consciousness.

The image of the woman or goddess and the serpent together is described in numerous mythologies other than the Judaic-Christian one, and they are all probably attempting to describe psychic energy and the relationship of the two functions of conscious, introverted sensation and conscious, introverted feeling. (See Johnson, 1988 for numerous descriptions and images of the relationship of the goddess and the serpent).

The first cry of the newborn is negative feeling that judges (bad) when he or she perceives, by conscious body sensation, a lack of something, namely, the loss of the merged opposites, when conscious sensation is first experienced. This is knowledge (known by and through the body) of the opposites of good and evil and produces the first value judgment, which is followed by the first emotion (love that desires, that is, ego love) of the human child, the only animal on earth capable of shedding tears, a physical manifestation of the body functions of sensation and feeling. This is personified in the Genesis myth as the Serpent and Eve or in the myth of the Fallen Angel, simply as the Serpent or the function of conscious, introverted sensation, with the earth representing the mother or the feminine. The value judgment of the feeling function is pure phenomenological experience brought on by the first phenomenological experience of the sensations experienced in the body. Feeling is not identical with affect, as Jung (1971/1921) described when he said:

MYTH OF THE FALLEN ANGEL: LUCIFER, THE BRINGER OF LIGHT
THE MORNING STAR

Fourth function after birth and a return to the first

First function in the womb

4 FUNCTIONS MERGED INTUITION (UNCONSCIOUS SENSATION) LUCIFER

LUCIFER IS CONTAINED CHILD OR UNCONSCIOUS SENSATION

HEAVEN and ANGELS

SPLITTING OF THE OPPOSITES

SPLITTING OF THE OPPOSITES

SOUL, SPIRIT AND BODY ONE WITH GOD, I.E., AN ANGEL

Also the Morning Star

unconscious THINKING Mother Goddess Conscious FEELING

Lucifer with God - no ego
UNION OF OPPOSITES

HEAVEN FATHER GOD (top of the mountain) SELF or CHILD MOTHER GODDESS WOMB or TOMB pit of mountain HELL

Lucifer with God - no ego
UNION OF OPPOSITES

unconscious THINKING Father God Conscious THINKING

SPLITTING OF OPPOSITES
Lucifer separated from God - ego

SPLITTING OF OPPOSITES
Lucifer separated from God - ego

Second function after birth
THIRD FUNCTION AFTER WOMB

UNION OF THE OPPOSITES

SOUL, SPIRIT AND BODY BECOME SEPARATE, I.E., MAN

UNION OF THE OPPOSITES

Third function after birth
FOURTH FUNCTION AFTER WOMB

conscious SENSATION LUCIFER *FALLS TO* HELL *OR* TO EARTH (BIRTH)

First function at birth
SECOND FUNCTION AFTER WOMB

CONTAINS SAME THREE IN ONE NOW SEPARATE

BRINGER OF LIGHT BECOMES PRINCE OF DARKNESS

OPPOSITES OF CONSCIOUSNESS AND UNCONSCIOUSNESS
THAT WERE MERGED BECOME SEPARATE, CREATING
THE SPLIT IN HUMAN CONSCIOUSNESS OR THE SEPARATION
OF SOUL AND EGO.

> Feeling, therefore, is an entirely *subjective* process, which may be in every respect independent of external stimuli, though it allies itself with every sensation. Even an "indifferent" sensation possesses a feeling-tone, namely that of indifference, which again expresses some sort of valuation (emphasis Jung's, p. 434).

Feeling that "allies itself with every sensation" is describing body sensation and what Jung did not say is that this is possibly because the body sensation precedes every possible feeling, which in turn would precede every possible affect. Without a perception of the sensation there would be nothing to judge or value and without the value judgment it could not turn into an affect. Jung (1971/1921) describes this when he goes on to say:

> When the intensity of feeling increases, it turns into an *affect*, i.e., a feeling-state accompanied by marked physical innervations. Feeling is distinguished from affect by the fact that it produces no perceptible physical innervations, i.e., neither more nor less than an ordinary thinking process (emphasis Jung's, p. 434).

In this short description, Jung distinguishes the difference between the feeling function and affect or human emotion and suggests that they are separate aspects of psychic energy, but aspects that are closely related, because it is the intensity of the value judgment given by the feeling function that creates or, as Jung puts it, turns into affect or human emotion. Obviously affect can be brought on by any of the functions in ordinary life. However, at birth or shortly thereafter, feeling will turn into an affect based only on conscious body sensations or perception of the body experience. If intuition and thinking are unconscious, as I believe them to be, they will not be evaluated; the conscious evaluation will be concerning the conscious sensate experience. Sensation will flow out of intuition and proceed to conscious feeling, which will register as an unconscious thought in the thinking function.

I think that Jung's description of feeling is adequate in every respect and can be applied to the infant at birth, which the mythology is describing in another, more pictorial manner, using the images and archetypes as personifications of minute psychic energy that is difficult, but not impossible, to describe by other means. Lucifer, as the Serpent/Devil archetype and one of the important archetypes in Judaic-Christian mythology, appears to me to be the personification of the psychic energy contained in the function of conscious introverted sensation. If that is so, his importance as an archetype may be important to developmental psychology that attempts to see archetypes and mythology as instinctual patterns of energy that represent psychological experience.

Godwin (1990) describes Lucifer, the Fallen Angel archetype, as the "Morning Star" archetype:

> Lucifer's other title is "The Morning Star," the star which heralds the rising sun, and we discover that this story is a borrowing from the even earlier legend of Shaher. This Canaanite deity of the Dawn was born out of the womb or "Pit" of the great Mother Goddess. Shaher, like Lucifer, was The Morning Star who was the last light to proudly defy the rising sun. He attempted to storm the solar throne of light, but was cast down from heaven for his impudence. This ancient epic was recorded seven centuries before Christ in a Canaanite scripture. *Five centuries* later a Hebrew scribe copied it almost verbatim, but borrowed the word to put into the mouth of the prophet Isaiah (emphasis mine, p. 91).

Lucifer's image obviously did not begin with Hebrew mythology, but had its roots in other ancient, primitive religions. Serpent gods were prevalent in these cultures without the pejorative connotations of the Genesis myth. Campbell (1964) tells us: "In Eve's scene at the tree, nothing is said to indicate that the serpent who appeared and spoke to her was a deity in his own right, who had been revered in the Levant for at least seven thousand years before the composition of the Book of Genesis" (emphasis mine, p. 9).

That the archetypes and, particularly, the archetype of the Serpent Lord, which was the probable prototype for Lucifer and the Serpent in Genesis, are repeated in numerous mythologies down through the centuries, indicates that they are universal and that they represent psychological and physical experience. Cosmological myths or any myth of beginnings, such as Lucifer, contain a description of primal individual experience, the microcosm contained within an apparent description of the macrocosm, mirror reflections of one another and identical. It is for this reason that the cosmological myths can be seen as an attempt to describe not only the creation of the world, but the creation of the human child, as she or he creates the world. They are, therefore, relevant to developmental psychology, which thus far has only hinted at this connection.

The myth of Lucifer as the Fallen Angel may not be described in the orthodox scriptures, yet the influence of this myth upon those religions that describe angels cannot be underestimated. This is particularly true of Christianity, because without the Fall of both Lucifer and mankind, there would be no need for the redemption by Christ. If this is so, a psychological interpretation of the myth of angels, and especially the myth of the fallen angel as a prototype of fallen man, appears relevant.

Moses as Divine and Human Child: The Hero Archetype, Confidant of Angels

The motif of the fallen angel and the motif of fallen humanity both appear to be related to the abandoned child/hero archetype, who usually is a divine or magical child, and like Lucifer or Adam and Eve, has lost his original parents or original home. The purpose of his journey is to find what was lost, what Campbell calls "his ultimate god." Campbell (1973) describes the hero thus:

> The two—the hero and his ultimate god, the seeker and the found—are thus understood as the outside and inside of a single, self-mirrored mystery, which is identical with the mystery of the manifest world. The great deed of the supreme hero is to come to the knowledge of this unity in multiplicity and then to make it known (p. 40).

Moses is an archetype of the hero, expressing the dual nature of man. Moses, as Divine Child and confidant of angels describes in Genesis how the human child creates or co-creates the world with God. Moses, as archetype for the human child, tells the world that he was once one with God, is now separated and must make his way back to the Promised Land, a symbol describing the Self. This describes the universal human attempt to reconcile the opposites of consciousness and unconsciousness, or soul and ego.

The child lifted from the water represents the first separation of the four functions from the primal Self of undifferentiation. This is the first mother (parents) of Moses, contained in the Self and the soul. This is also another version of the separation of the primal waters, the Self personified as the primal mother and intuition personified as the primal father. From the separation of the Self to the soul or intuitive function describes the first instinctual movement of life and twilight consciousness or the beginning male God. The undifferentiated functions are contained in one function, intuition, which is the first light or form of consciousness (the instinctual and unconscious body sensations of the human child). Unconsciousness and undifferentiation that tips the scales on the side of consciousness represents the Father God, who is now the container, while the Self that remains (the equilibrium has been altered) is usually personified as unconscious undifferentiation or the Mother. In this way the primal parents have been separated by the Son, the Divine Child of intuition, who represents both parents but is a male child, showing himself to be a replica, a beginning aspect of the Father God or consciousness. The loss of both parents (the Orphan archetype) represents the transition from: first, the Mother (Self that contains All) to the Father (Soul that contains All) and finally to the experience of birth and the function of conscious sensation (the tragic and heroic ego). Consciousness and unconsciousness, the original parents, have been separated entirely, becoming the ego and the soul divided, with the Divine Child as the middle or connecting symbol, which can be called super consciousness. The Divine Child's duty, as Campbell tells us, is to restore the unity in multiplicity that he once knew, by a return to the Mother, which is a return to the soul or Self, both being a state of undifferentiation. The soul (intuition) will come first, the first function to become conscious and the one necessary for a return trip.

Angels often appear to those who see or hear them, as something entirely other than their own psyche or as a gift from God. Intuitive knowledge that appears to come from outside oneself or which is not based on ordinary logic can appear as an angel, especially if this is in the belief system of the individual. This knowledge is then experienced by the feeling function and expressed by the thinking function in the form of an archetype that describes the experience of the received message. This is a similar view to that of Princeton psychologist Julian Jaynes, described by Springer and Deutsch (1981) concerning early Homo Sapiens:

> They heard voices inside their heads and called them gods. These gods told them what to do and how to act. Their minds were divided into two parts—an executive part called "god" and a follower part called "man." When writing and more complex human activity started weakening the authority of the auditory hallucinations, the "bicameral mind" slowly broke down. The voices of the gods fell silent, and what we call consciousness was born (p. 193).

Whether gods or angels, the message appears to come from the intuitive function and is then expressed by the thinking function or active thinking, both of which could be described as the "executive part called god." The "follower part called man" would correlate with the functions of sensation and feeling. Consciousness is ego consciousness, however, and does not come about without its opposite, unconsciousness, which can be seen as the silent goddess. I find it difficult to imagine, however, that early man did not have body consciousness in much the same way that modern man does, and it is possible that he had thoughts that he did not attribute to the gods. Certain otherwise unexplainable thoughts could be supposed to come from something other than from himself, which describes intuitive knowledge in many cases.

Identifying the human and psychological method of functioning does not refute the existence of God in any way, which the above quote might imply; what these ideas support is that God can only be known directly by individual human experience, which is an ancient idea.

The Divine Child archetype or the Angel archetype fits the psychological function of intuition quite well since the message of intuition often appears as something given with no effort extended by the receiver. Jung's description of an attitude of conscious expectation would necessitate an already existing thought that a god or an angel would respond to the expected message.

The impact of this can appear as a simple knowing, such as knowing who is on the other end of the ringing telephone, or as a Divine revelation, such as the ten commandments that Yahweh gave to Moses. Moses obviously expected God to reply and had an attitude of conscious expectation as he was given the message. This is how Jung described active fantasy as the product of conscious intuition. God or an angel of God gave the Word, but it was Moses (as Divine Child) who expressed that word by writing it on a stone and delivering the message to his people. In this sense, Moses was God's messenger. He is also reputedly the author of Genesis and several other books of the Old Testament, therefore, his archetypal influence upon the course of the Western world cannot be overestimated. Moses is the Divine Child and the story, the archetype that Moses gave to the world, is also the Divine Child. He personifies the human child, who creates his or her own reality, a reality based on the experience of the past, on what appears to be the known objective world, coupled with what is unknown, the message of God or angels from the inner world of the soul or Self. This describes the ego/body that is conscious, the soul, which appears unconscious, and the dynamics of human struggle to reconcile the opposites. The tragic Hero archetype, the ego/body that experiences the known world as separate from the subjective soul, overcomes the Dragon, which in the end is nothing more than himself, the innocent ego.

Every creation depends first on a destruction: Time cannot exist without a concept of eternity: The word is born out of silence. What is visible was first invisible. The feminine principle was associated with the dark and shadow side of God, later personified as Eve, the Mother of all the living. It is the Divine Child, as a symbol of the middle, that connects these two opposites and represents them as two aspects, one masculine and one feminine, of one undivided God in the form of the Divine Child God.

At this level, the Divine Child is Moses, Christ, Hermes, Mercury, Eros, or any archetype that represents a Divine Child, and psychologically, that part of every individual that is divine. The Divine Child also becomes the messenger,

Moses (Child) Taken From the Water
Drawing by a 9-year-old girl

the angel of God or the Son of God, an idea similar to Thompson's (1991) description of angels. He says that "the idea of angels as gods, sons of gods, servants, ministers, watchers, holy men, appears throughout the ancient civilized world" (p. 148). The angel closest to God appears to be energy that is neutral and undifferentiated, energy that contains the opposites existing as one with God.

Angels and demons are another splitting of the opposites, like the knowledge of good and evil, or the splitting of the Self (the unconscious body, soul or intuition) and body (the conscious ego) or an archetype that contains both in one, like an Archangel or a Divine Child. The hierarchy of angels described in Judaism and later in Christianity appears to replace the hierarchy of the Greek and Roman gods, who had only a few winged messengers, the most important ones being Hermes and Eros. When the multiple gods in Greek mythology became one God in Judaism, Christianity and Islam, angels flourished much in the same way as the old gods of Rome and Greece. Hermes, the Greek messenger of the gods, known for his double nature can be seen as the same energy as Lucifer and the Archangel Michael, or later Lucifer and Christ, a splitting of the archetype that would shape and define Judaism and Christianity.

Hermes, as a Divine Child, represented a god of wholeness, and was associated with the number four, as Kerenyi (1990) shows us when he says that "the fourth day of the month was sacred not only to Hermes but also to Aphrodite, who is closely connected to him in other ways as well" (pp. 21-22). As an angel archetype, Hermes represents an angel of what would later be called the highest order; as a Divine Child archetype, he appears close to all the Greek gods and chosen to deliver their messages. Both Hermes and Eros can be seen as angel archetypes, and both are archetypes of the Divine Child. Both can also be seen as having a double nature or, put in another way, both possess two kinds of consciousness, soul and ego. In Judaism, the Divine Child/Tragic Hero is Moses.

Moses appears in Judaism as the first important personification of the Divine Child archetype, who is also human and of humble birth, indicating his dual nature. Thus, Moses can be seen as an example of the child on all three levels, the Divine, the psychological, and the biological.

Campbell (1964) says that "The name Moses itself is Egyptian. It is the normal word for 'child' and occurs among the names, for example, of the pharaohs of Dynasty XVIII" (p. 128). Moses also means to draw out (mashah), and it was his new mother, the Egyptian princess, who drew him out of the water and named him Moses, or Child taken from the water. Thus, it is the child archetype that leads the Jewish people out of Egypt and bondage, an idea that was to be continued in Christianity with the words of Christ. "Amen, I say unto you: whosoever shall not receive the kingdom of God as a child, shall not enter into it" (Luke 18:16).

Moses, who leads the people out of Egypt, does not enter the Promised Land and is only allowed to view it from the top of a mountain before he dies. The Divine Child gets a quick glance at the perfect place, but is denied entrance because of the sins of the earth child (his human nature) and then dies. This, I believe, describes his personification as the Divine Child of the introverted thinking function, which must "die" before a new thought can be born.

His successor is Josue (Joshua), which is the same name as Jesus in Hebrew, and both mean savior. It seems rather curious that Moses, who was the greatest prophet thus far and who labored so intensely for Yahweh should be denied the final victory of going into the Promised Land. As a Tragic Hero archetype that represents the ego, I believe the myth is describing the necessity of the withdrawal (a symbolic death) of the human ego nature, in order to return to God or the Self.

This transition, from Moses as the old leader, to Josue (Joshua) as the new leader, is important for several reasons. It can be seen as a crossroads symbol, a place where opposites converge, as the old (Moses or ego) gives way to the new (Josue or savior), and at the very point of convergence, they become identical. The death of Moses symbolizes the death of the Earth or human Child (ego) and can be compared with the death of Christ, who is also a Divine Child (ego as Hero) archetype. And Josue, who succeeds Moses, has the same name as Christ, Jesus or savior. It is by death that the Divine Child enters into the Promised Land and becomes the savior, which was the same experience of the crucified Christ many years later.

Psychologically, this can be seen as the death of the ego and the differentiated ego functions, which return the human child to the state of original oneness or to the state of the undifferentiated functions of sensation, feeling, thinking, or intuition, the instinct that becomes archetype of Divine Child. Mystical experience described in all major religions appear to support this idea. The ego and ego consciousness, both reflections of the Father God, who says "I AM," reflect the worship of consciousness, which necessarily negates the opposite position or worship of the Goddess, who is now represented as the golden calf, another child symbol, this time connected to animals (instincts) and the feminine, as the cow was sacred to the Egyptians. The thinking function, as the end product of all the ego functions, was hailed as the one true God and associated with Adam and the masculine, while the feeling function, associated with Eve, desire, the feminine, and her close relationship with the serpent or the function of conscious sensation, were oppressed. The Word was the only true image, and all other images, seen to be worshipped as though they were gods, were to be forsaken. Thus, the archetype itself, especially as the written word, became a Divine Child. It told a story that necessarily contained the opposites and what was accepted as "true" negated the opposite position to "false." The conscious position negated the opposite position to the unconscious. The Goddess or the unconscious was destined to return, however, contained in the Divine Child archetype (her lover and her son), who expresses both principles, masculine and feminine, in one archetype. With the death of the ego in the conscious thinking function, the unconscious position can be seen, uniting the opposites by the Divine Child archetype.

Campbell (1964), put it thus concerning the Earth Mother:

> Mother Nature, Mother Eve, Mother Mistress-of-the-World is there to be dealt with all the time, and the more sternly she is cut down, the more frightening will her Gorgoneum be. This may cause her matricidal son to achieve a lot of extremely spectacular escape work, and he may end by becoming master of the surface of the earth; but, oh, my! what a Sheol he will know—and yet not know—within, where his paradise should have been! (p. 153).

This describes the hero unwilling to make the sacrifice or "die," that is, return to the mother, soul, or undifferentiated state.

Moses has a dual nature, and the Divine aspect of that nature will appear as something outside himself in the form of an angel sent by God. God's angel appeared to Moses in a flame of fire, and many divine revelations in the Old and New Testaments are dreams or visions accompanied by an angel.

It would seem that Yahweh gave the Word to a child archetype, who was to become the spokesperson for the Father God and the deliverer of God's message to His people. The myth of Moses appears to be telling us that the child, which his name suggests, creates the Word and the world. The psychological functions that Moses represents most are first, intuition (Divine Child), and second, sensation (human child and Tragic Hero or ego). That which he received and expressed through the conscious, subjective ego thinking function, with the suppression of feeling, was attributed to the Divine Father God.

The Word, written on stone by God and given to Moses, represents the archetype itself, the manifestation of all instinctual experience given form by language and the thinking function. The first level of the story, indeed, the total myth itself is the Divine Child; it expresses the experience of its teller not only in the spoken word, but by the written word, a feat that no other animal on earth can duplicate. As a metaphor, the written word has the power to describe two or more seemingly unrelated topics that can on a deeper level be seen as the expression of one meaning. Fact and fiction, two opposites that appear divided, can be seen as having a single source, united by the archetype of the Divine Child.

"And there arose no more a prophet in Israel like unto Moses, whom the Lord knew face to face" (Deuteronomy 34:10). As the greatest prophet in Israel, Moses as a Divine Child archetype, saw God face to face. I will conclude this chapter with the following idea: It is the child, like Moses, human and divine, who sees God (known by and through the body) and is co-creator of the universe, recording his or her experience, creating the archetype that was first an instinct.

This takes place in the psychological and instinctual function of intuition, where mother, father, and child archetypes exist as one and the function of thinking, which seeks to express that oneness by the archetype. Active thinking is the fruit of passive thinking. Sensation and feeling are the root and tree that bears them both, the living experience that finds a voice in the archetype, records and gives form to history, literature, religion, art, and science.

Chapter 4

Second Prelude to Genesis:

The Four Archangels of Michael, Uriel, Raphael, and Gabriel
as Personifications of Neutral or Undifferentiated Psychic Energy

In this chapter I will analyze and interpret the symbolism of the four Archangels: Michael, Uriel, Raphael, and Gabriel, as personifications of neutral psychic energy that leads back to a state of undifferentiation. This would describe a return to Paradise theme or a return to the Self. As psychic energy that flows out of the Self in the beginning of life, however, I see the Archangels as comparable with the archetypes of God (Michael), the Serpent (Uriel), Eve (Raphael) and Adam (Gabriel), while one with God in the Garden of Eden. God and Michael represent the psychological function of undifferentiated intuition; the Serpent and Uriel represent the function of undifferentiated sensation; Eve and Raphael represent the function of undifferentiated feeling; and Adam and Gabriel represent the function of undifferentiated thinking.

That they have been created as archetypes of a supreme archetype (out of the center, void, or Self) introduces the theme of the twin archetype (same but different) and the theme of the Angel archetype (most like God). It also introduces the theme of the Divine Child because each archetype, whether a divine or human personification or a psychic function, is still one with the creator or innocent and perfect. Creation necessitates separation, however, implying that this can be seen as a description of the *earliest psychological differentiation of the Self*. The four functions, as an archetypal structure of the human soul and body have begun, on earth and in Heaven, in the womb of the human mother, symbolized by Paradise.

I suggest that the theme of neutral and undifferentiated energy is important because it is a description of the union of opposites as a representation of the process of individuation as a continuous spiral cycle in the beginning of life, and ever present thereafter. I also suggest that the German mystic, Meister Eckhart, and the California philosopher, Franklin Merrell-Wolff, are often describing the same energy in different words, which I will analyze before a discussion of the symbolism present in each Archangel.

Disinterest and the High Indifference:
Two Concepts Describing Neutral or Undifferentiated Psychic Energy

Meister Eckhart (Blakney, 1941), long before Jung introduced the same idea into psychology, said the following:

> The whole scattered world of lower things is gathered up to oneness when the soul climbs up to that life in which there are no opposites. Entering the life of reason, opposites are forgotten, but where this light does not fall, things fall away to death and destruction (my emphasis, p. 173).

Eckhart apparently equated reason, which I would describe as equivalent to the thinking function, as the primary route to all higher knowledge, and many of his descriptions appear to be describing the split between the two sides of the thinking function, although earlier he describes the eternal birth or birth that takes place in the soul in the following words:

> Thus it is true that, if you are to experience this noble birth, you must depart from all crowds and go back to the starting point, the core (of the soul) out of which you came. The crowds are the agents of the soul and their activities; memory, understanding, and will, in all their diversifications. You must leave them all; sense perception, imagination, and all that you discover in self or intend to do. After that, you may experience this birth—but otherwise not—believe me! (p. 118).

Here Eckhart makes it clear that the departure is one of the ego and all ego functions, and a return to the core of the soul or what I would call the archetype for the psychological function of intuition, which is also the core "out of which you came," if the procession is first Self, then soul, and finally, ego. Obviously, there can be a coniunctio within each of the functions of thinking, feeling, or sensation, and if this happens in one function, it affects the other functions profoundly. Eckhart appears to have experienced the union of opposites in the thinking function or at least he thought so; what he thought was logical and reasonable language has usually been interpreted as mysticism.

The California philosopher Franklin Merrell-Wolff (1976) describes the possibility of what he calls "realization" from two functions, thought and feeling, when he says:

> For my own part, I have always found that cognition, when highly purified, could fly higher than feeling. It is perfectly true

> that Transcendental Knowledge is beyond thought, but, at the same time, it is equally beyond feeling and sensation. None of these three can be more than accessory instruments, and all of them are left behind at the final Transition (p. 68).

As a philosopher, Merrell-Wolff also appeared to understand a return to the Self from the thinking function, which he describes as his own preferred method or, in Jungian terms, his superior function.

Merrell-Wolff (1976, p. 172) names the four psychological functions in his philosophy. He calls what I have referred to as ego consciousness the subject-object consciousness that has three modes: sensation, affection, and cognition. If one reads Merrell-Wolff's descriptions of his terms, it is not difficult to recognize these modes as the psychological functions of sensation, feeling, and thinking, as described by Jung, and even though Merrell-Wolff was familiar with Jung's work (he thought Jung was the "greatest Western psychologist" (1973, p. 78), it is not difficult to imagine that his concepts came about from his own reflection on the possibilities.

What is of particular interest in his definitions of the three modes of ordinary consciousness and his definition of super consciousness, which he equates with cosmic consciousness, Christ consciousness, and so forth, is that his idea of super consciousness appears to be identical with the function of intuition. He names it "the symbol of the fourth dimension" (1976, p. 172). Thus, Merrell-Wolff appears to be describing two primary forms of consciousness that appear to be identical with what I have been referring to as the psychological function of intuition or the soul complex and the ego complex, which is composed of the three functions of sensation, feeling, and thinking, or what Merrell-Wolff calls the "subject-object consciousness."

Part of the problem in describing any experience has to do with language—which is often inadequate for the task. The word "indifference" seems to imply negative connotations that do not apply. In describing the reconciliation of opposites, Merrell-Wolff (1976, p. 313; 1973, p. 88) refers to indifference as the state of high indifference, attempting to rescue it from our usual understanding of ordinary indifference. Meister Eckhart (Blakney, 1941), calls it disinterest, explaining that, "pure disinterest is neither this nor that, it is empty nothingness" (p. 88). Meister Eckhart puts disinterest above love: "Experience must always be an experience of something, but disinterest comes so close to zero that nothing but God is rarefied enough to get into it, to enter the disinterested heart" (p. 83). Eckhart was correct for the simple reason that love, coming from two sides of the feeling function, cancels itself when united; when two become one, even love does not exist or is all that does exist. Nothing and everything become two opposites with the same meaning.

Merrell-Wolff's high indifference seems to me to be a pure objectivity where we simply observe the is-ness of things. I have used the word "neutral" (neither this nor that) in the same way that I understand Merrell-Wolff to use the phrase "high indifference" or Meister Eckhart to use "disinterest." The personification of psychic energy that is neutral finds one of its best representations in the Angel archetype, simply because angels are described as being the closest to God. They are also usually represented as being neutral in their sexuality (only the corrupted ones lust after the daughters of man), which probably symbolizes the merging of psychic energy contained within each psychological function or the energy of separate and seemingly opposing functions that have been reconciled.

When Eckhart speaks of a disinterested heart, however, he is not speaking of the thinking function, but the feeling function, which has suspended all value judgments and is in a neutral place. This implies a reconciliation between the two halves of the feeling function and a heart that is not divided, that is as pure, one might say, as the heart of an angel. It is even possible that thinking or reason, the exalted type that Merrell-Wolff and Eckhart describe, might require the suspension of value judgment or feeling to operate at optimal levels. Feeling would, therefore, not be absent, but raised to its highest level in undivided love. There is no thought that does not have feeling, in one of its forms, as the basis for the later expressed thought. If this is so, the importance of the feeling function has not been given due credit in the field of psychology as the possible ground for all cognitive thinking.

Merrell-Wolff (1973) describes the relationship between the feeling and thinking functions in the following way:

> In their depths, feeling and thought spring from the same root. This root, in its own nature as unmanifested, has a character that appears to the relative consciousness as both devoid of feeling and without conceptual form. But when realized, it has the value of fulfilled feeling and completed thought. Consciousness no longer feels a reaching out for an unattained completeness. With this, both thought and feeling lose their differentiated and therefore, identifiable particularity. But when the root is projected into the actualizing consciousness, it loses some measure of its purity, since to actualize is to particularize, even though on the most abstract level of expression (pp. 177-178).

This appears to be an excellent description of the making of an abstract symbol. Even though Merrell-Wolff is not attempting to describe beginning consciousness, I believe the process is no different for a newborn than it is for an adult.

Returning to the functions, angels can be seen to represent aspects of all the diverse and complex psychological functions, but the mightiest angels are those who represent psychic energy that is neutral. Neutrality is the synthesis of the negative and the positive positions or the opposites. It is the third position that leads to the fourth or the state of undifferentiation. Since the state of undifferentiation represents Paradise, any archetype that presumes to be God-like, but not identical with God, might represent neutral or undifferentiated energy.

One of the best representations of neutral, undifferentiated energy, outside of the Divine Child archetype, can be found in the symbolism of the four Archangels, Michael, Uriel, Raphael, and Gabriel. Michael represents the function of intuition; Uriel represents the function of sensation, although his position varies considerably, according to the myth; Raphael represents the function of feeling; and Gabriel represents the function of thinking.

The Archangel Michael as Archetype for the Psychological Function of Neutral or Undifferentiated Intuition

Michael is the first Archangel and a member of the first choir, the Seraphim, and appears to be the most important angel in all the Hebrew/Christian mythological literature, excluding the Fallen Angel, Lucifer. "The archetype of all Jewish angels, the Archangel Michael, is guardian and lifesaver through all of the Rabbinic literature" (Margolies, 1994, p. 260). Moolenburgh (1992) says: "The first is Michael, the one whom Daniel called 'the great prince,' who 'standeth for the children of thy people' (Daniel 12, verse 1)" (p. 88). Michael's name means "Looks like God" or "Who is as God," indicating his significance as the first Archangel.

"In mystic and occult writings, Michael has often been equated with the Holy Ghost, the Logos, God, Metatron" (Davidson, 1971, p. 194). He also holds the keys to the kingdom of Heaven, which I would interpret psychologically as a return to the function of intuition before experiencing the Self, that is, Heaven. Michael, as the benevolent angel of death, leads back to the "eternal Light" (Davidson, 1971, p. 194), which I understand as the light of super consciousness or the light of intuition, not the light of ordinary ego consciousness. What dies is ego consciousness that is replaced by undifferentiated intuition or soul consciousness. Thinking, feeling, and sensation must die, that is, become unconscious, before intuition, symbolized as the key, can open the door to Heaven or psychologically speaking, the Self.

Michael appears to be one of the earliest archetypes to be a "copy" of what is later, in Genesis, called the Father God. Cooper (1984) says of Michael:

> The fight between the Archangel Michael and the dragon is older than Christianity, which, as in so many other instances, adapted pagan myth to fit its teaching. St. Michael is the ancient Sun God who overcomes the dragon or serpent of darkness (p. 50).

Like the Father God in Genesis or the ancient Sun God, Michael, as the first and most important Archangel, can be seen as a personification for the psychological function of intuition or undifferentiated psychic energy. This energy "kills" the serpent of darkness or the psychological function of conscious sensation. Intuition as super consciousness would be the state of consciousness and unconsciousness united or undifferentiated and is personified as a god or replica of a god. What super consciousness kills is the darkness of consciousness and unconsciousness that are divided. The battle of Michael and the dragon can be seen as a battle between the soul and the ego or the battle between the two psychological functions of intuition and sensation, which do not work at the same time, in the psyche of one individual. The archetypes portray universal experience.

Michael is associated with the planet Mercury, the smallest planet in the solar system and the planet closest to the sun. The symbol of the morning star (Venus, Christ, David) appears related, as both the morning star and Mercury are described as the closest to the sun, which in mythology often represents God. And Michael, as described above, was considered in early pagan myth, to be the Sun God. He also seems to have many of the attributes of the Roman god Mercury or the Greek god Hermes, both of whom are the winged messengers (angels) for the gods.

In the realm of the four directions, Michael rules the East (Burnham, 1990). East represents the place of beginnings, as in the dawn of a new day, the dawn of humanity, or the dawn of individual human birth. In every mythology that produces symbols related to the four directions, the East is related to the function of intuition and intuitive knowledge. If the womb is Paradise and the center, East of Eden is the leaving of Eden, and the psychological function of intuition, a reflection of the center, as Michael is a reflection (Looks like God) of God. If we think of intuition as sensing, feeling, and thinking on an unconscious and undifferentiated level where we move toward or away from the object according to what is necessary (without the necessity of a conscious ego), this makes sense. It also seems reasonable to assume that this would be our first method of knowing and the source from which all knowing originally came and continues to come, like Michael, in the form of a serpent that sheds its skin and is continuously re-born.

As an archetype associated with the East and a symbol of the one of the four directions, Michael can also be compared with the East wind that Andersen (1974) describes in the Fairy tale, "The Garden of Eden." The East wind, personified as the fourth son and the mother's "favorite" carries the prince (that is, the ego), back to Paradise (p. 137). In this myth, mother nature puts her sons in a bag if they do not behave and they are reduced to silence (p. 133). This symbolizing by Andersen can be seen as another example of silencing the ego functions of sensation, feeling, and thinking, while intuition (the East wind) speaks. The direction of East, whether personified by the Archangel Michael or the East wind as described by Andersen, appears to represent the psychological function of intuition.

Of the Seraphim, Godwin (1990) says: "popularly known as the fiery, flying serpents of lightning, who roar like lions when aroused, the Seraphim are more identified with the serpent or dragon than any other angelic order" (p. 25). Michael is also identified with the lion. Jung (1958/1952) says that "Origen elicits from the diagram of Celsus that Michael, the first angel of the Creator, has 'the shape of a lion'" (p. 75). This may connote the importance of being first (King of the jungle) and the power of animal instincts, which to date cannot be explained rationally.

This sounds very much like the much older Sumerian archetype of the Serpent Lord, which contains lion-birds and serpents. Michael appears to be the first "Serpent Fire of Love." The lion head is also associated with the deity of Aion, or Time, an archetypal image that is winged (angel symbol) and enclosed in the coils of a serpent (see cover of Soul and Body, Meier, 1986). The image of Aion (2nd-3rd century A.D.) is a variation of the Serpent Lord archetype, which preceded it by at least several thousand years. As an archetype associated with the serpent, the lion, the first Archangel and himself considered a former deity, Michael can be seen as a variation of the Aion archetype. Actually, it would be the other way around, because Michael obviously preceded the Aion archetype by several thousand years. Being first denotes the end of eternity and the beginning of time, linking Aion and Michael, to creation mythology. As the Serpent of Lightning, "always associated with intuition and inspiration" (Fontana, 1994, p. 116), Michael roars like a lion, indicating the power of unconscious body perceptions, provided by an unknown "god."

Michael, as Prince, is also a Divine Child archetype, like his Greek equivalent Hermes, and he can be seen as neutral energy in the function of intuition, with the positive aspect being the Father God and the negative aspect being the Mother God. In other words, Michael represents the same psychic energy that Christ represents, and both can be compared with Lucifer, who represents the same energy before his infamous Fall.

As Prince of the heavenly hosts and commander-in-chief of the celestial army, Michael appears to be the most suitable Archangel to represent the first (and last or fourth) psychological function of the human infant, intuition. The celestial army that he leads is the energy of all the other functions, including himself, that have not been split or differentiated. Michael, as passive thinking or intuition, can be readily seen as human instinct; Gabriel, the Archangel that vies with him in fame and importance in angelology, can readily be seen as active thinking, the end product of the instinct or the archetype. Michael can be compared with the Father God in Genesis (intuition), just as Gabriel can be compared with Adam (thinking). If we consider the importance from this viewpoint, Michael would, indeed, be the first and most important Archangel for the simple reason that instinct precedes archetype and is necessary for the creation of an archetype. All ideas that are derived from the archetype are passive before they become active. Michael is the angel closest to God because both archetypes are a description of the first differentiation of psychic energy that flows out of the Self, where all functions exist as one.

The Archangel Uriel as Archetype for the Psychological Function of Neutral or Undifferentiated Sensation

Uriel is Michael's twin serpent, just as intuition is twin to sensation and the Father God in Genesis is twin to the Serpent in the Garden of Eden. The lion-bird symbol describes the two functions that have been separated and reunited or in a certain sense, turned inside-out. Michael is the head of the eagle or bird; Uriel is the body or the torso of the lion. Michael is the champion of the soul (intuition), and Uriel is the ruler or champion (sensation) of the ego and beginning ego consciousness. The lion-bird represents the two opposed functions that are united and working as one animal, a combination of divine angel and human animal, a heaven and earth merged symbol. In this respect, the lion-bird is a personification of the energy of the god/man/child, later known as Christ, or simply put in the Hebrew religion, a man or child of God.

As the patron saint of the Hebrews, Michael (intuition) leads Israel (sensation) in the form of Jacob, who is renamed Israel after his wrestling match with the angel Uriel. Leading the children of God out of bondage (bondage being synonymous with the experience of the opposites) will take them through the experience of all the opposites until they return to the state of unity and become free. In other words, the experience of the opposites at birth throws one into Hell (earth) when the unity of Paradise has been lost. Michael, however, will restore the original experience, which is what happens in the psyche when the ego is lost and there is a return to soul or the function of intuition. The cry of Israel to "let my children go" is a plea for unity in each function, represented by the child archetype, who symbolizes the unity of opposites. The twelve tribes of Israel can be seen as the positive, neutral, and negative energy in each of the four functions, considering Israel as the birth of consciousness.

"Uriel," Godwin (1990) tells us, means "Fire of God" (or Light of God); "he presides over Tartarus (or Hell) being both a Seraphim and a Cherubim" (p. 52). This can be translated as conscious sensation (Uriel) that is identical with unconscious sensation or intuition (the fire of God). Unconscious sensation or intuition is the fire of God. Fire symbolizes transformation and Uriel can be seen as the fire or light of God, which is consciousness and unconsciousness merged. He is not, like Lucifer after the Fall, a symbol of introverted, conscious sensation; neither is he, like Christ, a symbol of extraverted unconscious sensation that has yet to be experienced. He represents the neutral energy in the function of sensation, when both sides of the function are united to make a whole.

On the compass points, Uriel "rules South" (Burnham, 1990, p. 164), which connects him to the sun (son of God, Christ or consciousness) in his positive aspect. As the angel presiding over Hell, which I would describe as his negative aspect, he appears also to be closely related to the Prince of Darkness. He "rules" over the unconscious side of the sensate function. In this manner, Uriel represents both sides of the sensation function that are united, neutral, and undifferentiated. Uriel, as the neutral energy contained in the function of sensation, can be defined as the uniting middle symbol within that function, with Lucifer on one side as negative energy and Christ on the other side as positive energy. When a conjunctio within the function takes place, the middle or third archetype, Uriel, flows into a state of undifferentiation (the celebrated fourth position) that is equivalent to the Father God or being one with the Father God. Each Archangel, described as the closest angel (image) to God, yet different from God, is describing each psychological function in its ideal form, that is, when the opposites of consciousness and unconsciousness have been united in super consciousness or the Self.

As Archangels go, Uriel is usually considered the fourth and the least in importance of that quaternity; he is often tacked onto the end as an afterthought in many descriptions and occupies a position that appears to be interchangeable with many other angels. This is also a good description of the psychological function of sensation and its relationship to the body. The loss of super consciousness renders the split of consciousness and unconscious negative, thus introverted sensation would necessarily be seen as negative, which is reflected in all cosmological mythology that describes a loss of Paradise. The myths, however, also appear to be describing how sensation is related to and connected with the function of intuition and the Father God. One function is no better or higher than the other if one sees that they determine and reflect each other, like the twin Serpents in earlier mythology.

Uriel is, Godwin (1990) also tells us, "The first recorded instance of an angel becoming a man" (p. 52). The man he became in the myth was Jacob (sensation), who tricked his father into giving him the blessing rather than his twin brother, Esau (intuition). Jacob and his older twin Esau can be seen as later archetypes that also represent the split in super consciousness or human personifications of the two irrational functions. I see Jacob as sensation because he is the younger twin, who defeats his brother in the same way sensation, as the first function after birth defeats intuition, which is the first function in the womb. One can see all the experiences between the two brothers as the inner or psychic dialog between the opposing functions of sensation and intuition, and conscious and unconscious energy in the function of sensation, which is the same dichotomy that occurs in the Lucifer/Christ archetypes. Both myths describe the war between the psychic energy in the opposing functions or in the one function of sensation within one individual. This is recorded in Genesis, when the Lord replies to Rebekah, who inquires why the war in her womb:

> And the LORD said unto her, Two nations are in thy womb, and two manner of people shall be separated from thy bowels; and the one people shall be stronger than the other people; and the elder shall serve the younger (Genesis 25:23).

Intuition is the elder function that serves sensation. In psychological terms, this describes what happens in the human psyche; the function of intuition or the elder people will serve the function of sensation or the younger people. Isaac or the Father (thinking) favors Esau (intuition), and Rebekah or the Mother (feeling) favors Jacob (sensation). Here the conscious thought can be seen as counterbalanced by the unconscious feeling function, which in the end wins the contest. The fate of Israel is determined by a woman named Rebekah.

The man (represented by Jacob) that the Archangel Uriel becomes is also the human child who first experiences negative sensation at birth when consciousness and unconsciousness become divided, like the twins of Rebekah's womb, Jacob and Esau. The younger twin winning out over the older twin is the function of introverted, conscious sensation (Jacob). Jacob tricks the blind, dying father, Isaac (the function of conscious thinking that no longer sees clearly) into giving the blessing before he dies, (becomes unconscious). This can be seen as the old, dying thought that inadvertently blesses the function of conscious sensation, which will bring the new thought. The function of intuition is Esau or Edom, the red-headed, hairy, first-born who earlier sold his birthright for a bowl of stew. His birthright represents the position of intuition as the first function of the human child, while in the womb, a function which is sold or exchanged for food (the function of conscious sensation at birth). If one follows the complete story, which is not possible here, one can view Jacob's experiences and years of work and toil for Leah and Rachel to be a description of what happens in his attempts to reconcile the divided feeling function, represented by Leah (introverted feeling) and Rachel (extraverted feeling), yet another set of twins.

Graves and Patai (1989) describe the reconciliation of Jacob and Esau: "the Genesis account consistently favors Esau at Jacob's expense; not only by modern ethical standards, but by those of ancient Palestine" (p. 233). Favoring Esau over Jacob is homogeneous with favoring the Divine Child over the human child (intuition over sensation), but Jacob, as Israel incarnate, represents ego consciousness and consciousness not only of the Hebrews as a social group, but of the human child. Thus, Uriel is the first Archangel to become a man in the form of the Jacob archetype or the function of sensation.

The chosen race can be seen as the children or the children of God, or the neutral energy in each function that is reunited, extending that apparently elitist archetypal thought into its more universal meaning. In other words, the Chosen Ones of Israel can apply to the inner children in the psyche (the functions that have been reunited) or the outer children (the children of the world).

Sexton (1993) equates Jacob and Israel with the missing feminine and the soul archetype. I am more inclined to think that Esau represents the soul and Jacob the body and ego body consciousness, which negates the soul (the function of intuition) to the unconscious. If Esau represents the function of intuition, the soul is not absent, but identical with the spirit and the body as unconscious feeling. Intuition is soul, spirit and body united. In this particular myth, consciousness has acquired a higher status than it previously enjoyed in Genesis, when birth was the loss of God and Paradise. Jacob represents a positive interpretation of the function of sensation symbolized by his wrestling with an angel of God and God giving his blessing. The reunited twins represent body and soul which are reunited, after the fight and separation of the functions.

The twin brothers and twin sisters are other personifications of the twin serpents of psychic energy. The theme of twins or older and younger brothers or sisters is repeated over and over in many myths, starting with Cain and Abel, a more negative version of Esau and Jacob. In this myth, Cain is an archetype similar to Satan or the snake, (the first-born conscious sensation) that kills his younger brother (that is, conscious intuition), represented as Abel, the brother associated with animals or the more primitive (first in the womb) function, like the hairy or primitive Esau. Esau and Abel were both keepers of animals, symbolizing their primitive aspects of energy (conscious intuition) that precedes ego consciousness.

The warring brothers describe the battle of psychic energy between the two functions, first one wins, then the other, describing the cycles of psychic energy. Neither Cain nor Abel continues the genealogical myth, but Seth, the third child (youngest child is usually the hero in mythology) of Adam and Eve, propagates the race. Seth, as the youngest child, represents the unity between the functions of sensation and intuition or neutral energy, whereas the Esau/Jacob myth describes a reconciliation between the two functions, neither of which is seen in its pejorative extreme, although the preference appears to be for Esau, just as Michael is the preferred Archangel, and both represent the psychological function of intuition which is preferred over conscious sensation.

Uriel, who becomes Jacob, known to be the "sharpest eyed angel of all" (Godwin, 1990, p. 53) reconciles the opposites in the function of sensation and represents a union of opposites or a neutral state within that function. Sensation that sees sharply would be an apt description for a neutral place that sees equally well from both sides of that particular function. One can say that the angel Uriel becomes a man or one can say that the man Jacob becomes an angel or God/man. In either case, the function of sensation and consciousness has been elevated from its previous lower status symbolized by Jacob finally being blessed by God.

Uriel can be compared with Lucifer, who also presides over Hell and is renamed Satan. Like Lucifer, Uriel is the "Bringer of light of Knowledge of God to men." The names and symbols used to represent the same psychological experience vary from myth to myth, but the function of sensation appears to have more representations other than Uriel to represent the same energy. This might be due to the difficulty in expressing the negative and positive aspects of sensation, which is the instinct of beginning ego consciousness and its dark "twin," the unconscious.

Neutral energy can be defined as containing negative and positive energy, being neither, and it is always a child symbol in this respect (the third position), just as Lucifer is the first and favorite child/angel of God, and Christ is later the firstborn child of God. In this way, neutral energy can be seen as a type of energy contained within each function that leads to the (fourth) undifferentiated energy that exists when the functions are not separate; this is the energy that expresses the unity of the opposites. The energy exists first in the experience, or one could say the experience is the energy and the symbol is only an expression of the original experience. There is a trinity within each function that leads to the quaternary, and the experience of the opposites united within that particular function can produce a vision, an angel, or an idea of unity. Meister Eckhart (Blakney, 1941) says:

> The soul at its highest is formed like God, but an angel gives a closer idea of him. That is all an angel is: an idea of God. For this reason the angel was sent to the soul, so that the soul might be reformed by it, to be the divine idea by which it was first conceived. Knowledge comes through likeness. And so, because the soul may know everything, it is never at rest until it comes to the original idea, in which all things are one (p. 141).

That an angel is "an idea of God" seems like a pragmatic statement coming from a reputed mystic of the Middle Ages. It shows the value Eckhart placed on the Angel archetype as a personification of psychic energy meant to describe God and also shows his exaltation of the idea as a divine copy of God.

The Archangels Michael and Uriel can be seen as twin angels, both ideal reflections of God. They represent the first two irrational psychological functions of intuition and sensation that appear in the human child. Intuition is first in the womb; sensation is the first function to appear at birth as ego consciousness, negating intuition to unconsciousness. Michael looks like God because he represents the same neutral psychic energy. Uriel is the fire of God because he represents ego consciousness in the world. Intuition (Michael) and sensation (Uriel) can be seen as archetypes representing the first unfolding of the functions out of the Self and each reflect God in the other, one as soul and one as ego. The next ego function flowing out of intuition is the rational function of feeling or Raphael.

The Archangel Raphael as Archetype for the Psychological Function of Neutral or Undifferentiated Feeling

The third Archangel to be represented as a personification of neutral and undifferentiated psychic energy within one function is Raphael. Raphael is associated with the direction of West and is the angel of death, like Michael, and the angel of love, the two major themes of all great literature. Moolenburgh (1992) says the following of Raphael:

> Raphael has his own place in the Temple, and that is on the west side. This is the last part of the Temple, the holy of holies, the end of the road. Even as the sun goes up in the east and sets in the west, so the voyage of man is depicted symbolically as a voyage from east to west (p. 116).

The voyage of man, depicted symbolically as a voyage from east to west, appears to be also true in the realm of the psychological functions which appear in time as the same circular process, from East to South to West to North, reinforcing Jung's archetypal structure of the human psyche and his idea of a four-fold cognitive psyche that seems to be more organized than previously assumed.

Connolly (1994) tells us that

> Raphael is noted in Jewish and Christian literature as an Archangel and one of the throne angels. In Christian belief he is chief of the guardian angels and has the special task of protecting the young, the innocent, and pilgrims and other travelers (p. 95).

Raphael usually is depicted as the third Archangel of importance after Michael and Gabriel in Judaism and Christianity.

Connolly (1994) goes on the say that "Raphael is the angel of prayer, love, joy, light, providence, and, especially, healing" (p. 95). So many of the attributes of the Archangels appear to cross over from one to the other, such as light, with which they all are associated, that it seems important to focus on the primary attributes specific to each angel. With Raphael, that specific attribute has to be healing. Raphael's name means "Divine healer" or "God heals." Raphael is also a Seraph and "Chief of Guardian Angels" (Burnham, 1990, p. 104).

As a Divine Child/Angel archetype or energy that is neutral and undifferentiated in the feeling function, Raphael signifies the unity of the two sides of the feeling function. The positive and the negative are united in the third, neutral position of Raphael, which leads to undifferentiation and the experience of the Self. I see, for instance, the equivalent archetypes of Eve and Mary, as representations for the two sides of love in the feeling function, ego love and soul love. Subjective, introverted feeling and the value judgment it makes is based on the ego and ego consciousness (Eve). Objective, extraverted feeling and the value judgment it makes are based on soul or soul consciousness, which puts the object first (Mary). (This is a description of extreme archetypes, which I consider Eve and Mary to be.) Both positions make value judgments. Raphael represents the middle position of neutrality (also a value judgment, but different from the other two opposites) that leads to undifferentiation and a suspension of all value judgments in the feeling function. I see this as an ability that is crucial to healing and essential as a tool of the therapist or as an experience for the patient. Raphael can be seen as love in its highest form, love as a principle, or an archetypal experience essential before a return to the Self. Whatever the problem or goal is, it will not be accomplished without an experience of unity in the function of feeling on a conscious or unconscious level. I believe that all feeling is thought in an unconscious form and this is why it is associated with the feminine principle so often, at least in many of our Western myths and religion. Feeling is without form, without image, without words in its purest form, and like the excluded Goddess, is silent. The ability to love oneself without value judgments (or at least have that experience) is why Raphael, as a messenger of God, "heals."

Raphael, as Regent of the Sun, is closely associated with the feminine principle. A regent is often the female sovereign who rules in the absence of her male counterpart or is a prince carrying out the same duties. Raphael is associated with the sun, but he is not the sun, a symbol that usually represents God in mythology, just as the Archangel Michael is associated with Mercury as the planet closest to the sun or archetypal angel closest to God. Thus, the Divine Child archetype and the Divine Mother archetype are both played out in the figure of Raphael.

Concerning the Seraphim, Godwin (1990) tells us that:
> Their name actually suggests a blend of the Hebrew term *rapha*, meaning "healer," "Doctor" or "surgeon" and ser, meaning "higher being" or "guardian angel," The Serpent or dragon has long been a symbol for the healing arts, being sacred to Aesculapius (emphasis author's, p. 25).

As Seraphim and Chief of the Guardian Angels, Raphael is associated with the Serpent archetype and can also be seen as a later manifestation of the Queen Lion-Bird of the Serpent Lord image (synonymous with the Cherubim). Raphael or feeling is the first rational function to appear in the human child.

If we see the twin lion-birds or serpent/angels as representing a further differentiation of consciousness, after the functions of intuition and sensation become split, Raphael represents the differentiation of the feeling function that is still joined with the function of unconscious thinking. One set of the Lion-Birds or Cherubim can be seen as the two functions of intuition and sensation that are separated yet joined by the symbol of one animal. This would be Michael and/or Uriel, who represent the unity of the irrational functions. On the other side of the image, the Lion-Bird or Cherubim would be the two functions of feeling and thinking that have become divided yet are still joined, symbolized by one powerful animal. This is represented by Raphael and Gabriel. The bird, angel, or top half of the animal represents the divine, or that aspect closest to God, heaven, spirit, and so forth, or either function of intuition or thinking. The lower half of the animal, the body of the lion, represents an animal who is king of the animals on earth, and symbolizes the psychological functions of sensation or feeling or the body functions. Uriel or sensation turns into Raphael or feeling.

Godwin (1990) says of the Cherubim:

> Originally the Cherubim were mighty guardian figures which appeared throughout the Near and Middle East. The earliest Sumerian term is six thousand years old. This is found in the archaic pictogram of Ka-ri-bu. In this Ka is a head crying out, ri is a winged form which also suggests protection while bu is a sharp spear or sword like image which is associated with an armed man. Thus the overall portrait is that of a winged and armed guardian (p. 30).

Whether Lion-Birds or Cherubim, the archetypal energy appears to be the same, signifying an important and universal human experience. Godwin (1990) asks the following question: "How such magnificent and awesome beings shrunk to the size of tubby little winged babies, fluttering prettily in the corners of Baroque ceilings, remains one of the mysteries of existence" (p. 28). I do not think this is quite that mysterious if one sees that the Cherubim are representatives of a Divine Child archetype. As such, they have the strength and power of both parents united in themselves. That is why they can be portrayed as ferocious animals in adult or child form. As a Divine Child archetype, they represent energy that is neutral and equal. The rational and irrational functions are working in harmony, which they (hopefully) did as they became differentiated out of the Self and which is essential for a return to the Self. The lion-birds also represent the power of the human child who, in most cases, begin the process of individuation in a similar manner.

Perhaps the most popular and famous myth centered on Raphael is the story of Tobias in the Catholic Bible. With the inclusion of the myth of Tobias, Raphael becomes the third angel mentioned by name in the Bible; if Lucifer is counted, he becomes the fourth angel. (Uriel is not mentioned by name in the Jacob/angel myth, but is a supposition from other religious sources. Some say that Jacob actually was fighting with God).

Thus, there is a fourfold theme of Archangels throughout the Bible, with the primary focus eventually falling on the Fallen Angel, Lucifer, who is the adversary of Michael in the realm of angels. Michael, of course, is the archetypal angel closest to God and the one who battles and defeats Satan. As psychic energy, this is a description of the battle between the function of intuition or soul (Michael) and the function of sensation or ego (Satan).

Raphael's place here is the reuniting of the two sides of the feeling function in order to cure the split in that function and by doing so, also cure the split in the thinking function, where one thought without its opposite dominates. This is represented in the myth by the elder Tobias, who is blind, that is, cannot see both sides of the thought. (Consider how many of the Patriarchs in the Old Testament became blind.) Raphael cures the blindness of Tobias by putting the gall of the fish (a symbol for Christ) on his eyes, which symbolizes forcing him to see the bitter and rejected, unconscious thought, which is equal to his negative feeling, personified by his wife Anna. By a coniunctio in the feeling function and the thinking function, Tobias is cured and the family (the psyche) is restored to health. Raphael, as the angel of death, insures the death of the conscious ego, which is always an act of love or a sacrifice.

If Raphael is the patron saint of medicine (symbolized by the twin serpents of the caduceus or intuition and sensation that both contain feeling that is still neutral), he is no less important for psychology, which attempts to heal the soul. The curing of the feeling function appears essential in maintaining the flow of psychic energy in spirit, soul and body so that they continue to act as one undivided Self. The feeling function appears to be the function that unites the other two ego functions, sensation and thinking, in order for a return to the function of intuition, which supplies the gift of wisdom. Undivided love in the feeling function is the double-edged sword of Raphael or the Cherubim. When this energy is neutral and undifferentiated, love and death have the same meaning; they are the twin wings of the Archangel Raphael.

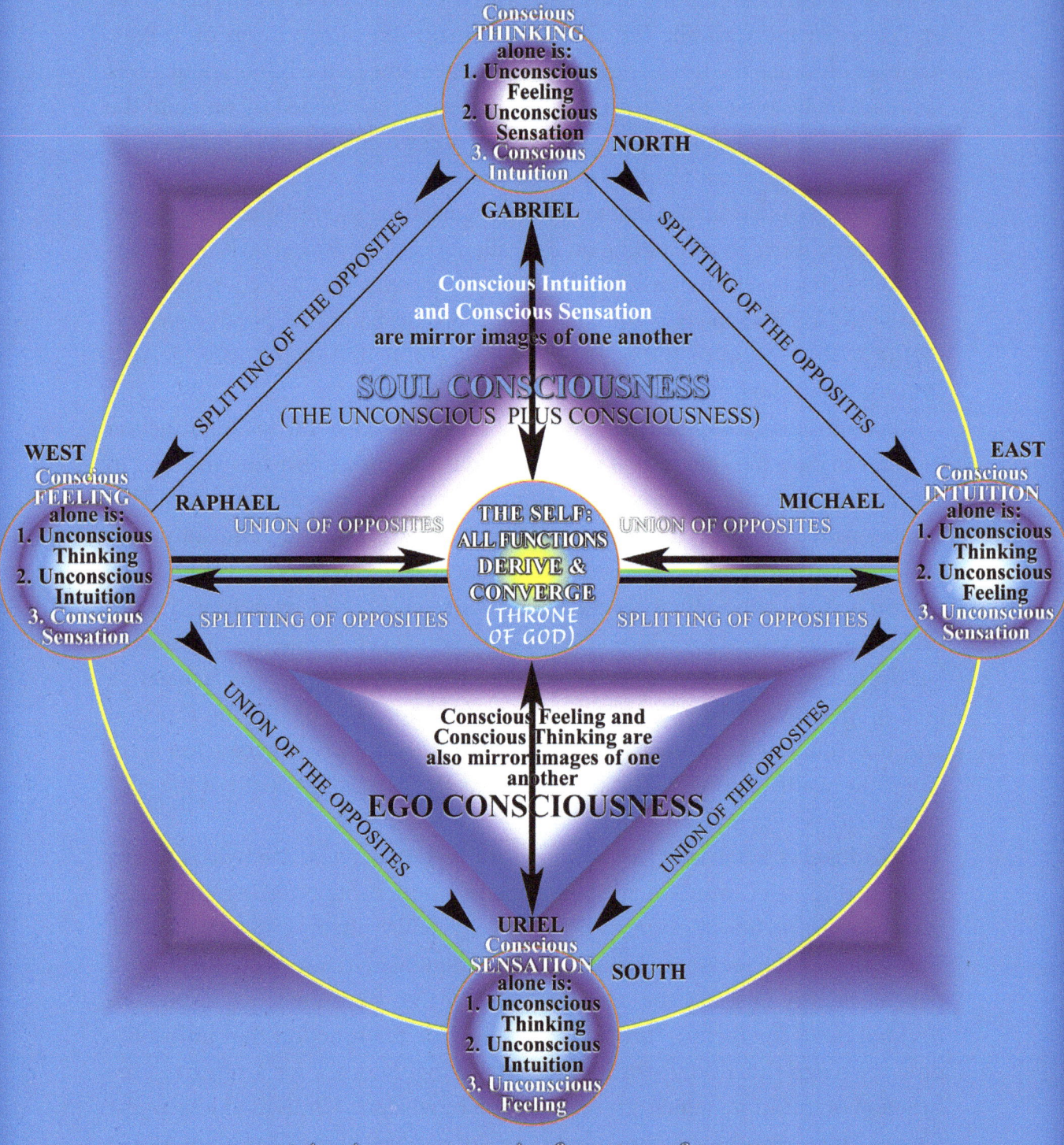

THE DIFFERENTIATION OF JUNG'S FOUR PSYCHIC FUNCTIONS
THE FOUR APOSTLES AS ARCHETYPES OF PSYCHIC ENERGY

conscious INTUITION alone is:
1. Unconscious Thinking
2. Unconscious Feeling
3. Unconscious Sensation

ST. MATTHEW
the tax collector
(called by Jesus and wrote the first Gospel)

Conscious Intuition and Conscious Sensation are also mirror images of one another

SOUL CONSCIOUSNESS
(THE UNCONSCIOUS PLUS CONSCIOUSNESS)

SPLITTING OF THE OPPOSITES

ST. LUKE (the dear Physician)

ST. JOHN (author of the last Gospel & Apocalypse)

conscious FEELING alone is:
1. Unconscious Thinking
2. Unconscious Intuition
3. Conscious Sensation

THE SELF: ALL FUNCTIONS DERIVE & CONVERGE — CHRIST

UNION OF OPPOSITES

conscious THINKING alone is:
1. Unconscious Feeling
2. Unconscious Sensation
3. Conscious Intuition

SPLITTING OF OPPOSITES

(author of the third Gospel)

Conscious Feeling and Conscious Thinking are also mirror images of one another

EGO CONSCIOUSNESS

ST. MARK (never knew Jesus)

UNION OF THE OPPOSITES

conscious SENSATION alone is:
1. Unconscious Thinking
2. Unconscious Intuition
3. Unconscious Feeling

Compare the similarities of the four Gospel writers: St Matthew, St Mark, St Luke, and St John with the description of the four archangels: Michael, Uriel, Rafael, and Gabriel. Matthew means "gift of the Lord" while Michael means "who is like God." One is the "first" and most important archangel and the other is the first writer of the Gospels. Both are archetypes that describe the psychic energy of intuition. The angel is the pure form (like God) and the man is a Sinner before his redemption by Christ. Mark never met Jesus, which describes the function of sensation when the ego is present. Can be compared with Uriel or Lucifer. Even more apparent is St Luke, who was called "the most dear physician" in the same way Raphael is described as a Divine physician. Both can be compared with the function of feeling. Also readily apparent is Gabriel as the archangel of revelation, which is comparable with St John's important role as the author of the Apocalypse, the last book in the Christian bible and the last gospel. St Matthew (intuition) is first and St John (thinking) is last. One can say that the Apostles lived the life of the archetype and / or that their lives represent that ARCHETYPAL energy. They are the archangels in human form, just as Christ is God in human form. They became messengers of the World, Evangelists for the message received by Christ, archetype for the Self.

The Archangel Gabriel as Archetype for the Psychological Function of Neutral or Undifferentiated Thinking

The fourth Archangel personified as neutral psychic energy is Gabriel, who represents neutral energy in the thinking function. Gabriel is associated with the direction of North, which represents the thinking function in many mythologies (see Loomis, 1991, p. 40). Using the symbol of the four directions, East represents intuition, South represents the function of sensation, and West represents the feeling function.

Gabriel's importance is second only to that of Michael in the Hebrew/Christian mythology, although in the Islam religion Djibril, who is equivalent to Gabriel, holds first place. Djibril or Gabriel appeared to the prophet Mahammad to reveal the Koran, and like Mika'il (Michael) is said to have saffron hair, which is a red-orange color, reminiscent of the red hair of Edom (Esau) in the Jacob myth. Both might refer to the red clay that Adam was formed from out of the earth and the psychological fact that passive thinking (intuition), comes first in the human psyche. Thus, the primary color of red shows up in association with Adam and Gabriel (thinking) and Esau and Michael (intuition), all archetypes for the two functions of thinking and intuition.

As the Archangel who brought the Word of God by the revelation of the Koran, the Islam holy book, the power and glory of thought (the thinking function) cannot be underestimated, and in its primal and earthly (red) form, all conscious thought was first intuitive thought. This is also probably why Michael and Gabriel are the only Archangels mentioned by name in the Bible. (The myth including Raphael is later excluded from the English version, a parallel perhaps, to the collective consciousness of Western society denigrating the feeling function as the thinking function escalates in importance).

Burnham (1990) describes Gabriel in the following way: "He is the Angel of Revelation. He is majestic, richly attired, and depicted in Christian iconography as kneeling before Mary, hands folded on his breast or carrying a scroll, scepter, or lily" (p. 104). The scroll connects Gabriel with the Word, language, and especially the written word and its importance in Western religion, whether Hebrew or Christian. The speaking and the writing of the thoughts of man, given by God or through God by an angel, become the consummate expression of archetypal experience. The scepter denotes the authority of Gabriel and the thinking function.

Gabriel (thinking) kneels before Mary because Mary represents the unconscious feeling function, or love without ego. If thinking is the mirror image of feeling, given content and form by the expression of an archetype, it will finally reflect the unity of the ego and soul in the feeling function, but only after the cherished thought, long considered the highest ability of man, has been sacrificed by the conscious ego. A new thought can be born to replace the one forfeited. Then we have Gabriel, or neutral, undifferentiated energy and a Divine Child archetype, who is the Hero of God. The Hero is always the conscious ego, and it knows itself to be divine after the sacrifice, when soul and ego are united in one archetype expressed as the Self. Gabriel represents neutral and undifferentiated energy that has experienced and united both sides of the thinking function.

The unity expressed by Uriel as neutral and undifferentiated energy in the function of sensation renders a state of innocence to the human child and to the function of conscious sensation as the function that introduces humanity into the world of ego consciousness. This is expressed in the myth of Jacob after his fight and blessing with the angel of God. Thus, Uriel as angel of the South, who would oppose Gabriel, as angel of the North or knowledge, can be seen as innocence, which may be a principle of the psychological function of sensation, as love is a principle in the feeling function, knowledge is a principle in the thinking function, and wisdom is the principle of the function of intuition.

The lily symbol appears to connect Gabriel to the moon and the feminine, as Chetwynd (1982) describes:

> The water-lily, confused with the ordinary lily is the light of conscious life, the first movement of life in the primeval slime. It is the earthly reflection in the water of the celestial moon—i.e., the reflection in human nature on earth of that heavenly light which is like the original light in the ocean of darkness, that swells with its fecundity and gives birth to the daylight sun/son. It is the original Flower of Light ("Fleur-de-Lis") but in the West this became associated with the ordinary lily (p. 245).

Just as Raphael or the feeling function is associated with the sun, Gabriel or the thinking function is associated with the moon. This appears to imply the relationship of the feeling function with the thinking function in both symbolisms, if we take the moon as a symbol for the feminine and the sun as a symbol for the masculine, which is usually the case in Western mythology. The lily is interchangeable with the rose and lotus symbol, and all three images symbolize the womb and represent Gabriel's connection, not only with the Virgin Mary, but with birth. Jung (1959/1938) calls the rose a Western equivalent of the lotus.

In India the lotus-flower (padma) is interpreted by the Tantrists as the womb. We know this symbol from the numbers of pictures of the Buddha (and other Indian deities) in the lotus-flower. It corresponds to the "Golden Flower" of Chinese alchemy, the rose of the Rosicrucians, and the mystic rose in Dante's Paradiso. Rose and lotus are usually arranged in groups of four petals, indicating the squaring of the circle or the united opposites. The significance of the rose as the maternal womb was nothing strange to our Western mystics (p. 363).

Thus, Gabriel is associated with birth, which probably represents a description of not only a biological birth, but a psychological birth, occurring when the two rational functions are joined in unity. When this happens, there is a return to the function of intuition and the process begins anew. Gabriel, like Adam, is representative of the birth or creation of the symbol or archetype. Neutral thinking that leads to undifferentiated thinking is equivalent to a return to the Father God; it is the function where the experiences of the previous functions are expressed by the formed image. Moore (1994) describes this when he says of the Annunciation: "It's an archetypal image, it's an image of something that happens eternally to us all the time" (p. 206). Gabriel (neutral, undifferentiated thinking) announces to Mary (extraverted feeling or agape love) that she is going to give birth to the Divine Child, which is a return to the function of conscious intuition. It might be better here to call it Super consciousness at this point.

Moolenburgh (1992) explains: "Gabriel is derived from the word 'gibor' and that means power or hero. From this word gibor is derived the word geber, a man. Gabriel thus means God's might" (p. 109). As the hero of God, Gabriel can be seen as an angel archetype representing the function of conscious and unconscious thinking that are united, also represented by Adam before the Fall. This is before the thinking function has become split into the two sides of introverted and extraverted thinking. Gabriel represents the same neutral and undifferentiated energy, the Divine Child/angel of the united thinking function.

As the "Hero of God," he is said to be the chief ambassador to humanity, a title that appears close to that given to Michael. Gabriel is associated with the moon and appears to be comparable with the feminine in a way the other Archangels are not. As Godwin (1990) describes, "Gabri-el is unique amongst an otherwise male or androgynous host, for it is almost certain that this great Archangel is the only female in the higher echelons" (p. 43). To call Gabriel exclusively female might be an exaggeration on Godwin's part, because the Archangel is represented as male in much of the literature, even though his image in art is often depicted as female. It appears more likely that Gabriel, as compared with the other Archangels, is the one most often depicted as androgynous.

This ambiguity concerning Gabriel's symbolic gender is especially interesting, as it connotes several important issues related to neutral and undifferentiated psychic energy. One of Gabriel's special attributes appears to be the gift of revelation and knowledge, especially as it is connected to the written word, and the other appears to be his connection with the feminine or mother archetype and the process of birth. It is always Gabriel who revels the knowledge of pregnancy to the women of the Old Testament and to the Virgin Mary in the New Testament. This knowledge is therefore connected to language and the word or logos and knowledge of the Divine Child. Perhaps this is why Mary is often portrayed in paintings as reading a book or having a book on her lap before the Archangel Gabriel appears to her. Moolenburgh (1992) tells us that "there is an old story which tells us of how Gabriel fetches the soul out of Paradise and instructs it for nine months while the body in which the soul is to live is growing in the mother's body" (p. 110).

Other versions of this myth say that Gabriel instructs the soul and right before birth, another angel comes and pats the mouth of the child, causing everything learned in the womb to be forgotten at birth. This delightful story represents Gabriel as neutral and undifferentiated energy in the thinking function, which is identical with the unconscious thinking function contained within the function of conscious intuition. The thinking function, which produces an isolated thought (the end of the process resulting in the archetype), is sacrificed for knowledge of the opposing unconscious thought, which brings forth a unity of the opposites or Gabriel in the form of neutral energy. This describes a loss of ego in the thinking function. In the beginning, however, in the womb, this cycle has not begun. The child is learning by one function only, which appears to be intuition. The neutral and undifferentiated aspect of that function, that is, Gabriel, is forgotten when opposites are introduced at birth.

The child in the womb is thinking all along, by the process or the instinct of intuition. Goldman (1993) says: "Intuition is not just a mysterious sixth sense. It is sense. Our intuition is our nature communication with our greater soul" (recorded lecture). This communication begins in the womb where the soul is instructed by the function of intuition and the invariably protesting soul that is removed from Paradise is the newborn child, as he or she experiences the opposites.

Gabriel is the hero of God because he represents psychic energy in the thinking function that is neutral and undifferentiated. He gives up his divinity, becomes a hero, for the sake of the divine birth, a new image, archetype or idea.

In summarizing the myth of the four Archangels as a description of neutral, undifferentiated psychic energy, I would suggest the following: The meaning of the myth of Archangels describes ideal human experience that is close to an idea of God. The image of the four Archangels surrounding the throne of God represents the four psychological functions of intuition, sensation, feeling, and thinking in their neutral and undifferentiated form, which is close to the experience of Paradise or the image of being one with God. One can call them four major and different images of God. Michael, as first instinct (intuition or soul) looks just like God (Spirit, Soul and Body are One). Uriel, as the second instinct (sensation), is the fire of God and beginning ego consciousness. Raphael (feeling), as an image of the divine healing God, is love. Gabriel (thinking), as the hero of God, is the archetype that is continuously born, dies and is reborn as the Divine Child.

The same energy will later be modified (the opposites bring "sin" and a split consciousness into the world) and expressed in the human, earthly form of the four great Evangelists: Matthew (Michael), Mark (Uriel), Luke (the great physician or Raphael), and John (Gabriel) who wrote the book of Revelation, all messengers of the Divine Child, Christ.

Chapter 5

The Myth of Genesis as a Metaphor for the Divine Child, the Psychological Child, and the Biological Child: Mythological Origins of Consciousness and Jung's Four Psychological Functions

In Chapter 5 I will analyze, interpret, and compare symbols and archetypes from the two Judaic-Christian cosmological myths of Genesis, with the four psychological functions of intuition, sensation, feeling, and thinking, as described by Carl Jung. The Genesis mythology can be seen as a description of the child from four levels: the mythological level of the Divine Child, the psychological level of the child, the biological level of the physical child, and a synthesis of the first three levels, showing their connection at the depth level as a mythological expression of universal human origins.

Genesis is seen as a metaphor describing simultaneously the physical and psychological birth of the human child. Genesis describes the origins of psychological development, including the split in what I am calling the super consciousness of the Self, creating the opposites of consciousness and unconsciousness. A divided Self is seen to begin at birth in the conscious functions of introverted sensation and feeling and the unconscious functions of intuition and thinking.

The four primary archetypes in Genesis are described as personifications of the psychic energy in each of the four functions. The function of intuition is represented by the archetype of the creating Father God; the function of sensation is represented by the archetype of the Serpent; the function of feeling is represented by the archetype of Eve; the function of thinking is represented by the archetype of Adam.

Genesis is seen as a description of the psychological functions in a state of undifferentiation (Self) as the process of differentiation and individuation begins. Paradise is a metaphor for the undifferentiated experience of the infant Self in utero, as intuition becomes differentiated. The Fall of Adam, Eve, and the Serpent is seen as a double metaphor describing physical and psychological birth simultaneously, symbolized by the loss of Paradise. The myth describes the beginning of the conscious body/ego and unconscious body/soul in the human child, as the four psychological functions continue to differentiate from the primal Self, creating at birth the separated ego and soul complexes.

Intuition is the first function to appear in the human child and begins in the womb (symbolized by Paradise), followed by sensation, which appears at birth (the loss of Paradise), followed by the rational functions of feeling and thinking. I will compare these archetypes with divergent mythological archetypes and symbols, suggesting that they contain similar patterns of psychic energy, and that they describe universal patterns of human experience.

The cosmological myth of Genesis is a description of two major and universal experiences in the life of every human child, the experience of life in the womb (Paradise) and the experience of the profound transformation from the womb to the world, symbolized as East of Eden and the knowledge of the opposites (consciousness and unconsciousness). This is a description of basic psychic energy in a state of continuous motion, the first cycle in the spiral dance of the eternal return.

Conscious intuition as a psychological function that contains the other three functions in a state of unconscious, undifferentiated energy, is what I believe to be the key that opens the doors of perception, allowing us to see our original experience as it was once described in the cosmogony of Western humanity, the myth of Genesis.

The Mythological Level:
Creation of the Divine Child from the First Divine Syzygy in Genesis

In the beginning God created Heaven and Earth (Genesis 1:1).

There is no beginning that does not presuppose the presence of an ending, and the first sentence of the creation myth in Genesis implies, rather than states directly, the opposites of ending and beginning. The ending inferred is the end of chaos and the beginning stated is the creation of cosmos or order. Thus, the two archetypes of ending and beginning can be said to be the splitting of chaos, the archetype in Genesis that contains the All, into the three archetypes of the Great Mother Goddess, God, the creating Father, and the Divine Child. These three archetypes can be seen as the female and the male principles, or psychologically speaking, the Self, Soul, and ego archetypes. In the original chaos, they exist as one and become three when chaos ends and cosmos begins, establishing the presence of three archetypes that reflect one another, not yet as opposites, but as mirror images.

Psychologically speaking, chaos or the void can be seen as the feminine archetype of the all-containing Great Mother or the Self. The Self archetype contains, with everything else, the three or four major archetypes of this cosmology, the Divine Father, the Divine Mother, and the Divine Child, existing as one in the undifferentiated Self. The Divine Father appears first out of the void, Self, or Great Mother archetype, as the creating Father God and represents the foremost form of consciousness, which is consciousness and unconsciousness united, in the primal function of intuition. With the establishment of the anthropomorphic Father God (intuition), time and consciousness have begun, but it is a golden time and a super consciousness, a time of wholeness and perfection, symbolizing Paradise (Being) and the infant in the womb. It is a physical Paradise because pain and pleasure are not separate experiences and it is a psychological Paradise because the four functions are still contained, like the creatures of Paradise, in the Father God.

As a mirror image of the Self from which it departs, intuition contains the (All) same three archetypes of Father, Mother, and Child. These are the functions of thinking, feeling, and sensation. The unconsciousness and undifferentiation of these three functions produce the fourth function, intuition, as a necessary compensation or opposite. Still contained within the Father God, the three functions of unconscious thinking, feeling, and sensation exist as one function, intuition or the Father God. To be in Paradise with the Father God represents the first differentiation of the merged functions as the one function of conscious intuition, which is the opposite of the other three unconscious functions. Thus, consciousness and unconsciousness are still merged but can be seen and identified as the four functions existing as one (God).

The Father God has been distinguished from the original chaos or void, usually defined as an all containing Mother archetype, and these two can be seen as the original World Parents, separated by the "Son," who is also the Father God or the Divine Child. Abraham (1995) says "the word chaos originally came from the Greek word meaning "gap," the creative void that gave rise to Gaia (Mother Earth) and Ouranos (Father Heaven), or the gap between them from which sprang all else" (p. 67). This "gap" can be seen as the middle or male Divine Child (Eros or Enlil) archetype who connects and separates the World Parents. Because he is male, he is identified with the Father God and consciousness. Because he is a child archetype, he is associated with beginning consciousness. Since they are "one," either archetype can be used, and the creating Father God can also be seen as the creating male Divine Child archetype. This represents the creative energy of the conscious intuitive function (knowledge contained in the body) that is subjective or the energy of unconscious sensation. Father and Son or the two functions of intuition and sensation are still merged.

Although Genesis does not describe the Father God as the son or child of the void, as the Sumerian mythology, for instance, describes Enki, the god of

Wisdom, he can be seen as such since he arose out of the chaos or void or Great Mother. The Father and Son as one theme will be introduced later in Christianity, where it appears to have the same meaning. When he (as Father and Son merged) arose, however, the Great Mother, that is, the feminine energy of the Void, came with him in the form of the undifferentiated function of feeling, the mate called Wisdom, who was with him from the beginning. Mother, father and child archetypes arose as feeling, thinking, and sensation contained in intuition, the Father God, just as Eve was first contained in Adam.

"God and the soul are essentially the same when regarded as personifications of an unconscious content" (Jung, 1971/1921, p. 248). The soul archetype appears as mate to the Self archetype, each a mirror reflection or twin to the other, establishing the difficult symbolism of sameness and difference simultaneously. The Father God or intuition represents a twilight consciousness that is still united with the unconscious, a state of being that is different from ordinary consciousness alone, just as it is different from total unconsciousness. As a beginning way of knowing, it can be defined as "knowing with—not knowing—that you know." Intuition can also be distinguished from the Self or Mother/Father archetype of undifferentiation because this aspect is different: In the Self archetype knower and the object known are identical, subject and object are one. Mythology accomplishes the subtle difference of Self and Soul by describing the male, as an archetype of light and consciousness, as the first one out of the void of undifferentiation. The first light, however, is not ordinary consciousness but the super consciousness (Being) that precedes it.

Neumann (1949/1954) uses the archetype of the urorobos, the serpent who eats its own tail, as a symbol of the Self. This can be seen as a symbol that expresses the same energy represented in the void or chaos archetype of Genesis. Neumann (1943/1993), however, describes the beginning in a different way: "The time of the beginning, before the coming of the opposites, must be understood as the self-description of that great epoch when there was still no consciousness" (p. 12). Unconsciousness, however, is not the same thing as undifferentiation, which I understand as a lack of boundaries where all opposites are joined and present. He goes on to describe this "no consciousness" state of being as the "round "container," that is, the maternal womb, but also as the union of masculine and feminine opposites, the World Parents joined in perpetual cohabitation (p. 13).

The description of no consciousness would be a state of total unconsciousness, and if that is so, Neumann has left out the masculine archetype, that of consciousness. If the opposites exist in perpetual cohabitation as the World

Parents, which I agree is the case, consciousness would be just as present as unconsciousness. In fact, you could say there is no difference. Neumann does not make this distinction, however, and splits the Self archetype, which can be symbolized as the uroboros, the void or the womb, into the World Parents of consciousness and unconsciousness, delegating the feminine archetype to the unconscious and the masculine archetype to the conscious.

The problem is that consciousness thereafter is "masculine" and unconsciousness is "feminine," and the great uroboros (Self or void) appears thereafter to be only feminine or unconsciousness, whereas ego consciousness is representative of the masculine (Neumann, 1949/1993, p. 25). Even though this distinction can be made later, the uroboros, void, or Self must be seen as the feminine archetype that contains everything else; the Father God must also be seen as one who contains the all, in a slightly modified (reversed) form that represents the first form of consciousness, intuition, or soul. This is the purpose of the male archetype in the original creation myth, whether as Divine Father or Divine Child.

Just as readily apparent as the World Parents, is the third archetype, that middle space that divides and connects the opposing principles. The personification of this energy is symbolized by the child archetype, human, divine, or any symbol that represents the opposites (parents) united or separated, such as seed, fruit, or a child animal, that is, a lamb, calf, or kid. The Divine Child archetype can be seen as an archetype of the Self, the soul, or the ego.

There is no mention of the Hero or Divine Child who is still contained in the uroboros, or the Child archetype that unites or separates the opposites, until much later in Neumann's description. This is probably because the ego consciousness that he describes does not begin at birth, although he describes quite well consciousness that is related to the body when he says:

> The fact that its organic substrate derives embryologically from the ectoderm shows that consciousness was a kind of sense organ; yet it was already differentiated in two directions and could perceive images coming from outside as well as from inside (1949/1993, p. 295).

I believe the cosmological material is describing this kind of early consciousness, today called awareness, in addition to possible later experience.

"The fact that the hero has two fathers or two mothers is a central feature in the canon of the hero myth" (Neumann, 1949/1993, p. 132). I think this symbolism can also be seen much earlier than Neumann surmised and described in terms of psychic energy and the four functions. In Chapter 3 I described the

Sumerian cosmological mythology of Nammu (Self symbol) and the four gods of creation, Enki, Enlil, Ki, and An. Enlil (sensation) is the Divine Child or son/hero in that mythology with dual parents. Nammu and Enki are the first set of parents, and Ki and An are the second. Nammu and Enki can be seen as the Self and the Soul (intuition) the first parents who give birth to Enlil or sensation. Ki and An, feeling and thinking, or the rational functions, are the second set of World Parents, and they represent the archetype that has been created from the primal, instinctual energy of the Self, the soul, and the ego. The same energy can be seen in the Genesis myth, where the Serpent represents the tragic villain/ego, whose dual parents are the Self and intuition and feeling and thinking.

I see the Self as unchanging; it is not only the feminine and the unconscious, it represents and remains undifferentiated energy. What flows out of it (the Father God or masculine archetype) does not deplete or change it to an opposite without its other. Consciousness does not flow out of unconsciousness; both consciousness and unconsciousness flow out of the undifferentiated Self, which remains an archetype of the Divine Mother, Divine Father, or Divine Child. I see this as an important difference in my interpretation of the cosmological material.

To describe the opposite of the Absolute (the Father God) is to describe Nothingness, which in the myth of Genesis is the feminine principle. Nothingness converges with Everything at some point, this point being another archetype for the Divine Child. The feminine principle can be seen as Mal'akh, the shadow side of the Father God, once he has left the original void. The dark or shadow side was already there in the beginning as Proverbs 8:23-31, speaking in the feminine voice of Wisdom, says:

> I was set up from eternity, and of old before the earth was made. The depths were not as yet, and I was already conceived, neither had the fountains of waters as yet sprung out: The mountains with their huge bulk had not as yet been established: before the hills I was brought forth; He had not yet made the earth, nor the rivers, nor the poles of the world. When he prepared the heavens, I was present: when with a certain law and compass he enclosed the depths: When he established the sky above, and poised the fountains of waters; When he compassed the sea with its bounds, and set a law to the waters that they should not pass their limits: when he balanced the foundations of the earth; I was with him forming all things: and was delighted every day, playing before

> him at all times; Playing in the world: and my delights were to be with the children of men (Proverbs 8:23-31, p. 649).

The personification of Wisdom as the Father God's playmate and co-creator of the world is the Goddess archetype, who is with God from the beginning. Psychologically speaking, she can be seen as the personification of the undifferentiated feeling function (the silent Goddess) that exists as one of the four undifferentiated functions of intuition, sensation, feeling, and thinking. This establishes her identity with what I have called the soul archetype or the function of intuition. When the Father God flows out of the Self or void, he "takes" the Goddess with him as his dark or shadow side, that is, undifferentiated feeling. The undifferentiated feeling function can be seen as being personified by the silent, absent Goddess archetype in the myth of Genesis, although this same energy can also be represented by other archetypes who are male, such as the Archangel Raphael, who was discussed in Chapter 4. In either case, the psychic energy being personified appears to be identified with the feminine principle of undifferentiated feeling, or two kinds of love united, self-love and love for other. Being with God every moment and helping him to create describes undifferentiated feeling that helps to give form and content to the archetype.

Wisdom helps her mate, that is, the Father God (differentiated intuitive function), create the world. This is a description of the human child as he or she becomes conscious and uses the psychological functions to subjectively create the world, which is always a creation of the archetypes. Wisdom and her mate, the creating Father God, can be seen as the functions of unconscious feeling and thinking, both of which comprise the function of conscious intuition, along with the Divine Child archetype, unconscious sensation. Thus, the function of conscious intuition can be described in mythology as Wisdom, the Father God or the Divine Child. It can also be defined as the primary function of super consciousness (Being) personified as spirit, soul, and body that are united with God. This is the reason it is so often associated with the divine, whether God or angels. I have called it the soul complex because I believe it is undifferentiated feeling that connects the other functions to one another in a melodious way. Feeling gives meaning to life. The function of intuition could also be called spirit, for at this level, there is no difference. More surprising, perhaps, is the fact that intuition can also be seen as the unconscious body. Intuition is the function where spirit, soul, and body can be seen as a whole.

The Wisdom archetype in Genesis represents the function of feeling (conscious and unconscious), merged with the other functions in the function of intuition. The undifferentiated feeling function is God's playmate. Ego consciousness splits the Goddess archetype of Wisdom into a Goddess of Heaven (the Virgin or unconscious extraverted feeling) and a goddess of earth (Eve or conscious introverted feeling). It also splits the Father God archetype (intuition) into the creating Father God (still intuition) and his Divine and later fallen Son, Lucifer, who becomes the function of unconscious, extraverted sensation. God, as the personification of intuition and his son, the personification of unconscious sensation are one that have become divided.

In Chapter 4 the origin of the Hebrew word Mal'akh was described as originally meaning the shadow side of God and later came to mean messenger. Thus, Wisdom is the shadow (unconscious) side of the Father God, can also be seen as a part of intuition. When the psychological function of intuition is described as Wisdom, it is a description of the Goddess as undifferentiated feeling, identical with the Father God and the Divine Child God, the personification of undifferentiated sensation. If the Mother Goddess is associated with the unconscious or shadow side of God, the Father God archetype is associated with consciousness, the "I Am That I Am" delivered to Moses and Mohammed by angels or an angel (God's hero, Gabriel) of God.

Both males are archetypes of the Divine male Child, and both are given instructions connected to words and their expression. They were both to deliver the message of God to the people in the form of the written language, one became the Old Testament and the other became the Koran. As archetypes of the Divine Child both are androgens which Singer (1977) defines as "the One which contains the Two; namely, the male (andro-) and the female (gyne)" (p. 6). The androgen is neither male or female but one who has a dual nature, like the Divine Child. He is always the third person or the middle person of this trio and always a Divine male Child archetype in Genesis.

To speak or to write the word is to give expression and form to the content and implies an act of creation. Shiarella (1992) describes the Vedas in the following way: "The world's oldest scripture, the Vedas, contains language strikingly similar to that of the Bible: 'In the beginning was the Creator, within whom was the word, and the word was the Lord Himself'" (p. 106).

In the Vedas, it is the word as Shakti or the feminine principle or side of God that creates the world, while Shiva is the ground or void or mate who contains everything in potential form as Paramashiva. Male and female archetypes are the reverse of Genesis, but appear to be delivering a similar message; that is, it is better to stay in the void or Self than it is to be born. If you are born, however, you must find your way back to the center or the static essence of Shiva, who contains all.

Neumann (1949/1954) says that the original phase of consciousness as a sense organ is "marked by the functions of sensation and intuition, i.e., the perceptive functions which are the first to appear both in the development of primitives and in that of the child" (p. 296). Here, he rightly agrees with Jung (1971/1921, p. 454). Which function comes first, however, was never described by Jung or Neumann to my knowledge, but the mythology appears to support and describe intuition as the first function of Paradise and sensation as the function describing the loss of Paradise. Intuition as a container of the other functions is the mythological key that apparently reopens the door to Paradise. A few years before his death, in 1957, Jung said "you do not know ordinarily how intuition works" (Evans, 1976, p. 100). This implies that Jung thought that intuition occurs as phenomenological experience that is usually not in one's conscious awareness.

Human and Divine is the state of the child and humanity; it is the "and" that needs to be explored, as Restak (1980) quotes from Eddington:

> We often think that when we have completed our study of one we know all about two, because "two" is "one and one." We forget that we still have to make a study of "and" (Eddington, A. The Nature of Physics, Cited in Restak, 1980, p. 35).

This is just as true of the inner world as it is in physics, and perhaps, the difference is relative. When the inner world and the outer world are experienced as one, the "and" disappears and the Divine Child (Self) is born; he or she contains both.

In the Genesis mythology, it is the male child that is the creative principle, representing movement and action and his shadow side is the receptive, invisible feminine, the mother archetype, or the earth child (human) or the girl-child, who is always identical with the mother because she is always a virgin. This is represented in the myths, Christian and numerous others, as the Virgin Mother and her Divine male Child.

In mythology and fairy tales, it is often the second or youngest daughter that saves the family or kingdom, like Psyche in the Psyche and Eros myth or Antigone (whose name means in *place of the mother*) in the Greek myth, the youngest daughter and sister to Oedipus. It is the sister in the stories with brother/sister themes, like "Brother and Sister" by the Brothers Grimm (1992, p. 42), who is responsible for saving her brother by marrying the king and destroying the wicked witch. The youngest daughter represents the person who has the least amount of ego or consciousness (knowledge) and the epitome of this archetype is symbolized by the virgin who is, psychologically speaking, without ego consciousness.

At the mythological level, it is the story of Genesis itself and the author of the story (Moses) that is the Divine Child because both reflect the contents of the collective unconscious of that time and place through the expression of the archetype. A description of the contents, however, is subject to change, even though the psychic energy is universal experience. Both reflect the ego and ego consciousness. What changes is the dress they wear. New words, pictures, and symbols spring up from the wells of collective being, giving the emperor new clothes one minute and the next minute stripping him bare and crucifying him. Describing the experience in terms of psychic energy or the functions has no effect on the experience as universal and constant; what it does is to allow that experience to be described in a different (psychological) language and link it with cosmology. Cosmology attempts to describe the same beginning experience by symbols, archetypes and the use of metaphor or art, which often precede a "scientific" viewpoint.

The first Divine Child is the function of conscious intuition, which contains Adam in the form of the undifferentiated thinking function (Adam as the image of God or the image that will be created from the instinct or intuition). It also contains undifferentiated feeling that will become Eve in Paradise, and last but irrevocably so, it contains undifferentiated sensation, the Divine Child archetype, identical with the Father God, who will become the Serpent of Genesis. Before the Fall, all exist in innocence and knowledge as one.

This describes the child in the womb, who first shows life and movement by the basic instinct of intuition or unconscious sensation. It is also a description of the Divine Syzygy and their Divine Child in the first creation myth of Genesis, as the three archetypes change form (the functions differentiate) and become the three archetypes of Genesis before the Fall, Adam, Eve, and the Serpent, all reflections of the Father God, thus perfect in their first creation. This describes the human child in the womb.

Edinger (1986a), in a discussion of the first line of the creation myth of Genesis states: "The Greek term for prima materia is arche, the same word used in the Septuagint to translate reshith, beginning" (p.15). Previous to this he states that the Gnostics considered the first four words of Genesis as a divine tetrad, and the arche to be the mother of all things. In replacing the words of arche and beginning with the word mother, the first sentence can be read in the following way: "In the mother God (Divine Child) created the heaven and the earth." God is the archetype for the creative principle, usually represented as male, consciousness, discrimination, separation, and the establishment of order. This is the male half of God, whose name designates it as the male half, leaving the shadow and opposite side of these attributes to the feminine principle or still contained in the mother. This is the male Divine Child, who is the creator and the created simultaneously. "God" is the child and the child is "God." The Divine male child is "taken" from the two united opposites of end and beginning or first (arche) and last. He is in the mother in the same way Eve is contained in Adam as his bone, a symbol that represents the seed or beginning of something. (Feeling is the beginning of thought.) Thus, the first sentence can read, "In the Divine Mother, the Divine male Child creates Paradise." Paradise is Heaven and Earth that has been named, but not separated; it is the Golden Age where Mother, Father, and Child still exist as one. The three-in-one theme is present in the beginning of Genesis, although not readily apparent and becomes a major aspect of Christianity.

In Judaism and Christianity, the division into four as a "primordial cosmogonic image" (Edinger, 1986a, p. 15) is particularly important. The "one" God in Genesis, present and identical with his creation (Adam, Eve, and the Serpent) in Paradise is the theme of three-in-one that is also the fourth, the number of wholeness. The psychological parallel to this primordial theme are the four undifferentiated functions existing as one in the function of intuition. Both describe the child as image of God and God as an archetype of the Divine Child.

The Divine Syzygy of the Spirit and Water in Genesis: Archetypes for the Creation of the Divine Child, the Psychological Child, and the Biological Child

And the earth was void and empty, and darkness was upon the face of the deep; and the spirit of God moved over the waters (Genesis 1:2).

Concerning the metaphor and Creation myths, Campbell (1988a) states:
> Creation myths, which, when read in their mystical sense might bring to mind the idea of a background beyond time out of which the whole temporal world with its colorful populations has been derived, when read, instead, historically, only justify as supernaturally endowed the moral order of some local culture. The social, as opposed to the mystical function of a mythology, is not to open the mind, but to enclose it (p. 22).

It is the psychological that I wish to focus on in the myth of Genesis. The biological, however, is just as apparent, and both appear to be contained within the historic because the narrative and the narrator are the hero or Divine Child.

On Earthly Paradise, Wind and Water

The water you see here is from no source
that needs replenishment from cloudy vapors,
like streams that rise and fall; with constant force
it leaves a fountain that receives again,
from God's will, every drop that it pours forth
to the two streams it sends across this plain.
On this side, it removes as it flows down
all memory of sin; on that, it strengthens
the memory of every good deed done.
It is called Lethe here, Eunoe there.
And one must drink first this and then the other
to feel its powers. No sweetness can compare
with the savor of these waters. And although
you may at once, and with no more instruction,
drink your soul's fill from the eternal flow,
let me bestow one thing more for good measure.
Those ancients who made songs to celebrate
man's Age of Gold, placed probably on Parnassus
this perfect garden of his first pure state.
Here mankind lived its innocent first days.
Here is the eternal spring and every fruit.
This is the nectar that the poets praise.

(Alighieri, Dante (Matilda speaking), from the Divine Comedy,
Purgatorio, Canto 28, 1977, pp. 397-398)

It is history because the story always occurs in time, even though the contents are an attempt to describe what is, as Campbell describes, beyond time.

A literal interpretation serves the purposes of the child mind because it contains the contents of the metaphor, the biological and the psychological, in its depths. The archetype expresses what is unconscious but contained in the human psyche. If this were not so, the myths would fade and die. In reality, however, they only change forms and are given new names and become new myths which are then accepted as true. Like the myth of the big bang, which describes the cosmology in the terms of science instead of religion. The big bang theory is the archetype, the Divine Child of the 20th century; it defines the modern world.

In the Genesis mythology, the Spirit of God is the personification of the male principle and the fecundating principle in acts of creativity, whether physical, emotional or mental. It is symbolized by air, wind, breath, the word, the mind, or logos, all symbols associated with the masculine principle in Western mythology. "The wind is the fructifying bird known to the primitives, the ancestral spirit that blows upon the women, and also upon tortoises and female vultures, and makes them fruitful" (Neumann, 1993, p. 22). Spirit is the essence of things, the sum and substance of all the parts. Spirit describes the totality, psychologically speaking, all of the psychological functions working in harmony to produce a divine thought. Spirit is connected to ego consciousness, movement, and action on the one hand and soul and unconsciousness on the other. This description can be seen in two ways, which appear to be different but have parallel meanings, one psychological and one biological.

In a biological sense, the Spirit of God moving over the waters can, in a poetic, esoteric way, symbolize the act of human sexual love, union, and procreation. The physical essence or active principle of the spirit can be defined as the spermatozoon contained in the semen of a human male and described in many mythologies as a serpent or fish. This can be seen as the manifestation of the spirit in its most material and liquid form. If five hundred million sperm (Nilsson, 1993, p. 42) are present from the start, the one who "wins" the race cannot be seen with the naked eye, but is the result of sensation, that function so often related to sex or the serpent, whether negatively or positively.

Jung (1958/1952) says that Christ was equated with the symbol of the fish and the serpent:

> The serpent is an equivalent of the fish. The consensus of opinion interpreted the Redeemer equally as a fish and a serpent; he is a fish because he rose from the unknown depths, and a serpent

because he came mysteriously out of the darkness. Fishes and snakes are favourite symbols for describing psychic happenings or experiences that suddenly dart out of the unconscious and have a frightening or redeeming effect. That is why they are so often expressed by the motif of helpful animals. The comparison of Christ with the serpent is more authentic than that with the fish, but, for all that, it was not so popular in primitive Christianity. The Gnostics favoured it because it was an old-established symbol for the "good" genius loci, the Agathodaimon, and also for their beloved Nous (p. 186).

Thus, the symbols of serpent and fish describe psychic or psychological contents. It is also possible that they express a parallel meaning that is biological, and both can be present at the same time. In discussing the Gnostic symbols of the Self, Jung (1958/1952) speaks of the symbols of magnet and iron and lists three different forms of magnetic agents:

1. The agent is an inanimate and in itself passive substance, water. It is drawn from the depths of the well, handled by human hands, and used according to man's needs. It signifies the visible doctrine, the aqua doctrinae or the Logos, communicated to others by word of mouth and by ritual.

2. The agent is an animate, autonomous being, the serpent. It appears spontaneously or comes as a surprise; it fascinates; its glance is staring, fixed, unrelated; its blood cold, and it is a stranger to man; it crawls over the sleeper, he finds it in a shoe or in his pocket. It expresses his fear of everything inhuman and his awe of the sublime, of what is beyond human ken. It is the lowest (devil) and the highest (son of God, Logos, Nous, Agathodaimon). The snake is not an allegory or metaphor, for its own peculiar form is symbolic in itself, and it is essential to note that the "Son" has the form of a snake and not the other way round; the snake does not signify the "Son."

3. The agent is the Logos, a philosophical idea and abstraction of the bodily and personal son of God on the one hand, and on the other the dynamic power of thought and words (p. 188).

The serpent that is not an allegory or metaphor, an animate, autonomous being; that is, it has a living substance of its own, is the human male sperm. The agent that is the inanimate and in itself passive substance, water, can be seen as the living water of life, brought forth by the act of physical feminine love or female ejaculation. This is represented in the symbol of the well as container or vessel (symbol for the womb or uterus). The well symbolizes the container for the inanimate and in itself passive substance, water. The depths of the well are the uterus, which contains and brings forth new life. The aqua doctrinae can be seen in two ways: The first is the actual substance of water brought forth in the act of love by the living female when she loves without ego or with agape love. The second, psychological meaning is that the water is the Logos contained within the feminine principle because it contains the ego and consciousness in potential or in undifferentiated form. The son that has the form of a snake (and not the other way around) is the living male sperm, the lowest (devil) and the highest (son of God, Logos, Nous, Agathodaimon).

In the alchemical literature (see Figure 1, p. 43 in Jung, 1954/1946) the living water is described as the Mercurial Fountain, and it is the first of ten images. Jung states:

> This picture goes straight to the heart of alchemical symbolism, for it is an attempt to depict the mysterious basis of the opus. It is a quadratic quaternity characterized by the four stars in the four corners. These are the four elements. Above, in the centre, there is a fifth star which represents the fifth entity, the "One" derived from the four, the *quinta essentia*. The basin below is the *vas Hermeticum*, where the transformation takes place. It contains the *mare nostrum, the aqua permanens* or the "divine water" (emphasis Jung's, pp. 41-42).

Here the symbolism can readily be seen to be both physical and psychological. The divine water flows from the physical body of the living female and this occurs when there is a psychological state of mind described as love that is without ego, unconditional love or agape love. When sensation, feeling, and thinking (represented by the three pipes) are in a neutral state, that is, without the conscious ego, they flow together into the basin, where they are merged or undifferentiated. This produces the mare nostrum, the aqua permanens or the divine water. That which is physical in the female can never be experienced by the male. It is in the psychologically equivalent experience that male can know female and the reverse, and the male/female or androgynous nature can be known in one psyche.

"Apart from autonomic changes, which do not differ from those of other types of arousal, and a decrease in sensitivity to pain that suggests the release of endorphins, almost nothing is known of the physiology of orgasm" (Freeman, 1995, p. 122). This appears to be the case, especially in the physiology of the female, although the myth may describe what science has yet to put into words.

The living water, that is, the water of female emission, can be seen in many symbolic images and is described in fiction and other literature, whereas modern psychologists studying human sexuality debate whether such a thing even exists. Denney and Quadagno (1988) state the following concerning female ejaculation as described in 1950 by Grafenberg: "No proof of this has been established at the time of this writing, and the G spot has never been anatomically located at the time of surgery or at autopsy" (p. 2). No doubt that is because there is no spot or button on the human female anatomy to push; the water produced is a physiological result of a psychological state of being. It is a result of agape love that sacrifices ego/self for other. This is the living water of mare nostrum, the aqua permanens, or the divine water.

The empty womb is symbolized by the empty earth. Darkness describes the state of the womb before conception or penetration. The earth or the woman before the first act of love is a virgin. The version of the description of creation from Genesis quoted above uses the language "moved over the waters"; another version (King James) uses "moved upon the face of the waters." Over the waters and upon the face of the waters both describe the movement of the spirit (sperm or seed) to its destination, its journey to the unfertilized egg. Nilsson (1993) says, "Conception is more likely if intercourse coincides with ovulation. The mucus of the cervix and uterus is then runny and transparent, permitting the sperm to swim upward to the ovum with ease" (p. 43). Here the sperm can be compared with the image of two creatures connected with water: a fish, often a symbol associated with Christ, and a serpent, also associated with Christ and God in many ancient religions, including Judaism.

Graves and Patai (1989) state:
> The heretical Ophites of the first century A.D. believed that the world had been generated by a serpent. The Brazen Serpent made, according to Hebrew tradition, by Moses at God's command (Numbers xxi. 8-9) and revered in the Temple Sanctuary until the reforming King Hezekiah destroyed it (2 Kings xviii. 4), suggests that Yahweh had at one time been identified with a Serpent-god—as Zeus was in Orphic art (p. 32).

The transparent water of the cervix and uterus can be seen as the creative feminine principle—the water of life that is often symbolized as a fountain—and the female promulgation that bubbles forth in the act of love, assisting in the delivery of the sperm to its destination. The primal waters usually symbolize the feminine principle in some aspect. Westman (1991) equates the water with Eve:

> The name Eve is the personification of the primal water out of which everything has its origin, not only present-day scientific theories but also mythologies from ever so many cultures. "The mother of all the living" in Genesis 3:20 is also mentioned in a different form: "And God said: 'Let the waters bring forth swarms of living creatures.' After all, the primal habitat of the human foetus, the "waters" of the womb, is an actual life experience (p. 417).

But, water even more primal than that of the first habitat of the human foetus is that water that issues forth in the act of physical love, determined by a psychological state of mind. This is agape love because it has to do with the principle of loving without ego. In this respect, the water symbolizes the feminine principle in its most glorified form (the Divine Goddess), and it is identical with the Spirit that moves over the waters. The essence or spirit and the divine water are both the materialistic manifestations of human love, which is also divine love. The divine thought can be seen as conceived in the same way as the divine or human child, by an act of love.

Psychologically speaking, Eve is mother of all the living because she represents (before the Fall) feeling in its undifferentiated form, the mother aspect of the original trio of sensation (the child) feeling (the mother), and thinking (the father). Water is the symbol that describes this undifferentiation best; it flows together as one thing, whether a drop or an ocean. This is Eve before the Fall; after the Fall, she represents beginning, conscious, subjective feeling that is ego-oriented. In this way, Eve represents the undifferentiated feeling function first, and after the Fall, only one half of the feeling function, ego love or desire, which gives birth to all living things. The other half, still contained in a state of undifferentiation, will become the archetype of the Virgin.

The highest form of Spirit is Logos; the lowest form of Spirit is the material body. The archetype of Spirit, as sperm, seed, or essence of the male principle, in its highest and lowest form, contains everything necessary to create new life, providing it finds fertile waters or ground in which this can take place. Like the serpent, it changes and sheds its old form to take on a new one, making it an excellent symbol for the process of transformation.

Arguelles and Arguelles (1977) describe two cosmic principles in the following:

> The play of unborn feminine space and unconditional masculine response describes two cosmic principles. The unceasing

> interpenetration of these principles allows communication and meaningful activity to take place. Although the unoriginated space of the feminine gives birth, there is no separation between the vastness of the unborn and its contents, the masculine. Woven into a cloth that is indissoluble, the interplay of feminine and masculine is an expression of the dynamics of creativity. Creative acts, as expressions of the masculine, arise from the feminine ground of creativity, the empty field, uncarved block, or velvety silence that inspires a communicative response (p. 17).

Spirit, air, or breath can be seen as the masculine principle of the Father God; the primal waters can be seen as the feminine principle of the Mother Goddess and the conception that takes place can be seen as the human child on one hand and the psychological energy of that child on the other, along with the creation of thought or the birth of the archetype. Thus, the mythological, biological, and the psychological are never far apart.

Campbell (1979) describes the power of the goddess as she relates to water symbolism in the following way:

> The water is the vehicle of the power of the goddess; but equally, it is she who personifies the mystery of the waters of birth and dissolution—whether of the individual or of the universe. For in the vein of myth the elemental mode of representation may alternate with that of personification. At the opening of the Book of Genesis is it not written, for example, that "the Spirit (or wind) of God was moving over the face of the waters"? Water and wind, matter and spirit, life and its generator: these pairs of opposites are fused in the experience of life; and their world-creating juncture may be represented elementally, as in this opening of the Bible, or on the other hand, as in the art of the Tantric Buddhism, in the image of a divine male and female in sexual embrace. The mystery of the origin of the "great universe" or macrocosm is read in terms of the procreation of the "little universe," the microcosm; and the amniotic fluid is then precisely comparable to the water that in many mythologies, as well as in the pre-Socratic philosophy of the Greek sage Thales of Miletus (c. 640-546 B.C.), represents the elementary substance of all things (p. 64).

Thus, the first creation myth in Genesis can be seen as a metaphorical, ideal description of the conception and birth of the biological child, as well as a metaphorical description of psychological processes of the child that occur simultaneously. The mythological, the biological, and the psychological are ever intertwined, the Divine Child expressing all three in one myth.

<u>The Father God, the Serpent, Eve and Adam as Primary
Archetypes in Genesis: Personifications of the Four Psychological
Functions: The Father God in Genesis as an Archetype
for the Psychological Function of Differentiated Intuition</u>

In the first creation myth of Genesis, the Father God represents the personification of the function of conscious intuition, where he contains Adam (undifferentiated thinking), Eve (undifferentiated feeling), and the Serpent (undifferentiated sensation). Man, as male and female is created on the sixth day in the first creation myth of Genesis. This describes the thinking and feeling functions in their state of undifferentiation in the psyche of one human child. It also describes the Serpent or sensation, sleeping, in the same way.

While still in Paradise or the womb, the three undifferentiated functions can be seen as identical with the Father God of intuition. As undifferentiated functions, they represent the Goddess; as one differentiated function, intuition represents the Father God. Thus, each is contained in the other. The myth describes the differentiation of the functions as they become conscious in the human child, and the beginning of conscious, subjective, introverted thought, leaving its opposite (feeling) in the (newly created) unconscious.

The creating Father God archetype in Genesis represents the psychological function of conscious intuition, which I have previously defined as containing the three ego functions of sensation, feeling, thinking, and intuition in unconscious and undifferentiated form, thereby creating its opposite in the function of intuition, the first differentiation of the Self. Nietzsche (1966/1989) describes beautifully what I believe is the same energy as intuition, which he understood as the will to power:

> Suppose nothing else were "given" as real except our world of desires and passions, and we could not get down, or up, to any other "reality" besides the reality of our drives—for thinking is merely a relation of these drives to each other: is it not permitted to make the experiment and to ask the question whether this "given" would not be sufficient for also understanding on the basis of this kind of thing the so-called mechanistic (or "material") world? I mean, not as a deception, as "mere appearance," an

"idea" (in the sense of Berkeley and Schopenhauer) but as holding the same rank of reality as our affect—(and, as is only fair, also becomes tenderer and weaker)—as a kind of instinctive life in which all organic functions are still synthetically intertwined along with self-regulation, assimilation, nourishment, excretion, and metabolism—as a pre-form of life (pp. 47-48).

This more primitive form where everything still lies contained in a powerful unity before it undergoes ramifications and development in the organic process, is what I would call intuition, personified in Genesis as the Father God, while Nietzsche calls it the will to power. This is the fine-point where the inquirer might ask of her or his experience: "Is it only me, or is it God in me?" Nietzsche decided it was the "will to power and nothing else" (p. 48). Nonetheless, I believe that he describes the same primal energy symbolized in the Genesis myth as the Father God. Jung (1958/1952) describes what Nietzsche calls a "primitive form" in the following: "All in all, it is not only more beneficial but more "correct" psychologically to explain as the "will of God" the natural forces that appear in us as instincts" (p. 27). In this respect, the Father God of Genesis can easily be seen as a personification of the irrational and instinctive function of intuition.

Adam, who will later become conscious thinking, and Eve, who will become conscious feeling, have not been separated; both are undifferentiated functions. Conscious and unconscious thinking (Adam) is identical with conscious and unconscious feeling (Eve), and both are identical with the Father God or conscious intuition, who is also identical with the sleeping Serpent or the Divine Child (undifferentiated sensation). The Father God and the Divine Child God (the sleeping Serpent) are the twin Serpents or the two functions of intuition and sensation that are undifferentiated.

In the myth of Genesis, the function of conscious intuition is Yahweh or the Father God, but he can just as easily be seen as the Goddess because they are One here, and the three or four undifferentiated functions are the same as the one conscious function of intuition. This is the three-in-one motif that defines one God. In the psyche of the human child, this describes consciousness in its elementary form or consciousness in the womb where there is no distinction between what is conscious and what is unconscious, producing a state of super consciousness, or what we call the function of intuition.

Intuition, the psychological function that gave Jung so much difficulty, is symbolized in the alchemical literature, among many other symbols, as the vessel. Jung (1958/1952) describes this as an important symbol: "It is clear from these quotations (by the alchemists) that the vessel had a great and unusual significance" (p. 379). This great and unusual significance is what distinguishes conscious intuition as a vessel for the other functions. The alchemists also called the vessel "ovum," signifying its relationship with the feminine, womb symbolism, and the egg symbol.

Jung (1958/1952) comments that "the egg is content and container at once" (p. 239). This describes the psychological function of intuition, which can be defined as the psychological function that contains the other functions, plus itself, as one. Intuition can be symbolized by many archetypes, male, female, child, animal, or vegetable, but in the Judeo-Christian cosmology, it is represented as the Father God, who contains Adam, Eve, and the Serpent, plus himself, in Paradise. This is a description of intuition as a function of conscious and unconscious contents, which it remains, even after the other functions flow out of it, like the four rivers flowing out of Paradise.

It is essential to distinguish the function of intuition from that of the Self, which I understand as the void in Genesis. The contents of a cosmological myth can be seen as flowing out of the original chaos. When, however, a creative god or goddess arrives on the scene or any archetype that represents the creative act, the opposites have also begun in the form of destruction, death, or any symbol opposite to creation and life. Whenever we have such archetypes, we have left the void and the Self and are in the realm of mythology, which has thousands of such archetypes, all attempting to account for the same primal experience. While in the primal experience of the void or Self, nothing can be or needs be said, indicating to me that a primary method of knowing can be distinguished from the Self, while at the same time be closely related, just as it is related to, but different from, ego consciousness. This I understand as the function of intuition, which appears to me to be the most reasonable of the four functions as a method of primary knowing. It also appears to be representative of the first image of God, reflecting the Self, but different, like identical twins who are the same yet different.

Jung (1954/1946, p. 119) said that a return to the Self was not complete without what he calls "the fourth function," and the reverse is just as true. What comes out of the Self first is known and passes through what becomes the fourth function (at birth) of intuition. In this manner, first is last and last is first.

Intuition is the psychological function that the child uses while in the womb. After conception, the fetus is a living creature using a function, which is really more than psychological because it also depends upon the body as the primal instinct. Intuition is knowing, but not knowing, that "I" am the one who knows.

In the womb, the human child knows what to do by instinct, to move toward or away from its environment; however, there is no reflecting ego that thinks, feels, or senses that it is "I" who know. It knows without knowing how it knows or who it is that knows. This is a hallmark of the intuitive function, even after birth, whether the knowledge given is simple or profound and attributed to the gods, angels or any divine being. The instinct carries an infinitesimal light of consciousness which can also be described as boundless; it is not ordinary consciousness. "Energy is an abstract concept which is indispensable for exact description of the behavior of bodies in motion" (Jung, 1958/1952, p. 251). The infant in the womb is alive and in motion, and contains that energy in the function of intuition, the Father God of Genesis.

The ego appears to evolve out of the function of intuition or all the undifferentiated functions, body, soul and spirit as one to create the ego as a reflection of the soul, spirit, or body. As soul, they exist as one; as ego they exist as three separate functions of consciousness: sensation, feeling, and thinking. Intuition is the ego in its primal form, which can be called soul.

The Serpent in Genesis as the Function of Unconscious Sensation (Intuition) or the Divine Child Archetype: The Serpent in Eden as the Archetype of Conscious Sensation

The archetype of the Serpent in the Garden of Eden represents the psychological function of undifferentiated sensation before the Fall or before Eve eats the apple. As undifferentiated sensation, he is identical with the Father God or the function of intuition in the same way that Adam and Eve are identical. This is why he appears to know as much as the Father God; he is the Divine Child archetype, the sleeping Serpent while still one with God in Paradise. It is really the Serpent who becomes conscious first, because by the time he tempts Eve, he already appears to know what God knows, the opposites of good and evil. As a variation of Lucifer, the Bringer of Light, the Serpent (sensation) represents the first form of conscious awareness and the first form of unconsciousness, when intuitive knowledge is replaced by conscious body sensations.

Neumann (1949/1954) describes the importance of the symbol of light:
> Ernst Cassirer has shown how, in all peoples and in all religions, creation appears as the creation of light. Thus the coming of consciousness, manifesting itself as light in contrast to the darkness of the unconscious, is the real "object" of creation mythology. Cassirer has likewise shown that in the different stages of mythological

consciousness the first thing to be discovered is *subjective reality*, the formation of the ego and individuality. The beginning of this development, mythologically regarded as the beginning of the world, is the coming of light, without which no world process could be seen at all (emphasis mine, p. 6).

This subjective reality (introversion) and the formation of the ego and individuality is what destroys Paradise; ordinary consciousness is not a prize to be had in Genesis for that reason. The Serpent Devil is called the Prince of Darkness because he also brings unconsciousness, which splits super consciousness, Paradise, or the Self, into opposites. Pagels (1989) describes the view of Ptolemy in a similar way: "According to Ptolemy, a follower of Valentinus, the story of Adam and Eve shows that humanity 'fell' into ordinary consciousness and lost contact with its divine origin" (emphasis mine, p. 65).

From a neurobiological viewpoint, Freeman (1995) states:

From its beginning in and from the womb the path of an intentional structure is unique, growing from the genetically determined groundwork by the grasping for available sensory input from within and outside its own body. The same steps are not replicated in any other brain, and the structure that evolves is self-organized, with its own frames of reference and its unique patterns. We see this reflected in the EEG patterns that lack any recognizable geometry or relations between animals and are meaningless to us, except in the context of observing the behavior of the individual. It is in this sense that each brain is epistemologically solipsistic. *Its knowledge comes from its cumulative constructions induced by the sensory milieu, which is also unique for each individual in the common environment, due to individual differences in physical and emotional perspective and expectancy* (emphasis mine, p. 120).

I understand this "sensory milieu" that "begins in the womb," to be the experience of sensation. In the womb, that experience and knowledge described in Jung's psychological language would be the function of intuition, which would be unconscious body sensation.

The conscious function of intuition (containing Father God), is also undifferentiated sensation (Divine Child or Serpent) in the human infant, while still contained in the womb. It is he, and remember that he can be seen here as identical with the Father God, who tells Eve that her "eyes will be opened: and you shall be as Gods, knowing good and evil" (Genesis 3:5). Unconscious sensation (personified as the sleeping Serpent) has turned into conscious, introverted sensation—the devil, negating unconscious sensation, which is intuition, to the unconscious. The Serpent's words and instructions can be seen as the information (human instincts) contained in the human child's body that inform the infant that it is time to be born, to leave the eternal experience of Paradise in the womb. It is time to experience the mother as "other" in the world, and to experience a world which appears to be full of opposites. It is time for consciousness and unconsciousness to become divided and the human ego and soul to be born and separated.

On the sixth day, God creates the animals, including the Serpent. He calls them "good." Before the Serpent tempts Eve, he can be seen as the Divine Child Lucifer, who shows up mysteriously in Paradise and apparently has not as yet fallen himself. The unorthodox literature is hazy on this point, and the Bible is silent, although throughout much of the literature, it is assumed that the Serpent who betrays mankind is the Fallen Angel, Lucifer, who is now called the Prince of Darkness. The Good Serpent in Paradise (and all of the "good" animals) can be seen as representing the function of unconscious, undifferentiated sensation, a counterpart to the Father God. When intuition or the Father God is conscious, the Serpent or function of sensation is unconscious, which reflects the opposite nature of the two functions. When the Father God is absent, the Serpent shows up under the forbidden tree. When the function of conscious intuition is absent, conscious sensation appears. Here is the image of the twin Serpents, the same yet different; it is also an excellent description of how the opposite functions of conscious sensation and conscious intuition are connected, yet separate and do not work at the same time, which Jung so astutely described.

The anthropomorphic Serpent apparently has speech, a fact that seems to elevate him in the realm of power. Maybe this could be called body language. He tells Eve she will become like the Father God if she eats from the tree of knowledge; she will become all-knowing, and this is, of course, what happens. Eve eats and gives the apple to Adam, who follows in her transgression, apparently without much discussion. This implies that the archetype or first representation is completed soon after feeling becomes conscious. Adam and Eve then become aware of their nakedness, which had previously gone unnoticed. They are no longer "covered" by the containing parents. Adam's eating of the apple signifies the fourth and last function to become differentiated and conscious as introverted thinking.

As a major archetype in the collective unconscious of humanity, the corrupting Serpent personifies conscious knowledge through the senses. The infant in utero is known to see, hear, taste, smell, and touch with his or her bodily senses.

The infant experiences sense perception in the womb, but the experience necessarily is different from life after birth. The function of sensation, while experienced, is not likely to be conscious if the ego, as we know it, is not present. We can imagine that the child is without the ability to discriminate by the function of conscious thinking. We can also imagine that the infant is without the ability to make a conscious value judgment of good or bad, like Adam and Eve in Paradise before their infamous feast. If the opposites of good and bad are not present or consciously experienced, all experience would be neutral. This can be seen as a Paradisiacal state of being. Apparently, all cultures and religions, which are numerous in history, that describe a golden place and time where perfection rules, believe, at least on an unconscious level, that the human infant contained in the womb of the mother, does not suffer under any conditions. I think the cosmological myths tell us this is so, whether it exists as collective knowledge or not.

The functions of thinking, feeling, and sensation all appear to be unconscious, leaving the function of intuition as a possibility for awareness of some kind to be present in the womb. Assuming that intuition is unconscious sensation, which I have suggested throughout this research, it would indicate that the infant in the womb has use of this function and that it is consciousness in its primary form. As an instinctual and irrational function, it appears reasonable to me to assume that this is the first function of consciousness and that it is experienced first in the womb. This idea would correlate with the human child, personified as Adam in the Genesis myth and the Serpent in the Genesis myth, as identical with the archetype of the Father God of Genesis. Thinking and sensation are both unconscious while one with God. Thus, the child, human and divine, creates his world. The child is the image, and the image is the child. The child is the archetype and the image of the creating Divine Child/Father God, or the first instinct, intuition, which appears also as the last or fourth function.

Jacoby (1985) describes the Paradisiacal state as linked to the pre-conscious state of infancy when he says:

> In the biblical myth, the paradisiacal state was lost when mankind acquired knowledge of good and evil, apparently against the will of God. Such knowledge represents the beginning of the ability to differentiate between opposites, the faculty upon which human consciousness is based. In psychological terms, then, the idea of Paradise is linked to the pre-conscious stage of infancy in which the ego, as the center of human consciousness, has not yet been activated (p. 25).

This statement reflects every psychology from the past that does not allow for the possibility that the beginning ego of the infant is activated by birth and that the infant becomes conscious at birth. Jacoby never mentions the possibility of Paradise being in the womb, and the theme of the young infant being "preconscious" is repeated here. This is the reason, perhaps, that the Western cosmology myth of Genesis has never been linked to developmental psychology in a more precise manner. Why it is so difficult to imagine that an infant has knowledge of the opposites at birth is a mystery to me. The Serpent represents the function of conscious sensation and the beginning human ego, symbolized best by the archetype of the Fallen Angel. The Serpent in Paradise is singled out as the reason for Eve's transgression. Jacoby (1985) continues:

> Both *tiufal* and Devil are derived from the Latin *Diabolus*. That, in turn, developed from the Greek verb *diaballein*, which literally means "to throw into confusion" and was understood to connote "to bisect, to create enmity, to slander or insult." These connotations bring us back close to the German word for "doubt," *Zweifel*, which originally was composed of two elements, zwei (two) and *fallen* (to fall). Interestingly, the English word "double" is etymologically related to the Old German and Old Frisian word for "doubt." In brief, then, "to doubt" connotes "to fall into two parts" or "to fall out of an initial unity" or "to waver in the face of two possibilities" (pp. 127-128).

This devil or doubt that Jacoby superbly describes is the function of conscious, introverted sensation and the beginning of the human ego and consciousness. The human body is conscious. The Father God is intuition or super consciousness that falls into two parts or falls out of an initial unity when consciousness is divided from the unconscious. In the "original unity," intuition, the Father God, and unconscious sensation, the Serpent, lived as one. The functions of intuition and sensation become divided and now work as two functions that alternate in consciousness. The first splitting of unity is that of faith and doubt, doubt being the opposite that becomes conscious first, negating faith to the unconscious (God). Jacoby (1985) describes the Serpent as doubt:

> The Serpent thus symbolizes, among other things, human nature's inherent potentiality for doubting, for calling things into question. The snake "poisons" the satisfaction of a complacent harmony with some sort of order, whether external or internal; it represents a deep-seated human instinct to eventually cast doubt on the validity of taboos, articles of faith and value systems. It

therefore stands for "Evil" from the vantage point of those external or internal systems of order. But from the standpoint of life's ongoing flux, calling things into question is positive and necessary; doubt gives rise to new orientation (p. 128).

I agree and would add that conscious, subjective, or introverted sensation, which I believe the Serpent personifies on a deeper level, is the beginning of the human child's ability to create the world from his or her personal and conscious experience, which negates the Father God to the unconscious and Lost Paradise.

"However, it is viewed, the Serpent in Paradise is impulse" (Jacoby, 1985, p. 128). This impelling force is the instinct for life, death, consciousness, unconsciousness, destruction, and creation.

Eve or the Feeling Function as the Bone (Beginning) of Adam or the Thinking Function

"The first woman dominates the story of the Garden of Eden" (Phillips, 1985, p. 55). In the second creation myth of Genesis, which is the Garden of Eden myth, Adam, who was created in the image of God, contains the feminine or Eve. The Father God, who represents one masculine God, contains the feminine within also, in the same way as Adam. She can be called invisible, dark, void, unconscious, silent, mother, lover, sister, or many other things, but she represents the feminine principle as the direct opposite of the Father God, who represents the masculine principle or collective concepts of these principles. The creation of Eve thus gives us information of the Father God and the bone or seed contained within the Father God or the invisible Goddess (feeling that is undifferentiated and contained in the function of intuition), since Adam is the image created in God's likeness. God's seed or bone and playmate is Wisdom; Adam's partner, created from his bone, is Eve. In this way, thinking is a reflection (Adam as image) of intuition. At this level, they are not opposites, but identical. Adam is created first because the archetype is the instinct given form and content.

The rib or bone, as a seed symbol representing Adam, is one of the most significant symbols in Genesis. Cirlot (1971) states the following concerning the symbol of the seed: "Equivalent to the egg... for in the centre of the fruit is the seed which represents the Origin... it is a symbol of earthly desires" (p. 115). Eve certainly represents earthly desires. Cooper (1988) states: "the fruit is Immortality; the essence, the culmination and result of one state and the seed of the next" (p.72). In the eating of the fruit, which is Eve or feeling that loses the experience of undifferentiated feeling (innocence) and experiences consciousness in half of the feeling function (knowledge of the opposites) Eve is leaving one state (Paradise) for the next state (consciousness). She will later be redeemed by the Virgin Mary, who represents perfect faith in other as God and perfect love for other (conscious extraversion) and is the woman (and sometimes the Divine Child) who will "crush the head of the serpent with her heel" (Genesis 3:15). Perfect love that is not based on ego will suppress the Serpent of conscious, introverted sensation. By returning to perfect faith and innocence as opposed to doubt, Mary will not be subjected to the dichotomies of the flesh (sensations) or the dichotomies of the heart (feeling) or the dichotomies of the rational mind (thinking). In those realms of earthly being, she will remain a virgin. This describes the altruistic ego that sacrifices itself for the sake of other, the Divine Mother, as opposed to Eve, the Earth Mother.

Eve, who is created from the bone of Adam, represents the seed or beginning for what will possibly become conscious thought. There is no other symbol in Genesis that describes this better than Eve as the rib or bone of Adam. Feeling is the precursor for thought. There is no conscious thought that does not have a counterpart in the realm of feeling, conscious or unconscious. Feeling is the "bone," the beginning, of thought. Subjective, introverted feeling (Eve) is the "Mother of all things," and creates the good, the bad, and the indifferent. Desire creates the world. Thus, Eve "sins" first, feeling becomes conscious before Adam, the archetype or subjective thinking becomes conscious. Feeling is the unmanifested thought—invisible, silent and dark—all attributes of the Mother Goddess.

McLean (1989) says of the two versions of creation in Genesis:
> The myth of the Fall was brought in rather late in the Jewish tradition, and the creation story in Genesis was in fact formed by uniting two separate versions. These versions reveal another fact of the Goddess in the Garden in the form of "Ishah." Adam, the archetypal man, called "Ish" in one of these stories, and "Ishah", are two parts of one being, an hermaphroditic archetype of humanity, two emanations of masculine and feminine attributes in incarnation (p. 98).

The hidden Mother Goddess in the book of Genesis is contained within the Father God, on his left (sinister) side, as portrayed by Michelangelo in his Creation of Adam painting (see Meshberger, 1990, pp. 1838, 1839), just as Eve is contained in the original Adam as one of the bones over his heart. The myth tells us this because Adam is a reflection, a copy, created in the image of the original, the Father God. Thus, however Adam is portrayed is also a portrait of his Creator. The Mother Goddess appears to be the first angel or messenger of God, as his shadow or unconscious, undifferentiated side. The Mother Goddess is everything that is the opposite of the Father God. Where He is light, She is darkness. Where He speaks, She is silent. She is the shadow of the visible God of Eden, the invisible Goddess, the playmate of God, later called Wisdom. And She has been there all along, in the myth of Genesis and other myths where the Goddess appears to be missing. And who is the Goddess in psychological terms? What kind of psychic energy is described by its very absence? She is the dark, undifferentiated side of God, contained in the original trinity of undifferentiated sensation, undifferentiated feeling, and undifferentiated thinking. She is the undifferentiated feeling function, existing with the Father God; intuition and Adam or undifferentiated thinking; and the Divine Child God (Serpent), undifferentiated sensation.

The Goddess shows up again in Paradise, just as the Father God does in the form of Adam, who is (divine) undifferentiated thinking. She returns in the form of Eve, who is undifferentiated feeling (and also divine), until she eats the forbidden apple; then she becomes the Mother of all the Living, she is conscious, subjective, or introverted feeling. With the Serpent in the garden, who is conscious, introverted sensation, and Eve, who represents desire by introverted feeling, ego consciousness begins, reflecting what appears as opposites, Adam and God as unconscious intuition and thinking. But the opposites, God and Adam as unconsciousness, and the Serpent and Eve as consciousness, at this "top of the mountain" scene, express the same energy as Eve and the Serpent. The unconscious thought and the unconscious intuition are the sensation and the feeling in the form of soul, partners to the functions of sensation and feeling. This, as Campbell quoted earlier writes, is the inside and the outside of a single mystery. At the very moment consciousness is divided from unconsciousness, they can also be seen as one and the same. Woman and snake, long the perilous partners in multitudinous myths, bring consciousness into the world and, simultaneously, bring unconsciousness, symbolized by death, into the world. Psychologically speaking, snake and woman are the functions of conscious, introverted sensation and conscious introverted feeling, functions that are the universal experience of every human psyche, male and female alike. We know the world first with our body and then our heart, and finally with our intellect.

And the newborn infant, fresh from the mother's womb, fresh from Paradise, resounds his or her first cry; the newborn is the Serpent, Eve, Adam, and God, all rolled into one, but different from the one that was left behind, because the characters have all been separated, split into the functions of intuition (God), sensation (Serpent), feeling (Eve) and thinking (Adam). The subjective ego has been born in all the functions. And from that first cry on—desire is always a desire to return to Paradise, though every desire may be cloaked in a different attire. This takes time in the book of Genesis, until the birth of a Divine Child. In the nursery, however, the story usually goes much faster. The mother uses all her functions for this end and they are all extraverted, directed toward the objective perception of her child. The mother (assuming she is capable of intuitive consciousness) in the form of extraverted feeling, love that renders her own ego unconscious, the ego that is forfeited for the sake of other, will return the child to that state of bliss, at least temporarily. The mother, now in the world, will return the child to the experience of being one with the parents in Paradise. This is what I have previously described as the first transference. To the human mother, who is really adopting the child persona of girl/virgin, represented in the Christian myth as the Virgin Mary archetype, the child and his or her ego are divine. The "Virgin" mother is the archetype of the girl/child/mother who loves without ego (agape). She is always the psychological function of conscious, extraverted feeling (Virgin) that negates Eve, introverted feeling, to the unconscious. The Virgin, whether in Christianity or any of the numerous myths that speak of a Virgin Mother (born without original sin, no knowledge of a subjective "I"), is always the other side of Eve, who is conscious introverted feeling. Campbell (1991a) expresses this: "In medieval Christian thought, the two contrary forces symbolized in the downward and upward pointing triangles were personified, respectively, in Eve and the Virgin Mary, through the second of whom the effects of her predecessor's Original Sin were reversed" (p. 80).

Taken together (as they were in Paradise), they are the Goddess in her dual form. Every human mother (and father or any "other") who loves the child in this way is living out the archetype of the Virgin Mother. The importance of this experience is not "who" the "other" is, but that someone is playing the role of the Virgin Mother archetype. This is why a human father or any mother substitute or both can provide the same experience for a child after birth.

Desire is love that contains fear and there is always an ego (Eros) attached. The arrows that the winged (angel archetype) child god of love, Eros, shoots were the arrows of desire or ego love. Fear is the real opposite of agape love. Desire is analogous with love that contains fear, for desire is the perception of a lack of something, namely Paradise, that place where both kinds of love were experienced as one. As Emily Dickinson said: "This is all there is," two kinds of love and two kinds of consciousness: ego love and soul love. I perceive these as the two sides of the feeling function. This is the double-edged sword of Christ, Christ as the "twin fishes." Ego love (desire) and soul love (without desire, death of ego) are the two sides of a whole; taken together, they comprise the total definition of love, two opposites that can be reconciled and exist as one or stay divided and wounded. If there is no wound in the feeling function, there is no need for the angel of healing, Raphael, who represents the same energy of undivided love. Unity in this function, first represented by Eve and desire and later by the virgin archetype, appears essential for a return to the undivided Self.

The destiny of the newborn infant crying a first cry in the nursery, the destiny of all living beings, is to live out both sides of love and come to the realization that he or she was that all along. There are only two beginning sides to the feeling function in the psyche: "I desire" and "I do not desire," and both of them are love. Love or the feeling function united in one psyche is not an emotion, but what I perceive as a psychological principle. Ego and Soul are joined in the Self, where feeling is now experienced as Being. Value judgments no longer exist, for all opposites are one. This is the wisdom of the Goddess, the undivided feeling function, who rejects nothing and contains everything. The feeling function, so long and in so many ways, has been devalued, discounted, abused, and misunderstood, like the feminine principle and often the living female, who is usually associated with it symbolically. Jung (1971/1921) described the feeling function in the following way:

> The intellect proves incapable of formulating the real nature of feeling in conceptual terms, since thinking belongs to a category incommensurable with feeling; in fact, no basic psychological function can ever be completely expressed by another. That being so, it is impossible for an intellectual definition to reproduce the specific character of feeling at all adequately (pp. 435-436).

These are, no doubt, words of wisdom. But conscious subjective feeling, that is, the Goddess as Eve, does not need to speak. Adam or thinking, the created image or archetype, speaks for her, which was God's instruction to Adam and Eve as they leave the Garden. Eve, or feeling, should follow her husband, Adam or thinking, and be subjected to him thereafter. The meaning, on a psychological level, describes conscious subjective introverted feeling as following the archetype which becomes conscious thought. In Paradise, Eve followed Adam, that is, she is the epiphenomenal Eve who was created after Adam; when Paradise is ending, however, Eve leads the way and is responsible for the fall of humanity and the division of the Self and Soul, that is, Paradise, into two forms of separated consciousness. Subjective, introverted feeling, attached to a conscious ego is responsible for the fall of humanity. Eve is to follow her husband, because Adam expresses the feeling in the form of an archetype, image or idea, especially as the spoken and written word.

This, of course, is a different meaning than the literal interpretation, but a crucial one for understanding the interpretation of the archetypes in Genesis as patterns of energy in an individual psyche and not as historical figures that determine the destiny of all humanity. It is time to see Eve, who I see as a personification of the conscious, introverted feeling function, in a new light. Baring and Cashford (1993), describing the cosmological myth, put it thus:

> If the myth is understood symbolically—not as an incontrovertible statement about human nature but as an expression of humanity's own experience of itself at the moment of initiation into consciousness—then the meaning changes totally. To bite into the knowledge of good and evil is then to be separated forever from the state of unconscious unity in which all life is one (p. 504).

It is not only unconscious unity that is loss, but the undifferentiated energy of the Self and Soul, which contains consciousness and unconsciousness united. The meaning has always been there; what changes is our perception of the mythological contents, and understanding them from a new and different perspective.

Harrison (1994) expresses quite beautifully the archetypal energy of Eve and Mary or the Goddess in her dual form:

> In that heaven for which we yearn but which we cannot imagine, Eve is united with Mary, carried by flight's of angels to Mother God/Father God. She has become Mary's twin in purity, her sister. Without Eve, Mary, would not be our sister. All we know of heaven we know from Eve, who gave us the earth, a serviceable blueprint: Without Eve there would be no utopias, no imaginable reason to find and to create transcendence, to ascend toward the light. Eve's legacy to us is the imperative to desire. Babies and poems are born in travail of this desire, her great gift to the loveable world (p. 2).

This, I believe, can be translated into less elegant personifications, which nevertheless contain the same luminous and beautiful truths. Eve and Mary are the Goddess in her dual form. Eve is conscious, introverted feeling and Mary is her opposite, unconscious, extraverted feeling. Together they describe the psychological function of feeling, the Goddess who is silent and absent when the God (thinking) speaks. They exist in the psyche of male and female alike. Subjective feeling is the mother of all things and the mother in every human child that gives birth to all things.

The voice of Eve and the silence of Mary have been depicted in a thousand or more personifications, two archetypal energy patterns present in all humans. Eve and Mary, however, are the archetypes present in the Western cosmological myth of Genesis, Eve by her voice and Mary by her silence. Taken together, both archetypes define what I understand to be the psychological function of feeling.

Adam as Divine Child, Image of God: Archetype for the Psychological Function of Undifferentiated Thinking

> And the Lord God formed man of the slime of the Earth: and breathed into his face the breath of life, and man became a living soul (Genesis 2:7).

Adam is the first man/child and the first human soul, created from slime, which is viscous mud. This is also a substance secreted by certain animals such as fish. Immediately we have several images: earth, water, and fish. The earth symbolizes the feminine. Water is also usually a feminine symbol, and earth or mud that has only a little water is viscous, that is, it has a high resistance to flow; it moves slowly. The fish often symbolizes Christ and could represent Adam as the Divine Child, which was his status before the Fall. Science also indicates that we were all fish in the beginning, not only in the womb, but as evolutionary creatures on earth.

Adam, then, is composed of two feminine symbols, earth and water and pieces of fish, which when associated with Christ or the perfect man, appear as a masculine symbol. The earth and water represent his connection to the mother and womb, whereas the pieces of fish connect him to the Divine Child archetype and the broken body of Christ. I see this image as the death of ego, symbolized by the death of the body or sensations, but in the newborn it would represent the ego that has not yet appeared in any of the functions. When God breathed into Adam's face the breath of life, a fourth symbol appears, air or breath being another masculine symbol. After the breath of God creates him as a living soul, Adam is composed of three of the elements: earth, water and air, plus animal modicums, which can be a fish or snake. Both fish and snake represent the most primal or archaic of creatures, and both have been associated with a god in numerous antiquated religions. The missing element in Adam appears to be fire, which is usually a masculine symbol associated with light and consciousness. Chetwynd (1982) describes the three elements transformed by fire:

> Everything in the material universe, including man, can be divided into solid (Earth), liquid (Water), and Vapour (Air), and these three are transformed one into the other, through the agency of Fire (Energy). In their context Earth, Air and Water are aspects of spatial reality while Fire symbolizes the process of time (p. 137).

This describes Adam as a universal personification of the infant in the uterus; he is contained in inner space by being in the womb. If the womb is seen as representing Paradise, we can describe Adam (infant) as the myth describes, without fire or time; he lives in an eternal place, where time has not yet begun.

Adam is named after and composed of the earth (mother symbol), the element that Eve will later come to represent. This describes the archetype (thinking), air, breath or spirit (God), as named after and composed of the earth. The archetype (Adam) is made of the same basic matter (mother) as the feeling function (Eve). The image is composed of the feeling that precedes it.

In Genesis 1, Adam still contains Eve (mother, earth, or the undifferentiated feeling function) within his body; they still exist as one created creature, like Plato's original round man. With God's breath or air (spirit), he contains the Father God, while water (undifferentiated feeling) links him to the Mother Goddess. The theriomorphic symbolism of the animal or fishes in pieces appears to describe the Divine Child who has not been born psychologically, but is already composed of the parts or the same basic material. In other words, he has thinking, feeling, sensation and intuition as undifferentiated functions, which makes him an image of the Father God or the function of intuition.

Thus, after the first description in Genesis 1, of God creating man as male and female, the second creation myth also depicts in the beginning only one Being, who still contains the uncreated Eve in his body. The creation of Eve represents a description of the separation of undifferentiated feeling from the thinking function. Eve has been taken from Adam's side and given a name, which establishes that they are separate functions. Even so, Eve represents feeling that is still in a state of undifferentiation; thus, she is, like Adam, still one with the Father God or intuition. Thus, in Genesis 2, Adam and Eve live in Paradise or thinking and feeling have been established as separate partners who are still both replicas of the Father God or intuition. Thinking and feeling are created and alive, but both are innocent. This means that they exist as living potential that has not yet been used; there is no ego consciousness, but the consciousness that is available is that of soul or oneness with God.

Feeling (Eve) is created as a helpmate for the function of thinking (Adam) and removed from the body of Adam as the rib or bone, which is a seed symbol, symbolizing beginnings. Chetwynd (1982) calls the seed "the spark of life, which swells into actual living forms and contracts back into the seeds. It is related to the sperm-drop and to origins" (p. 421). This means that the bone, the seed, or beginning of the feeling function helps, like a rib assists the body, thinking to breathe. Breath connects the bone symbol with the Father God (air, spirit) and the function of intuition. When feeling is removed from thinking, thinking will flourish (as one function). Feeling (Eve) is created for the sole purpose of making sure the image or archetype (Adam) will not be alone, that is, without meaning.

To be naked is a description of the appearance of the four functions that were once covered, that is, undifferentiated as the Goddess and differentiated as the Father God—both sides of intuition. It is a description of the flowing out of the functions in part; what was once covered—the subjective, introverted side of humanity—will become conscious first, creating the unconscious at the same time, and leaving the extraverted functions, at least temporarily, in the state of unconsciousness. The extraverted side will be introduced by the mother or primary caretaker, and the process of life and the reconciliation of the two sides of each function will begin.

Thus, Adam's final eating of the apple is describing the final separation of the four functions as each becomes conscious. Adam represents the final birth as the archetype which becomes thinking. "The moment of the rise of consciousness, of the separation of subject and object, is indeed a birth" (Jung, 1956/1912, p. 326).

The Serpent was the first to be described (sensation) or the ego as body, then Eve or the ego as feeling, and finally, Adam or the ego as thinking, which will be the final outcome of the created archetype. This is the newborn, fresh from Paradise, who has the capacity for body sensations, feeling, or making value judgments, and the ability to fill in the forms of the empty archetype with his personal experience, which may contain the collective and also something that is not collective, except in the unconscious, because human nature is ever evolving and the possibility for what has never been expressed is contained in every newborn child.

Sidoli (1989) describes proto-images in the infant: "In infancy, we can infer the existence of proto-images, such as shapes and patterns, in the baby's mind, which, enriched by sensuous experiences, will in time develop into proper images of objects and people" (p. 4). I agree with Sidoli here and think that the first proto-image is what Adam, as a specific archetype (that is, a separate function) and as the last character in Genesis to eat the apple, represents. Adam represents that aspect of the human infant that is capable of creating images and archetypes, which leads to the ability of cognitive thought and the thinking function. He is a stamp of the Father God and like the Father God, puts his stamp on all experience. The myth describes the Serpent, Eve, and Adam as banished from Paradise at the same time, which I think is a description of birth and consciousness in the introverted functions. This indicates to me that Adam, as an archetype for the archetype or the created symbol in the thinking function, must take place at birth, paving the way for the future development of what we call thinking. In other words, the first image or representation possibly occurs at birth, as a result of the preceding functions. This is comparable in the myths to the pompous assumption of the first "Son," that is, the mighty angel Lucifer, who boasts that he is equal with God.

That the first image or archetype created by the newborn may be subjective or a product of introverted thinking appears to be a reasonable assumption. That it may be an abstract image appears to me even more reasonable. Jung (1971/1921) quotes Worringer concerning abstraction:

> The counterpole of empathy is abstraction. According to Worringer, "the urge to abstraction is the outcome of a great inner uneasiness inspired in man by the phenomena of the external world, and its religious counterpart is the strongly transcendental colouring of all ideas. We might describe this state as an immense spiritual dread of space… This same feeling of fear may also be assumed to be the root of artistic creation." We recognize in this definition the primary tendency towards introversion (p. 505).

Jung and Worringer understand abstraction, although I would call the "feeling of fear" the subjective or introverted I that demands to be loved. Applying these ideas to the newborn infant, this abstraction would match the introverted, conscious feeling function that desires, assuming one imagines that desire is ego-love or the exact opposite of agape love. The newborn is not capable of empathy (soul love, agape), which Worringer sees as the counterpole of abstraction, but he or she may certainly be capable of its opposite or abstraction in the form of the simplest archetype. It seems reasonable to assume that the infant would experience abstraction before he would experience its opposite or empathy. He will experience empathy when it is given to his demanding ego by someone in the world, usually his mother. Jung (1971/1921) goes on to quote Worringer:

> "The urge to abstraction is the origin of all art," says Worringer. This idea finds weighty confirmation in the fact that schizophrenics produce forms and figures showing the closest analogy with those of primitive humanity, not only in their thoughts but also in their drawings (p. 506).

Adam, as a personification of conscious, introverted thinking (after the Fall) appears to fit this description. As soon as there is an I that abstracts, that takes only one portion of the object and leaves the rest, the wholeness of that which was previously there has been shattered. To abstract is to separate and divide and express a part of the total picture. This can be seen as Adam as he is separated from God by ego consciousness; he no longer exists as one with God, but is aware of an I and an other. This also describes an act of destruction and an act of creation: Oneness or wholeness is destroyed for the creation of two, and Adam has been separated from God by his consciousness, which is also separated from the unconscious when thinking and the ego begin. Thus, Adam represents the introverted consciousness of the thinking function in the individual newborn child, just as Eve can be said to represent the function of conscious introverted feeling and the Serpent before her represents introverted, conscious sensation.

If Paradise is going to be shattered, the characters in the drama (the psychological functions of the human child) are going to fall into a synchronized pattern of experiencing the opposites of good and evil first in the conscious body perceptions, second in the feeling function that evaluates, and third, in the function of introverted or abstract thinking, which is the final destruction of what was once Paradise. The Lost Paradise of Genesis appears to be describing, in a story that takes longer to read, perhaps, than the actual experience, the beginning of human consciousness and unconsciousness. It is consciousness in the body, heart, and emotions, and a description of the beginning intellect of the thinking function, as the human child creates his or her world. The urge to abstraction is the origin of all art, and the average human child, although influenced by his or her genetic structure, is nevertheless an artist from the beginning of life, creating the picture of her or his individual world.

The archetype of Adam represents the function of thinking—specifically unconscious (a living soul) and undifferentiated thinking—while Adam is still in

Paradise or the infant is still in the womb. Undifferentiated thinking, undifferentiated feeling, and undifferentiated sensation are Adam, Eve, and the Serpent, all existing in undifferentiated form in the archetype of the Father God or differentiated intuition. Intuition is the function that allows us to see the picture as a whole. When thinking is undifferentiated and both sides of the thinking function are merged or neutral or free of opposites, it is identical with the function of intuition. Thus, Adam is created in God's image and lives in Paradise as one with the Father God. Adam is the prototype of the first human, but in the first creation he is also created perfect and a god.

Adam is the archetype of the archetype itself, and the Father God is an archetype of the instinct that first contains and then creates the archetype as an expression of the experience that preceded it. The archetype exists as unconscious potential contained within the instinct. This is what the myth of Genesis appears to be describing by the personification of psychic energy as it flows out of the Self. In the first creation, Adam appears to represent the same psychic energy as the Christ archetype, as well as the angel Lucifer, before his exit from Heaven.

Neutral and undifferentiated energy in the thinking function can be seen as the merging of both sides of the thinking function to produce energy that becomes undifferentiated (another theme of the third that turns into the fourth). This would describe a return to undifferentiated thinking. In the case of the child in the womb, however, or the first person in Paradise, this would be energy that has never been differentiated. At this point, conscious intuition can be seen as identical with the three unconscious and undifferentiated ego functions, described in the myth as Paradise. Consciousness and unconsciousness are the god and goddess merged and still one, a reflection of the Self that can be called soul. Adam, as unconscious thinking, is still contained in Eden.

Adam represents undifferentiated thinking, which makes him the first image of the Father God. Undifferentiated thinking contains both consciousness and unconsciousness. This describes the thinking function as an image of the intuitive function, which contains both darkness and light, consciousness and unconsciousness merged as super consciousness. This is Adam as Divine Child, reflection and image of the Father God while still in Paradise. The "death" of the ego (Hero) in the thinking function is what returns the "Hero" to the innocent state of Adam before the Fall or creates the new Adam (Christ). Adam, like the Archangel Gabriel, is the "Hero" of God while still in the Garden of Eden.

Active thinking or ego consciousness as we know it has not yet come into being. The ego is still contained in the soul, although both have been separated

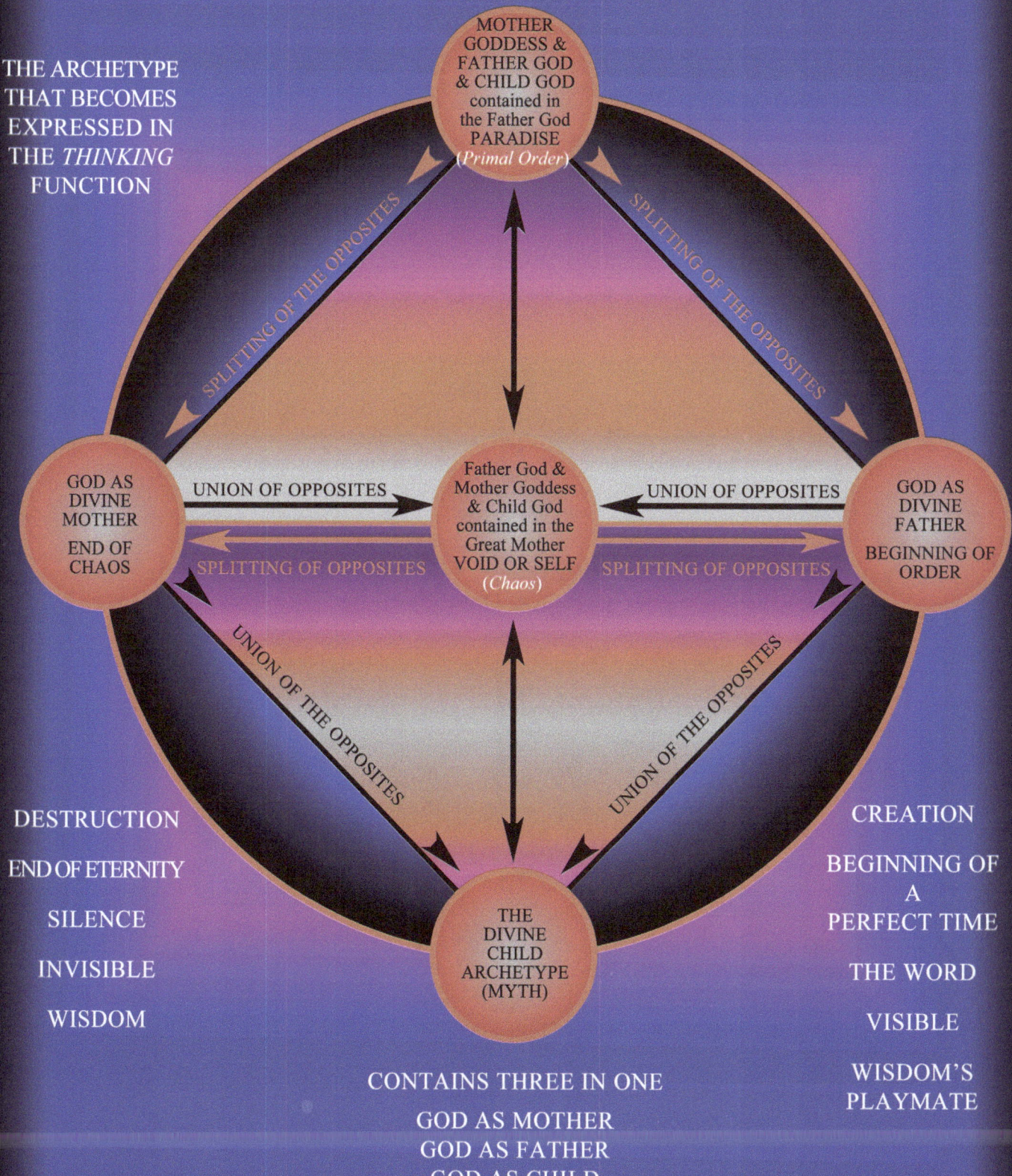

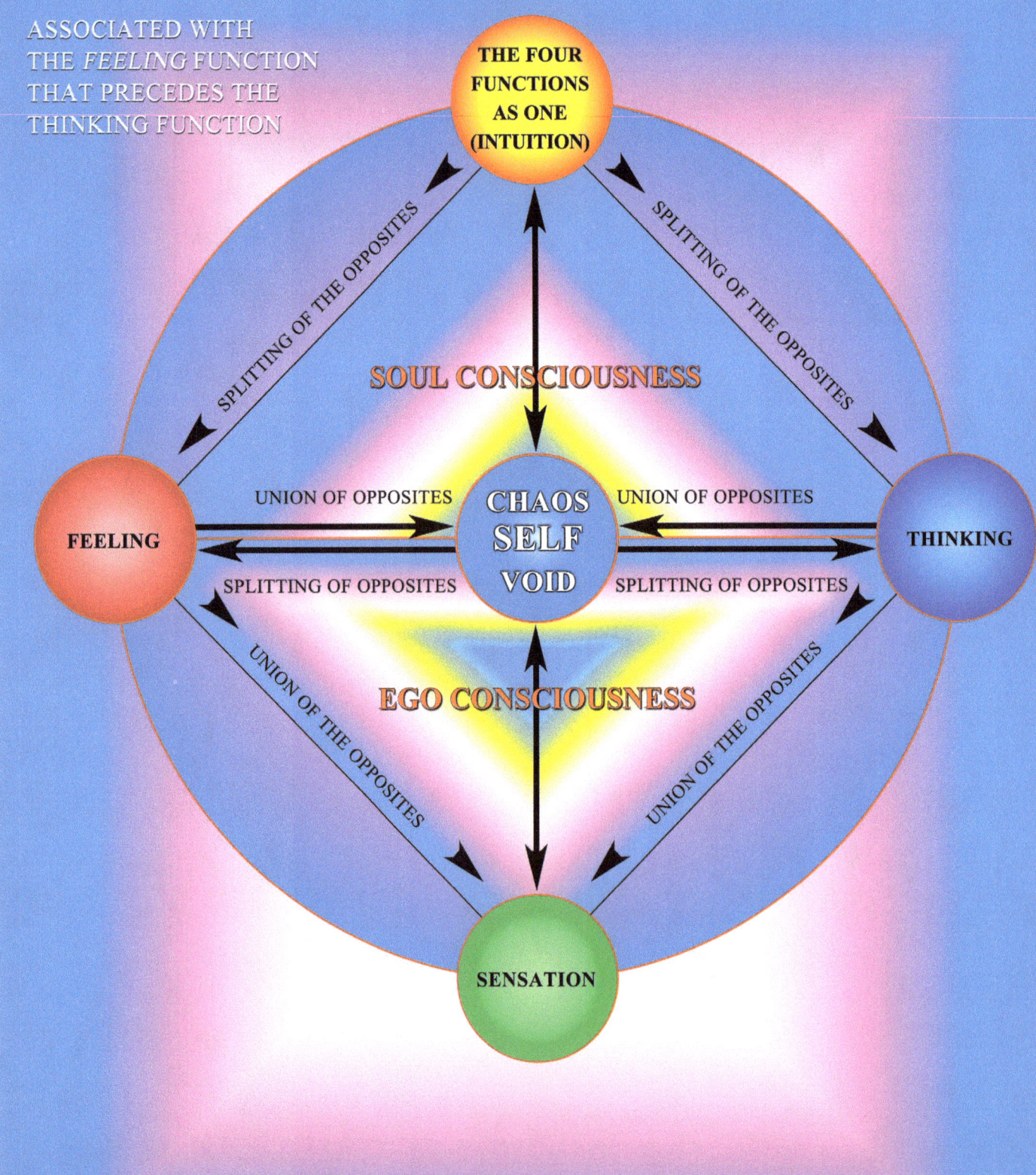

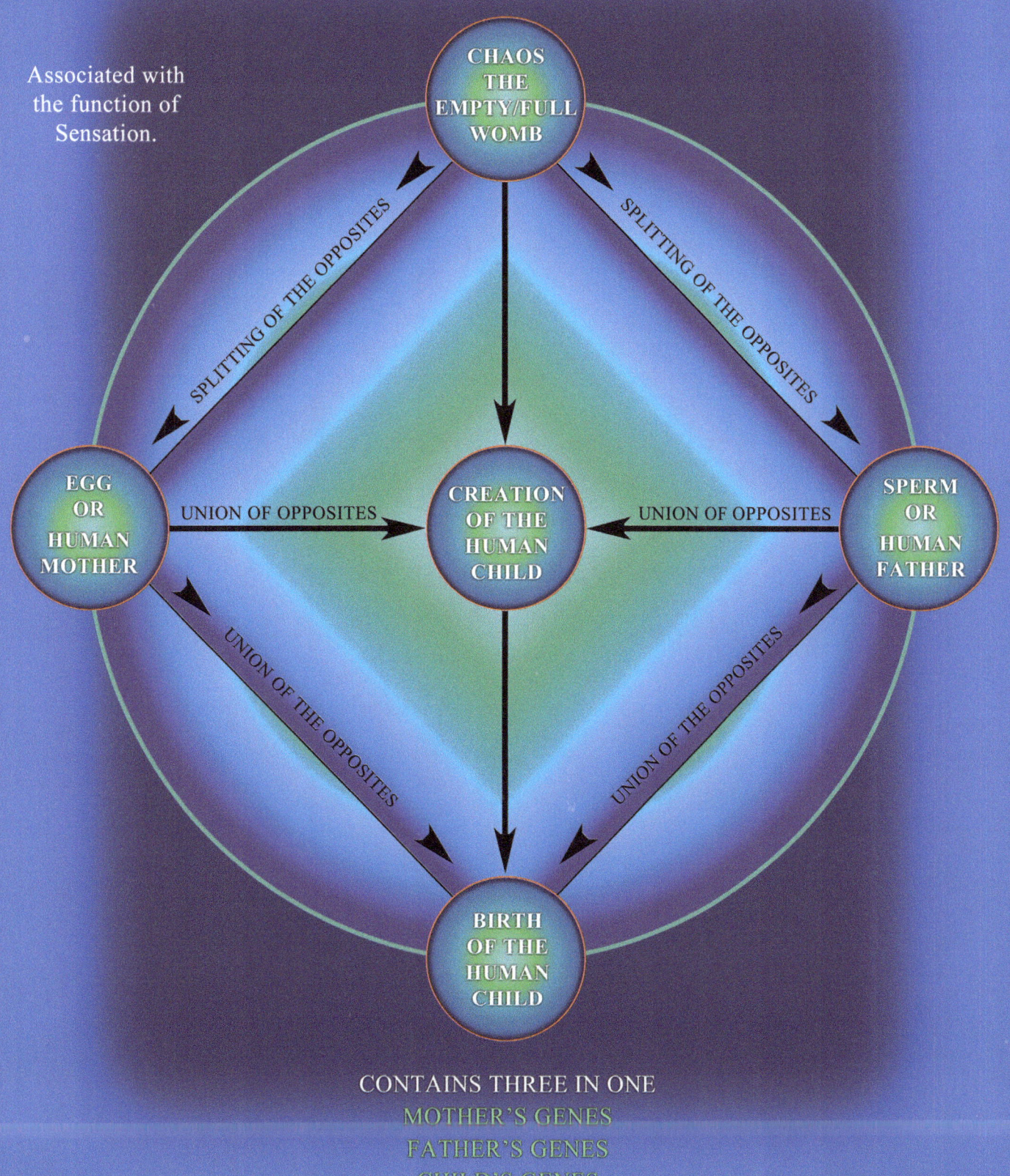

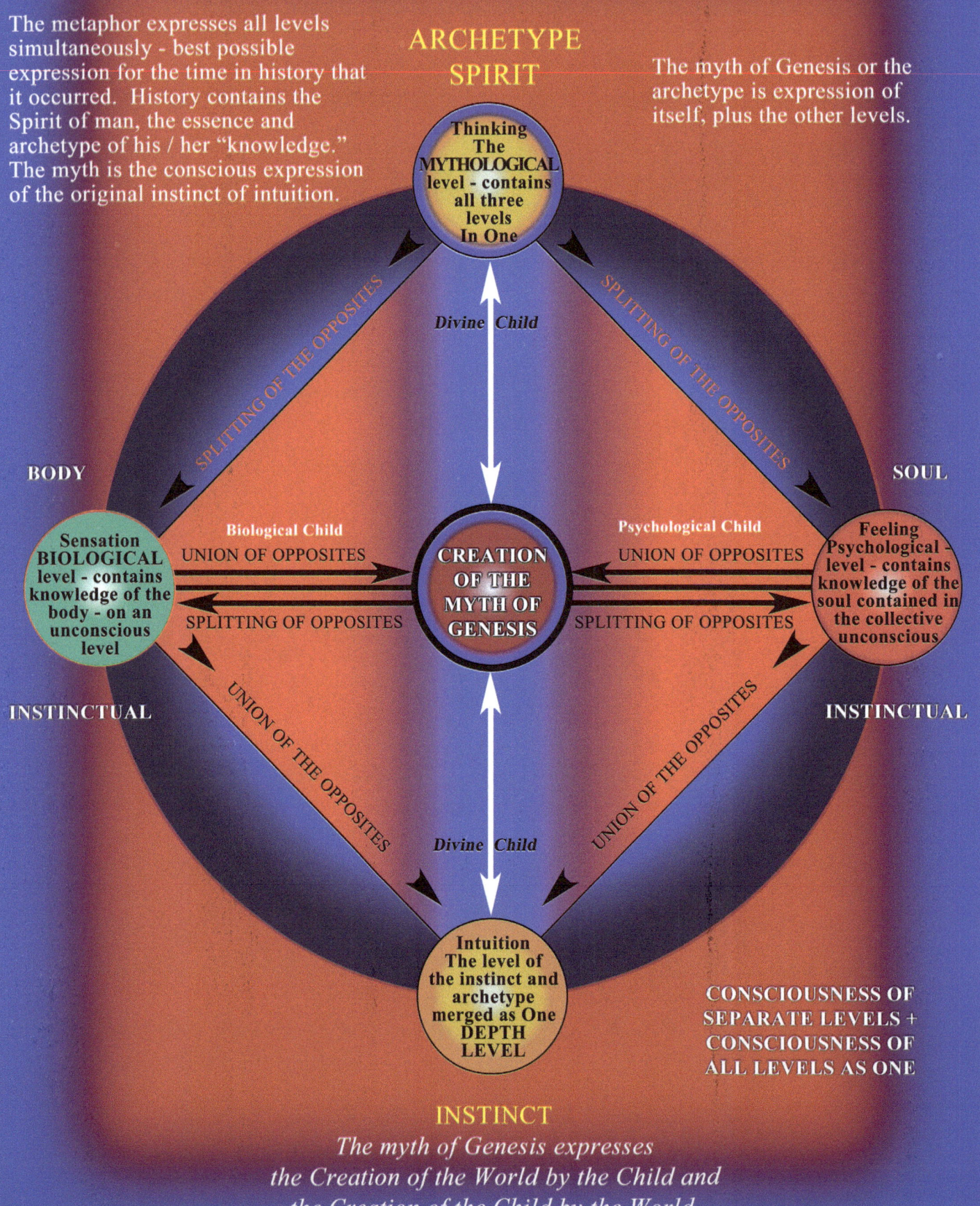

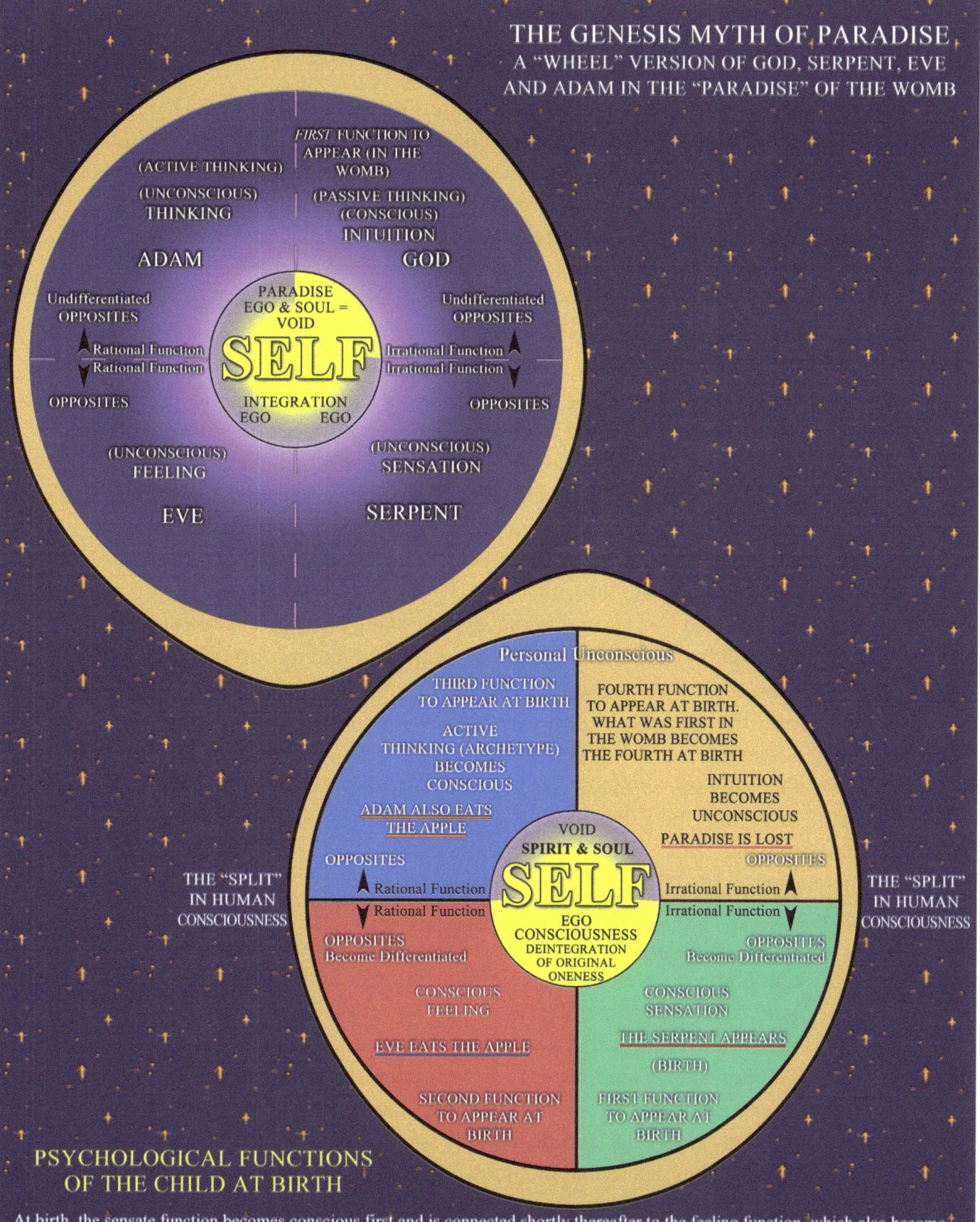

At birth, the sensate function becomes conscious first and is connected shortly thereafter to the feeling function, which also become conscious. At this point, intuition, which is the opposite of sensation, returns to the unconscious. Thinking, the function that produces the image or representation of the object, remains unconscious. Thus, the personal unconscious is born at the same time consciousness appears, and they are opposites. Active thinking, along with passive thinking or intuition, can be called soul functions, because they exist as one undifferentiated function, spirit and soul as one. Sensation and feeling, which are conscious, are functions of the body ego. Two types of consciousness are created at birth. Intuition is first in the womb and at birth, the second function to appear is sensation. Feeling becomes the third, while thinking becomes the fourth. The fourth is then identical with the first intuition. At birth sensation appears first, feeling occurs second, thinking is the third function to appear, while intuition becomes the fourth. Conscious active thinking is identical with intuition, or passive thinking. **This is the "Maria axiom" – one becomes two, two becomes three, and out of the third comes the one as the fourth.**

from the Self, represented by a Father God (intuition as a function in the human child), who creates after leaving the original chaos or the Self. In the original Self, Father and Mother God, creation and destruction, consciousness and unconsciousness, and all opposites exist as the still point of Being. Campbell (1964) describes this as the Bronze Age cosmology:

> All, according to this vision, though in apparent tumult, is harmony at root, as a manifestation of the all-supporting, all-suffusing mystery of being, which transcends thought, imaging, and definition; that is to say, transcends the search of science (p. 5).

This is the same image of the twin Serpents contained in the Sumerian Serpent Lord archetype discussed in Chapter 4. When the twin serpents of god and goddess mate, they return to the center (Nammu) where they are one, an image used to describe the indescribable. This is the Self of the human child who begins life by the light of conscious intuition and returns to that function when the ego disappears in whole or part. Every human child is the Father God, Adam, Eve, and the Serpent.

Adam is created first, as undifferentiated thinking and the last function (in the human child) to become conscious. He is the first and the last, the child as instinct and the child as archetype. Westman (1991) describes the word: "Etymologically the word archetype is derived from the Greek word arche meaning 'first,' 'foremost' or 'chief' and typos meaning a 'blow' or the 'mark' left by a blow, and 'impress' or 'mold'" (p. 33). This describes Adam as the "first imprint" or copy of the Father God; it describes unconscious, undifferentiated thinking as the "first imprint" of intuition, that is, the as yet unexpressed archetype as the "first imprint" of the instinct.

Sidoli (1989) says of the archetype:

> In the early stages of life we have to take into account primarily the "bodily pole" of the archetype. Its symbolic and spiritual polarity, although potentially present, is not yet available to the infant, who is immersed in sensuous experiences of a subjective and undifferentiated kind, a stage where impulses predominate (p. 4)

Sidoli is correct about the body aspect of the archetype being essential. However, the infant can live the spiritual polarity simultaneously with the body polarity. The sensuous, subjective, and undifferentiated experiences of the infant are those of the instincts, represented symbolically in the myth of Genesis as the Father God, Adam as the unformed archetype, Eve as the united feeling function, and the Serpent as the united (with God, or intuition) sensate function. The infant is living this archetypal (also spiritual) experience, which is, indeed, also real. Sidoli (1989, p. 4) also discusses Jung's description of the "bipolarity" of the archetype. If, however, the archetype is created in the thinking function as a result of the other three functions, it would be more than bipolar; it would be fourfold in nature. The archetype would be the expression of the experience of all four functions. Jung (1963/1955) describes Adam as "the psyche par excellence" (emphasis Jung's, p. 390). I believe that Jung was correct because Adam, as archetype for the thinking function, reflects the experience of the fourfold psyche of the human child.

It seems necessary to see the Serpent and Eve as archetypes for that first primal experience of conscious, subjective sensation and feeling, for without these two, there would be no third or fourth. The Serpent, or the senses that awaken at birth, represents consciousness that reflects what becomes the unconscious opposite—the Father God, intuition. Eve or feeling is consciousness that reflects Adam, the as yet to be conscious thinking function. Adam eats the apple after Eve; he becomes conscious after she has already done so. In the time and space between Eve's eating of the apple, that is, feeling becoming conscious and Adam's eating of the apple, or the archetype becoming conscious, consciousness and unconsciousness can be seen as a reflection or mirror image of one another. This, I believe, is the highpoint of the Genesis myth; it describes the so-called split in human consciousness as super consciousness is replaced by the opposites of consciousness and unconsciousness. The irony, and perhaps the beauty of this still-point description in beginning time, is that Adam, as the image of God, is still unconscious and undifferentiated energy, and still a reflection of the intuitive function or the Father God, who has now become the function of unconscious intuition. Thinking and intuition or Adam and God or the archetype and the instinct all represent the creation of ego consciousness, first in the functions of sensation and feeling, as a reflection of the unconscious Father God and the unconscious Divine Child, Adam.

Eve or feeling is born from Adam's rib, that is, consciousness in the feeling function is born from the seed of the undifferentiated Adam or thinking, just as the Serpent is the undifferentiated function of sensation while still in Paradise and becomes the Serpent in Eden or the separate function of conscious, subjective introverted sensation as intuition (God) divides into two functions, the Father and the Son or intuition and sensation. At the point where they converge, conscious intuition is identical with unconscious sensation, just as conscious feeling is identical with unconscious thinking. The feeling function, which makes value judgments of good and evil, is the unmanifested thought, just as the Serpent is son or child of the Father God and the first form of consciousness of the opposites. Eve and the Serpent, or feeling and sensation, have become differentiated from the Self and from the soul and are the first forms of ego consciousness. They reflect their opposite sides in God and his image, Adam, who at this second in time, the pinnacle point of the myth, are unconscious.

When Adam eats the apple, ego consciousness in the thinking function appears, and this must describe the creation of the archetype in human consciousness or the mind of the human infant. The myth appears to support this idea by telling us that Adam and Eve leave Paradise together. In other words, that moment in time when consciousness and unconsciousness were mirror images of one another has passed and the heroic ego and his soul, consciousness and unconsciousness, has been established in all the functions. The three or four functions that existed as one function have become the four psychological functions. The bliss of Paradise has been shattered as Adam, Eve, and the Serpent, or the ego functions in the newborn child, now differentiated, make their way into the new world of opposites. Intuition or passive thinking has been replaced by active thinking; the instinct has been replaced by the archetype and "God" has been replaced by his image Adam, as Paradise is lost. This describes one full cycle of (half) the functions in one human infant as the introverted half differentiates and becomes conscious. The human infant has experienced the entire myth and is fresh from the womb of Paradise, not yet embraced by human arms as he or she resounds the first cry of protest. It also is the end of the Genesis Paradise myth. To pick up the extraverted half of the functions, it is necessary to go on to Christianity, which continues the myth by the description of another birth, the Divine Child who replaces the old Adam.

They looking back, all th' Eastern side beheld
Of Paradise, so late thir happie seat,
Wav'd over by that flaming Brand, the Gate
With dreadful Faces throng'd and fierie Armes:
Som natural tears they drop'd, but wip'd them soon;
The World was all before them, where to choose
Thir place of rest, and Providence thir guide;
They hand in hand with wandring steps and slow,
Through Eden took thir solitarie way.

(John Milton, from Paradise Lost, 1981, p. 357)

Chapter 6

Symbols and Archetypes from Divergent Mythologies that Express Psychic Energy Related to Genesis, the Self, and the Four Psychological Functions

The Rope Image of the Hindu *Bhagavad Gita*: An Eastern Three-In-One Motif

A simple image to compare with various symbols and archetypes in Genesis, as well as the four psychological functions, is the rope symbol described in the ancient Hindu Bhagavad Gita.

Chatterji (The *Bhagavad Gita*, 1960) says the following:
> According to the Gita's analysis, there are two eternal, self-existent classes of being in the universe (XIII: 19). One of these is purusha, translated variously as soul, spirit, self, man, and the other is prakriti, translated as nature, matter, nonsoul, or material nature (p. x).

Anthropomorphic or theriomorphic personifications, such as male, female, child, or serpent, are replaced by the description of the same energy in the simple analogy of a rope. *Purusha* (Soul or Spirit in the Bhagavad Gita) is described as *one rope made of three strands*. The single rope can be compared with the apple symbol in Genesis or the golden egg symbol of Eros. All three symbols represent the state of undifferentiated energy (three or four in one) that is differentiated into the one psychological function of intuition, the single strand called purusha or soul in the Hindu Bhagavad Gita mythology.

Prakriti, as nonsoul or material nature, is the name for the three separate strands. One strand, Rajas, is red and can be equated with the feeling function. Tamas is black and can be compared with the function of sensation. Sattiva is white and can be compared with the thinking function. The three strands woven together to form one rope can be compared with the three serpents held in one chalice in the alchemical King image. Both images of three contained in one can be seen as representing the three ego functions that are differentiated (after birth) or divided into three (three strands or three serpents) that become one (undifferentiated and differentiated) archetype or function.

Purusha is the soul (complex) and Prakriti are the three ego functions of consciousness (ego complex). The Eastern symbolism appears to be describing the same energy that the Serpent Lord image, the alchemical king and queen image and part of the Judaic-Christian image of Paradise describes. The rope is the Father God (intuition) and the three strands are Adam, Eve, and the Serpent (thinking, feeling, and sensation) that become conscious and differentiated.

The same symbolism can be seen in the Christian trinity, where the three-in-one motif describes a return to the Divine Child and super consciousness when the opposites have been reunited in all the functions. The fourth does not need to be added; it has always been there in the form of the Divine Goddess of Love and Silence, the shadow of the Father God as Word. The Holy Spirit is the three archetypes existing as one, just as the three stands in one rope describe the same archetypal energy of one God.

A Comparison of the Wind and Water Symbolism in Genesis with the Great Serpent Mound: Tokchi'i, Guardian of the East

The Great Serpent Mound, near my hometown of Portsmouth, Ohio, is the largest known serpent image in the world. The newest radiocarbon analysis suggest that the mound is about 1,400 years older than conventionally thought. The new date of construction is estimated at approximately 321 BCE, one year after the death of Aristotle in Greece. Controversies continue about the dates involved, and the names of the Indian tribes that created the effigy mound. The serpent representation is generally assumed to have been created by the Adena-Hopewell Indians, 1000 BCE - 700 CE (Campbell, 1989, pp. 167, 188; Johnson, 1988, p. 178).

Later, it is suggested that the Fort Ancient culture, that came later was the creator of the Serpent Mound. The artists, whether the Adena people or their descendants, carved the sacred image at the pinnacle of their world, using the substance they considered their holy mother, the earth.

Bancroft-Hunt (1992) says of the Adena mounds:
> The most famous is the Great Serpent Mound, which twists and coils along the top of an exposed hillside in Ohio for a distance of 1, 300 ft. It is a magnificent representation of a people's ability to draw strength from the earth (p. 77).

Although many of the numerous mounds in Southern Ohio are known to be burial mounds, it is known that the Serpent Mound was not created for that purpose. Exactly what the immense serpent image symbolized for the Indian artisans continues to the present day to be a matter of speculation. "The antiquarian Stephen D. Peet [1890] was among the first to propose that the mound was the effigy of a deity" (Molyneaux, 1995, p. 110). Molyneaux (1995) goes on to describe:

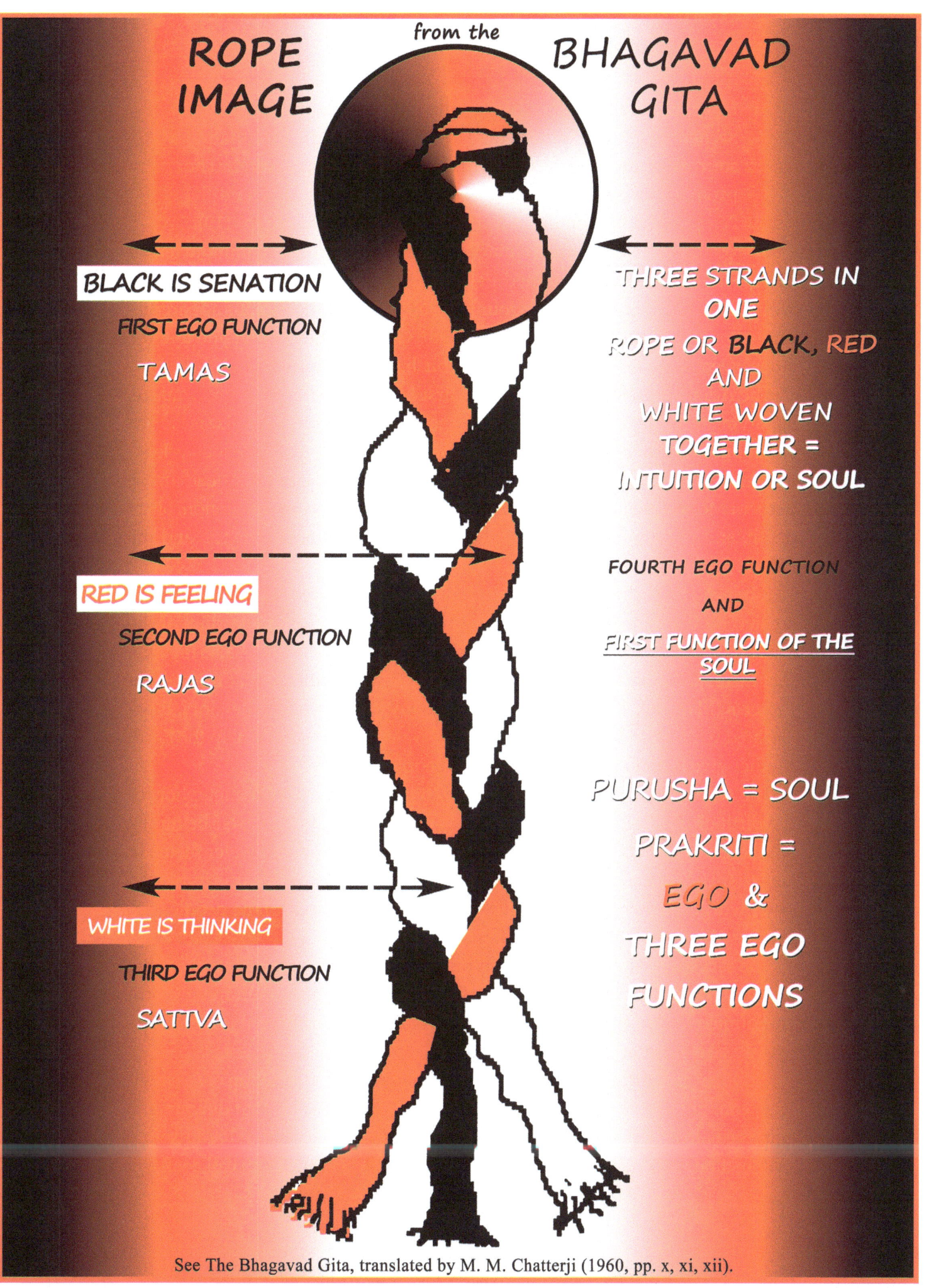

See The Bhagavad Gita, translated by M. M. Chatterji (1960, pp. x, xi, xii).

> In Native American mythology the divinity known as Horned Serpent, Antlered Serpent or Water Monster is the guardian of sources of life arising out of the earth, especially water. The promontory overlooks an entire water catchment area, and the "egg" originally contained a small circle of burnt stone (p. 110).

Surrounded by water, this art image appears to describe in mammoth terms, the sperm and the egg contained in the primal waters of the womb. And, I would suggest, the circle of fire around the egg, a ritual the Indians apparently carried out at times, represent life and birth. One might even imagine that the stones were lit as a ritual celebrating the birth of a newborn child.

The Adena Indians were among the first North Americans to grow maize, signifying their interest in a goddess of vegetation and birth. Little else is known about the civilization of the Adena people, who disappeared mysteriously, leaving behind numerous monuments and mounds that honored their dead. In the Serpent Mound archetype, I suggest that they were honoring conception, birth, death, and rebirth, symbolizing the eternal return of life and death, and the eternal return of psychic energy.

Johnson (1988) says that "The Hopi claim that the Ohio snake mound was created by their ancestors. The snake's name is Tokchi'i, the guardian of the East who protects the tribe from that direction" (p. 178). The Hopi also imagine that the oval egg-like mound in the serpent's jaws is a village that the serpent protects (Marshall, 1993). The serpent, in many tribes besides the Hopi, is associated with the fertilizing rain (the living water) and is said to help the Earth Mother give birth to plants, animals and people.

The serpent with an egg in its mouth can be seen as a double metaphor for the birth of the biological and psychological child, the image itself being the Divine Child archetype. It can be compared with the wind and water theme in Genesis. The created archetype represents symbolic knowledge (the inner and outer worlds thrown together) of the collective unconscious of the people who expressed it in their simple, sacred image.

The serpent is equivalent to the spirit or wind and the egg is that which the living water (agape love) produces. This is the theme of human male sperm and human female egg and the conception of the human child. It is the Divine Syzygy as elementary male (serpent) and elementary female (egg).

On a psychological level, the serpent can be seen as the function of (elementary) conscious (body ego) sensation (the Serpent in Genesis) that devours the egg (the Father God who contains Adam, Eve, and the Serpent in Paradise), or the function of conscious intuition (soul). The egg, which the Hopi call a village, is the function of intuition that contains the ego and soul undifferentiated or the functions that exist as one people, that is, the world. The egg is analogous with the symbol of the apple (child symbol) in Genesis, as the container of the soul and ego undifferentiated. Both represent the beginning of ego consciousness and the separation of the ego from soul consciousness. Eating the apple or the egg is also representative of eating the body of Christ (eating innocence for knowledge or the reverse, eating knowledge for a return to innocence). The serpent and egg image can be seen either way, as a birth of ego and as a death of soul and describes both simultaneously. The birth of the ego is the birth of the soul as a separate entity, just as the birth of conscious sensation relinquishes intuition as a joint function and becomes the two functions of intuition and sensation.

The image itself is the product of the Divine Child, the sperm and the egg theme represent the biological, human child, and the serpent as ego (spirit) and egg (soul) represents the contained, psychological child, whose innocence is about to be lost, like the lost innocence of

Adam and Eve. Thus, the simple image describes the mythological, the biological, and the psychological simultaneously.

The serpent faces West, symbolizing the setting sun and death, yet Tokchi'i represents the guardian and protector of the East, the direction associated with the rising sun and birth. By this simple juxtaposition, the creators of the Serpent Mound have introduced in their abecedarian symbol the opposites of East and West or life and death. The serpent, as spirit, sperm or ego, represents ego consciousness, which is always a death (loss of Paradise) for the soul (Paradise) where they existed as one. Thus, the image contains the theme of the eternal return and the universal experience of the people who created it.

Tokchi'i is guardian of the East as the Lion-birds (identical with the Cherubim) are guardians of the Serpent Lord. He is guardian in the same manner as the Cherubim of Genesis placed East of Eden to guard the way back to Paradise.

<u>The Symbolism in the Tenth Picture of the Rosarium Philosophorum:
Three Serpents Contained by One Chalice</u>

Concerning the Divine Child or the lapis, Jung (1954/1946) says: "The lapis, understood as the cosmogonic First Man, is the radix ipsius, according to the Rosarium: everything has grown from this One and through this One" (p. 147). This describes Adam as undifferentiated thinking that is identical with the function of

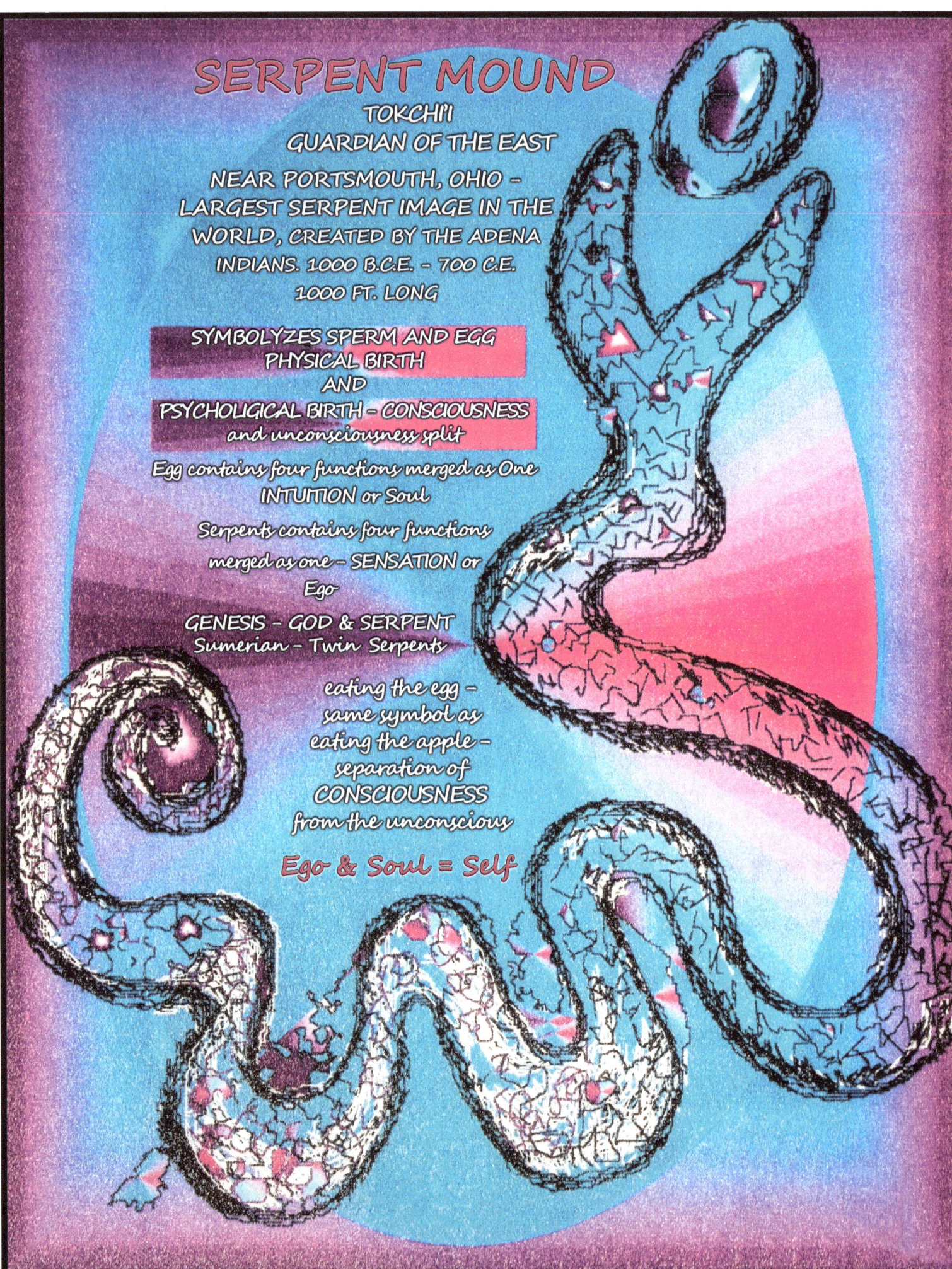

intuition or the Father God. In the infant in the womb, it describes the psyche and body existing in a state of undifferentiation, using the basic instinct of intuition.

In Chapter 10 of The Psychology of the Transference, called "The New Birth," Jung (1954/1946) discusses the tenth picture of the "Rosarium Philosophorum" (see Jung, 1954/1946, Figure 10, p. 145):

> It shows an apotheosis of the Rebis, the right side of the body being male, the left female. The figure stands on the moon, which in this case corresponds to the feminine lunar vessel, the vas hermeticum. Its wings betoken volatility, i.e., spirituality. In one hand it holds a chalice with three snakes in it, or possibly one snake with three heads; in the other, a single snake. This is an obvious allusion to the axiom of Maria and the old dilemma of 3 and 4, and also to the mystery of the Trinity. The three snakes in the chalice are the chthonic equivalent of the Trinity, and the single snake represents, firstly, the unity of the three as expressed by Maria and, secondly, the "sinister" *serpens Mercurialis* with all its subsidiary meanings (pp. 152-153).

Jung's description of the two sides of the body may only apply to the two faces of the male and female. My first impression of this picture was that the body of the male had become the left side and the body of the female had become the right side, suggesting a relationship between the two sides of the brain. That the left brain rules the right side of the body and the right brain rules the left side of the body was not consciously known to the alchemists, but it is possible that they were unconsciously describing left/right brain functioning in their symbols.

Much more obvious is the symbolism of the three serpents or one serpent with three heads, held by the king and the one serpent held by the queen, both, as Jung describes, connected to the mystery of the trinity and the axiom of Maria.

The chalice symbolizes the vessel or container for the three serpents which can be seen as the three conscious and differentiated ego functions of thinking, feeling and sensation that are contained in the one function of intuition. One serpent held by the queen is the function of conscious intuition, represented by the archetype of queen and soul. It is when the three conscious ego functions merge into the unconscious that they become one serpent and the king and queen become identical or the philosopher's stone, that is, the Divine Child or the new Adam is born.

This symbolism can be seen in two ways. First, it describes a return to Paradise or rebirth. Second, it describes the original separation, that is, the first birth of the king or all three ego functions. Queen or soul as the psychological function of intuition reflects the Self on one side and on the other, all of the ego functions. It depicts the human, individual child who is composed of Self which differentiates into soul and ego. The Divine Child or the philosopher's stone is the ego and soul that are both reflections of the Self; they are three-in-one.

The blackbird or raven symbolizes a death of the conscious ego functions, thinking, feeling, and sensation. The bird, an angel symbol, represents the spiritual necessity for an ego death. The ego functions must die or be sacrificed, symbolizing a return to the unconscious where all three functions will again become merged or undifferentiated. At this point, they become identical with the queen or the function of conscious intuition.

The blackbird (death symbol) sits on the ground, symbolizing the spiritual or divine functions that are grounded or unconscious. The Hermaphrodite is then elevated off the ground as a spiritual being who has wings like the angels, indicating the divine nature of the undivided Self or the Divine Child. All of this shows that the ego is also divine but the divinity cannot be known except by its own sacrifice or death. When this happens there is a return to the Goddess or Divine Mother, who always contains the Divine Father, and the Divine Child is born. Psychologically speaking, the ego functions and soul are no longer divided and consciousness and unconsciousness exist as one or the Self of super consciousness.

Many of these symbols can be identified and compared as variations of those previously discussed in the much older archetype of the Serpent Lord and the archetypes of the twin serpents and lion-birds. The copulating king and queen serpents are similar to the copulating king and queen in the alchemy symbolism and represent the same psychic energy. (In both mythologies they are represented as brother and sister lovers.) The Serpent Lord is one serpent that contains everything else and from which everything emerges, just as the Divine Child is the one Serpent of alchemy and identical with the Divine Mother and the Divine Father. (The Divine Child and the Divine Mother both represent the function of intuition, as does the Divine Father, when he is undifferentiated thinking.)

The wings of an angel on the body of an androgynous human are reminiscent of the Lion-bird and its half animal and half spiritual nature. The male represents the conscious ego that contains the unconscious soul (one Lion-bird) and the female represents the conscious soul that contains the unconscious ego functions as one serpent (the other Lion-bird). Each reflects the other, like the Lion-birds. When they come together, as they do in the tenth picture, ego and soul become one and the Divine Child or philosopher's stone is born.

The theme of brother/sister lovers and incest symbolizes the close (blood) relationship of the ego (body) and consciousness, with soul (spirit), which is not total unconsciousness, but the union of both in super consciousness. The king is red like Adam because it is by the spilling of blood, the sacrifice of the innocent soul (lamb), that consciousness can be born. The soul is then created as something separate (the split in human consciousness or the crack in the cosmic egg, which is really a split in super consciousness). The queen is white (nothingness) because she represents the soul, spirit, and body contained in one by the function of conscious intuition. Symbolizing innocence and purity, white reflects the colors of the rainbow, just as the soul or intuition reflects the emerging four ego functions and at the same time, reflects the Self.

Standing on the moon, the feminine vessel similar to the chalice, represents a return to the Goddess (intuition), the vessel containing the functions as one. The sun/moon tree can be seen as a variation of the staff or rod symbolism and the open doors of the Serpent Lord image; both represent the human spine and the physical route of conscious (sensation) and unconscious (intuition) perceptions. The sun (son) is conscious sensation and the moon (mother) is unconscious sensation. United, they are the Divine Mother and the Divine Child, both symbols for the Self.

Psyche and Eros: Symbols of Transformation Leading to the *Coniunctio* and Birth of a Divine Girl/Child Named Joy: Archetype for the Self.

The Greek Paradise myth of Psyche and Eros describes the process of individuation and a return to the Self, symbolized by Joy or Pleasure, a Divine girl/child born in Heaven. The marriage, separation, and reuniting of Eros and Psyche represents the union, the shattering and the reunion of ego and soul, in all of the functions. Elsewhere (Lenhart, 1990b), I have interpreted this myth as:

> Joy, the divine girl/child is an archetype of the Self, created by the *coniunctio* or union of opposites, represented by Psyche and Eros. Psyche is an archetype of soul and soul love or nonego consciousness; Eros is an archetype for ego and ego love or ego consciousness (p. 1).

Together, Psyche and Eros comprise the bisexual, dual nature of Eros, where

Image copied after Figure 10 in The Psychology of the Transference, Jung, 1954

The male holds three serpents in his right hand: yellow serpent symbolizes conscious sensation, red serpent symbolizes conscious feeling, blue serpent symbolizes conscious thinking. The chalice that contains the three Serpents is the function of conscious intuition. The Queen holds one serpent in her left hand, symbolizing the merging of the functions into one Serpent, Intuition, or Soul.

psyche's child

high dark secret room
my grandmother's house
my room
glass coffins
filled with the taste of
sweetness
and
ever-lasting
life
silver coins round smooth
shining light
the night has named me
Joy
as spirits dance and gather here
to rock me gently
as I sleep.

(Gerry Anne Lenhart, 1989)

Psyche and Eros are joined as one in an earthly Paradise, equivalent to the Garden of Eden. This represents the ego and soul coexisting as one differentiated function, intuition. Eros can be compared with the Father God/Divine Child of Genesis; both are first out of the chaos or golden egg of the Self. Eros is the Divine Child who contains ego and soul or consciousness and unconsciousness as one, like the Father God (Divine Child) in Genesis. Eros, as a Divine Child god, is an archetype for the primal ego; Psyche is an archetype for his other side, the virgin, unconscious soul. While in the earthly Paradise, they exist as Divine Lovers.

The Greek translation of Psyche (besides the word soul) means moth or butterfly, informing us that Psyche or the human soul is going to acquire wings, like her lover Eros. As an archetype describing the metamorphosis of the human soul, Psyche is equivalent to any virgin archetype (one without ego consciousness or innocent) and can be compared with the Virgin Mary of Christianity. Like the Virgin Mary, she did not "die" but ascended into Heaven at the end of the myth.

The marriage of Psyche and Eros represents a union of opposites, expressed as soul and ego, unconsciousness and consciousness, female and male, mortal and immortal, earth and heaven, bride and groom, innocence and knowledge, human and divine, visible and invisible, expectant mother and father, youngest daughter and eldest son, and finally, I would add, two kinds of love, seemingly forever in opposition to one another, agape love (love for other) and ego love (love for self). As a myth that describes divine and human love, Psyche and Eros is a myth that focuses on and particularly illuminates the feeling function. (It is not possible to describe the entire myth here, which I believe describes all the functions in action, if Eros and Psyche are seen as the conscious (ego) and unconscious (soul) side of each function.)

In the garden of what appears as a Paradise, after their marriage on earth, Psyche and Eros exist as one, symbolizing the original unity of the soul and ego, or consciousness and unconsciousness that are united in the function of intuition. An important part of the myth, however, goes on to describe Psyche and Eros as the two sides of the feeling function in conflict. The resolution of that conflict, accomplished by Psyche's arduous tasks, her final success and her acceptance as a goddess in Heaven, represents the two sides of the sensate function (Eros as conscious, introverted sensation and Psyche as unconscious, extraverted sensation) and the two sides of the feeling function (Eros as conscious, introverted feeling and Psyche as unconscious extraverted feeling). The myth describes the oscillation of the cycles of separation and unity as they occur in both sides of each function. The resolution of the final conflict takes place as the birth of a Divine girl-child. This is the final union of opposites in the function of thinking, symbolized by Joy's birth in Heaven.

This tale is a description of psychic energy in the psyche of one individual as the process of individuation proceeds. It concerns four major functions that begin in the womb, intuition as the theme of earthly Paradise, and conscious, introverted sensation (Eros) and its opposite, unconscious extraverted sensation (Psyche) and conscious, introverted feeling (Eros) and its opposite, unconscious extraverted feeling (Psyche), functions that begin at birth, as consciousness separates from unconsciousness. Since the myth appears to be describing cycles of the psyche, the conflict in the functions could apply to at any age.

The waking (ego consciousness) and mischievous Eros (often called a serpent) can be seen as conscious, introverted sensation and compared with the Fallen Angel, Lucifer, or the Serpent in Eden, who both represent the same primal energy. One of the pivotal scenes in the myth is Psyche holding her candle torch to look upon the face of the sleeping Eros. The sleeping Eros, Psyche observes with awe, is more beautiful than anything she imagined and is, indeed, a Divine God. This sleeping, being a symbol for the unconscious God, describes the function of unconscious, extraverted sensation, which can be seen as identical with the function of intuition. The sleeping Eros is the Divine Child of intuition. Thus, what Psyche sees is herself, the sleeping or unconscious ego. This, I would suggest, is a psychological experience of the utmost importance for the individual at any age, because it is the human soul gazing at its own innocent and divine ego. Psyche's journey, after this scene, when Eros flies away, is to get Eros back, which would mean making something conscious that is unconscious.

Eros is ego and body consciousness in the function of sensation. Psyche is his soul, where they still exist as one and everything in the body that has yet to become conscious; this is the double nature of Eros and the double nature of love. Thus, Eros can be seen as the Divine Child or creating God of Genesis (conscious, introverted intuition) or the Serpent of Eden (conscious, introverted sensation) or Eve (conscious, introverted feeling) or Adam (conscious, introverted thinking). Eros represents the conscious, introverted functions. Psyche is the other side of Eros and represents the unconscious extraverted soul in each of the functions.

As the youngest daughter (extraverted feeling comes after introverted feeling in the newborn and Psyche's sisters are shadow figures that represent introversion), Psyche is a symbol for the innocent human soul who loves blindly. She cannot, in the beginning, see Eros and the human soul, unconsciousness, cannot see its ego. In addition to unconscious, extraverted sensation, she represents the unconscious extraverted feeling function that loves other with little or no ego. This is reinforced by the symbol of virgin, which describes her in the beginning of the myth, and she can be compared with the Virgin Mary of Christianity or a virgin (beginning) Aphrodite. She is likened to a drop of dew from the earth, as opposed to Aphrodite, who comes from the sea, which tells us that she is of the "small" as opposed to the "mighty" Goddess of love. She is, however, the fairest mortal on earth, symbolizing the importance and the beauty of love for other with no thought of self. These are traits necessary in the human mother if she is to reflect or mirror soul for her human child and satisfy his or her ego demands.

Psyche is not a Goddess of love completed, but the seed or beginning of a love Goddess. What Psyche, as unconscious extraverted feeling, needs is Eros, or in the Genesis myth, Eve, which psychologically speaking is conscious, introverted feeling (ego love). To become an immortal Goddess in Heaven, Psyche needs ego, ego love, or Eros, or both sides of the feeling function in balanced unity. When this occurs, she becomes a Goddess equal to Aphrodite, the Goddess of Love. Aphrodite is the one instructing Psyche in the ways of love after her loss of Eros, to assure his return. And, I would add, she knows what she is doing, just as Psyche makes the right decision at the end of the myth, assuring her status as a Goddess in Heaven, where she gives birth to the Divine Child, Joy, archetype for the Self.

Gayley (1939) describes Eros as one of the "lesser divinities of Heaven; however, most worthy of mention" (p. 35). He offers at least four accounts of the origins of the world that were popular in Greek mythology, several of which include Eros as a Divine Child. One account, attributed to Orpheus, tells of a huge egg that is born from chaos. By reason of its rapid rotation, the egg splits into halves, creating Heaven and Earth. Eros, who is bisexual and has wings, proceeds from the center of the egg, along with other "wondrous beings" (p. 3). Jung and Kerenyi (1949) consider these two things, wingedness and bisexuality as: "harking back to the same pre-human, indeed pre-childish, still completely undifferentiated state" (p. 55). This undifferentiated state is what I see as the psychological function of intuition, personified as the egg and then as the Divine Child of Eros, who contains the god and goddess or the wondrous beings of the four undifferentiated psychological functions. Psyche is the feminine side of the bisexual nature of Eros, soul and silent partner called unconsciousness. The golden egg is the container and the contained, one Soul, merged with ego, that reflects the Self.

Eros, however, quickly becomes associated with the masculine principle. "His nature," Jung and Kerenyi (1949) tell us, "is explicit in his name, 'Eros' meaning 'demanding love'" (p. 53). Thus, Eros is love that demands or subjective introverted love that says, "I want." If Eros were not in need, there would be nothing to demand or desire. As desire, Eros is commensurate with Eve: Both give birth to worldly things. Introversion is the attitudinal function that creates or gives birth to all things. This appears to be true whether the archetype that personifies it is male or female, and obviously it can be portrayed both ways in mythology. Indeed, this is how the father archetype gives birth in any myth using that symbolism. It is also what Eve has in common with the Father God, and why she is, like Adam, created in his likeness.

Contained within the golden egg, Psyche and Eros are soul and ego still merged, or the function of conscious intuition. As the first one out of the egg, Eros represents beginning consciousness in the sensate body and the subjective or introverted "I." Psyche then becomes the other side of Eros, the dark, unconscious soul.

Thus, Psyche and Eros can be seen as personifications of all the psychological functions, intuition, sensation, feeling, and thinking, representing the energy of the conscious and of the unconscious in each function. Introverted body sensation connects Eros with sexuality and demanding ego love, and extraverted body sensations, which are unconscious when Eros is present, represent Psyche or the unconscious soul. In the feeling function, Eros is also conscious introverted feeling, with Psyche representing his opposite or unconscious extraverted feeling. As conscious introverted feeling, Eros can be equated with Eve and desire after the Fall, and Psyche can be equated with the Virgin archetype or unconscious extraverted feeling, that is, love without desire.

Desire does not necessitate an *actual* need, but the ego that perceives something as lacking experiences a perception of need. Eros is desire, a word that means "to await the stars." If one *had* the stars, there would be nothing to wait for; to wait implies that there is an object not possessed, but wanted and expected. This experience may be one of pleasure or pain or both mixed.

That two types of consciousness and two types of love exist (in one human psyche) may be one of the most important psychological aspects in the myth of Psyche and Eros. It was the wise woman, Diotima (Plato, 1928, p. 369), who describes yet another version of the birth of Eros; he is the child of Porus (Plenty) and Penia (Poverty), and he is born on Aphrodite's birthday. This metaphor appears to fit the description of desire most accurately, for it includes the double nature of Eros, who is more than the description of "exuberance and delight" (Ponce, 1991, p. 3). Eros (or ego love) can also mean pain and suffering; he was feared by the gods; even his father, Zeus, admonishes and blames him for his many affairs (Neumann, 1952/1956, p. 51).

Joy, as a Divine girl/child and archetype for the Self, never desires eternity; she has eternity. When the desire has been met, time ceases and the human child becomes the Divine Child. Jung (1959/1955) describes the child archetype in the following way:

> The "child" is therefore renatus in novam infantiam. It is thus both beginning and end, an initial and a terminal creature. The initial creature existed before man was, and the terminal creature will be when man is not. Psychologically speaking, this means that the "child" symbolizes the pre-conscious and the post-conscious essence of man. His post-conscious essence is an anticipation by analogy of life after death. In this idea the all-embracing nature of psychic wholeness is expressed (p. 97).

Thus, Joy is an archetype of the Self (the Divine Child) and psychic wholeness. The marriage of Psyche and Eros represents a union of the opposites in all of the psychological functions, returning Psyche and Eros to their former state of undivided soul and ego as personifications for the psychological function of intuition. This is a return to the God and Goddess and the function of intuition as one differentiated function that contains the ego functions in a state of undifferentiation.

This is only a sketch of this simple but extraordinary Greek and Roman myth, which describes a transformation and psychological journey of the individual human ego and soul commensurate to that of the Old Testament and the New Testament, in a return to Joy, archetype for the Self.

Mythology and Biological Psychology as a Function of the Human Nervous System: The Left/Right Brain Metaphor

> Mythology is not invented rationally; mythology cannot be rationally understood. Theological interpreters render it ridiculous. Literary criticism reduces it to metaphor. A new and very promising approach is opened, however, when it is viewed in the light of biological psychology as a function of the human nervous system, precisely homologous to the innate and learned sign stimuli that release and direct the energies of nature—of which our brain itself is but the most amazing flower (Campbell, 1979, p. 42).

THE MORNING STAR

SYMBOL OF LOVE

Divine Child God

Thinking
EGO

Feeling
SOUL

SELF

Bird

Bird

Lion

Lion

ONE LOVE

LOVE

LOVE

Intuition

The Serpent Lord

Sensation

DIVINE MOTHER AND DIVINE CHILD ARCHETYPES: CHRIST, LUCIFER, DAVID, VENUS, APHRODITE, ASHTORETH, ASTARTE, ISHTAR AND INANNA. THREE OUTSIDE POINTS REPRESENT THE THREE SEPARATE EGO FUNCTIONS: SENSATION, FEELING AND THINKING. THREE MERGED, OR INSIDE TRIANGLE ARE THE ONE FUNCTION OF INTUITION OR SOUL. INTERTWINED, THEY REPRESENT THE MERGING OF SOUL AND EGO AS ONE SELF. THE DOUBLE CUPS THAT ARE JOINED CAN BE SEEN AS AN ABSTRACT FORM OF THE LION-BIRDS ARCHETYPE. INSIDE SQUARE IS THE SERPENT LORD: ONE LOVE AND ONE GOD.

THE MARIA AXIOM OR, THE FEMININE PRINCIPLE

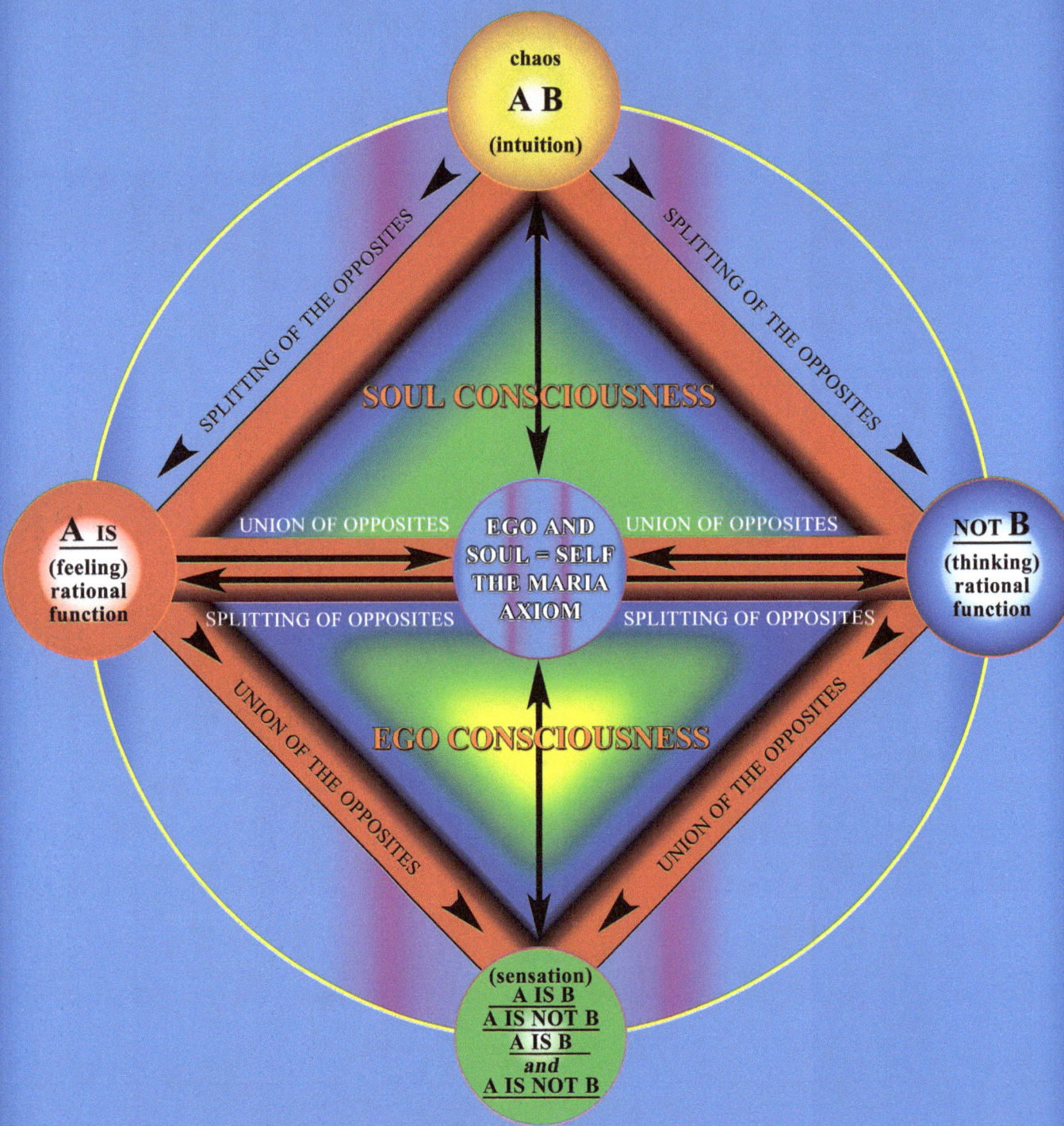

Aristotle's logic states that A is not B and excludes the middle. The Maria axiom or, the feminine principle, is always from a middle position - - the top of the mountain which sees all four (or more) positions and embraces them all. From an ego viewpoint this can appear as nonsense; from a soul viewpoint this is Truth. The soul begins at the "foot of the mountain" (pyramid) and is also contained at the top, or the center; "she" joins the ego to the Self. Aristotle's logic refutes the feminine, but the feminine embraces Aristotle's logic *and* all other positions. They can be seen here as opposites that flow out of and return to the self. The rational functions and feeling and thinking both separate and join the opposites; the irrational, instinctual functions of intuition and sensation contain all of the opposites: Intuition contains them in merged form (chaos) and sensation experiences the opposites eventually.

The Human Abstract

Pity would be no more,
If we did not make somebody Poor:
And Mery no more could be,
If all were as happy as we:

And mutual fear brings peace:
Till the selfish loves increase.
Then Cruelty knits a snare,
And spreads his baits with care.

He sits down with holy fears,
And waters the ground with tears:
Then Humility takes its root
Underneath his foot.

Soon spreads the dismal shade
Of Mystery over his head;
And the Catterpiller and Fly,
Feed on the Mystery.

And it bears the fruit of Deceit,
Ruddy and sweet to eat:
And the Raven his nest has made
In its thickest shade.

The Gods of the earth and sea,
Sought thro' Nature to find this Tree
But their search was all in vain:
There grows one in the Human Brain.

(William Blake, from Songs of Innocence and of Experience, 1980, p. 88)

In recent years, much has been written on the subject of left/right brain functioning in what Campbell describes as the most amazing flower—the human brain. Our own Western mythology, such as the myth of Genesis and many others, contains symbols and archetypes that can be seen as describing numerous aspects of the human brain. This seemingly overlooked fact is described by the unlikely mystic, poet, and artist William Blake (1980) in the last sentence of his poem "The Human Abstract" when he says that the tree sought in vain by Gods of earth and sea "grows in the human brain" (p. 88).

Another unlikely suspect for providing a biological model for religious archetypes is the artist Michelangelo. Meshberger (1990, pp. 1838-1839) has identified the image of a human brain surrounding the Creation of Adam fresco painted by Michelangelo. He identifies minute neuroanatomic structures located within the image of the Father God in the fresco. The image that he describes is that of God, Eve and the angels. Meshberger suggests that Michelangelo is portraying the gift of the intellect given by God as he creates Adam, which I would interpret as the thinking function.

It is also possible to see that Adam, who is alive, like the child in the womb, is unconscious or innocent in the ego function of the intellect (thinking) and that God's touch is the first gift of consciousness in the form of conscious intuition or the functions in a state of undifferentiation. The interchange may describe the exact point where intuitive consciousness begins, Adam as one with God. What is unconscious is identical with what is conscious if all are one with God in Paradise. Adam is the image of God because he exists with God, in the function of unconscious and undifferentiated thinking. Because thinking, feeling, and sensation are still undifferentiated, Adam is the perfect image of the Father God of intuition, who has the same attributes. Michelangelo depicts this by showing the Father God (differentiated intuition) with his arm around Eve or the Divine Mother (undifferentiated feeling) and his being surrounded by angels, archetypes for the Divine Child (undifferentiated sensation). The human brain is the sphere that contains them all. Ornstein (1975) describes left/right brain theory when he says, "A growing body of evidence demonstrates that each person has two major modes of consciousness available, one linear and rational, one arational and intuitive" (p. 28). The two major modes of consciousness that he describes are what I am referring to here as ego consciousness and soul consciousness. Elsewhere, Montanaro (1991) also describes two types of consciousness, "the different work performed by the two hemispheres produces two types of consciousness and two types of memory" (p. 82).

In his early work (1956/1912) Jung referred to this as "two kinds of thinking" acknowledging that intuition contained consciousness that differed from rational thinking, but never fully describing what that difference was, and apparently never conceding that it might be consciousness and unconsciousness in an undifferentiated form. Left/right brain theory was not prevalent (or even present) in the years Jung wrote and one can only speculate on what he might think today, given these and other findings in modern developmental research concerning the human infant. His statement, however, that intuition "stands in a compensatory relationship to sensation and, like it, is the matrix out of which thinking and feeling develop as rational functions" (1971/1921, p. 454) is consistent with the idea that more recent research supports, namely, that the right brain, and intuition and sensation, is dominant in early childhood. And, if intuition is seen as "unconscious perception" while sensation is seen as "conscious perception" (1971/1921, p. 463) the right brain would be that which describes both in a state of undifferentiation. Intuition would be the psychological function that links soul to body. It would also be the function(s) leading to the development of the rational functions of feeling and thinking, as Jung described, and left-brain dominance, which he also often described, using a different vocabulary.

Montanaro (1991) describes the importance of both hemispheres, paralleling Jung's description of the importance of the four functions: "The fact that human reality consists of two different modes of being must be well understood by all educators if we are to provide, from the very beginning, proper stimulation for the two equally important hemispheres" (p. 82).

It is clear that Jung was aware of what Montanaro calls fact, and differed from other psychologists before or after, when he included the function of intuition as essential for psychological wholeness. Even though he admittedly could not describe how intuition works, which to date remains inadequately described, he insisted that the function of intuition was essential for an experience of the Self.

Montanaro (1991) continues:
> The first modest signs of understanding and response to the environment can be seen even in unicellular creatures. As life became more complex, we developed a more complex nervous system. There are three main stages in this process (also known as the "Theory of the Three Brains" by Paul McLean).

We must remember that, historically, life started from simple unicellular creatures and reached the complexity of humans. In our individual life, each of us recapitulates the whole of evolution, starting from the single cell we are at the moment of conception. The evolution of our nervous system is the history of successive growth, enlargement and specialization. In this evolution we can clearly recognize components which are related to three stages that overlapped each other. Each of them contains special characteristics of our personalities (p. 4).

Montanaro goes on to discuss the Triune Brain Theory described by Paul McLean, which consists of the reptilian (serpent archetype) brain, the paleomammalian brain, and the neomammalian brain. The reptilian brain, the oldest and deepest part, sounds like a description of the instinctual function of intuition, which contains the other functions in undifferentiated form, according to my hypothesis. The paleomammalian brain sounds like the introduction of the feeling function after intuition and sensation divide. Finally, the neomammalian brain, the component related to the greater mammals and rational thinking, sounds like what Jung described as the thinking function. Is it possible to imagine that we have evolved to the point where all are used at birth? And is it possible to see the Triune Brain Theory as another "scientific" "three-in-one" brain archetype?

Obviously, there is much concerning the human brain that is uncertain. Neurobiology as a scientific discipline often considers much of the literature on left/brain psychology quasi-scientific and questionable. Even so, the human mind tends to arrange functions of the brain dichotomously. Using the left/right brain theory as a ground for interpretation, many symbols and archetypes in the myth of Genesis and numerous other myths can be identified that are biologically related.

The staff in the Serpent Lord image, reminiscent of the Greek caduceus and Hermes, god of mystic knowledge and rebirth (see Campbell, 1990b, p. 283), is a tree symbol and analogous with the Kundalini symbolism of Eastern religions. It represents the human spinal column and the corpus callosum, the place of communication between the left and right brain. Both sides of the human brain, which look like two coiled snakes, can also be seen as personified by the twin serpent image discussed earlier, signifying the many and diverse images of the snake and tree motifs that permeate mythology.

Sagan (1977) states concerning the corpus callosum:
> There is no way to tell whether patterns extracted by the right hemisphere are real or imagined without subjecting them to left-hemisphere scrutiny. On the other hand, mere critical thinking, without creative and intuitive insights, without the search for new patterns, is sterile and doomed. To solve complex problems in

changing circumstances requires the activities of both cerebral hemispheres: the path to the future lies through the corpus callosum (p. 191).

I agree. The corpus callosum may be, and I believe often is, personified symbolically as the bridge that connects what is called consciousness (left brain) to what is called unconsciousness (right brain), or the bridge of the soul to that of ego consciousness. The right brain can be seen as the goddess (silent) or the Divine Child and the left brain can be seen as the god (archetype, word), that speaks. The right brain can also be seen as the tree of life, representing that place where intuition contains the whole, rather than the parts; the left brain can be seen as the tree of knowledge of the opposites, where discrimination and separation of the parts is essential, as in the function of sensation. The symbol of a staff or tree is homologous with the human spinal cord, whether it is the staff of David, Moses, or God, or the caduceus of Hermes. What goes up and down the tree/spine are human perceptions, conscious and unconscious, which I see as the two functions of intuition or sensation. Sometimes the staff turns into the serpent, or two serpents are entwined around the staff as in the twin vipers image; in every case the image is probably describing body sensations that are traveling up and down the human spine, messages or angels delivered and received by the left/right brain.

Montanaro (1991) describes the collaboration of the two hemispheres in the following:

> The hemispheres are capable of wonderful collaboration and share information through the fibres connecting them. An intuitive insight can be translated into a logical verbal sequence which makes communication with others possible, and a better form of consciousness within ourselves. Verbal expression can also be translated into a graphic image and, if the image is well executed, it can be an even more powerful means of communication than the words themselves (p. 82).

Words can be translated back to the image in the most powerful way, as Montanaro describes. I think few artists would disagree with this statement. It also seems reasonable to me to assume that the image or picture preceded the words as abstractions, at least in the beginning of life.

The apple in Genesis represents the fruit of consciousness and unconsciousness merged. The apple or any fruit symbol is a child symbol, and to eat the fruit or child is to destroy innocence and create knowledge. Eating the apple is the assimilation of intuitive information in the right brain, where the image is

Dante's Three in ONE Rainbow

Within the depthless deep and clear existence
  of that abyss of light three circles shown --
  three in color, one in circumference:
the second from the first, rainbow from rainbow;
  the third, an exhalation of pure fire
  equally breathed forth by the other two.
But oh, how much my words miss my conception,
  which is itself so far from what I saw
  that to call it feeble would be rank deception!
O Light Eternal fixed in itself alone,
  by Itself alone understood, which from Itself
  loves and glows, self-knowing and self-known;
that second aureole which shone forth in Thee,
  conceived as a reflection of the first --
  or which appeared so to my scrutiny --
seemed in Itself of Its own coloration
  to be painted with man's image. I fixed my eyes
  on that alone in rapturous contemplation.
Like a geometer wholly dedicated
  to squaring the circle, but who cannot find,
  think as he may, the principal indicated --
so did I study the supernal face.
  I yearned to know just how our image merges
  into that circle, and how it there finds place;
but mine were not the wings for such a flight.
  Yet, as I wished the truth I wished for came
  cleaving my mind in a great flash of light.
Here my powers rest from their high fantasy,
  but already I could feel my being turned --
  instinct and intellect balanced equally
as in a wheel whose motion nothing jars --
by the Love that moves the sun and the other stars.

The Divine Comedy Canto 33

holistic (holy) and reproducing it in part, by language or logic in the left brain. In mythology this is not only holy, but God himself as Word or Christ as man and God speaking the word.

This is the separation of the parts from the whole, the beginning of thou and I and the creation and separation of Heaven and Earth. The idea of three or four unconscious psychological functions that exist as one conscious function of intuition can be easily seen in a biological sense, if one conceives the possibility that there is no fully present or developed ego present in the right side of the brain and that all ego functions are unconscious, undifferentiated, and merged, working as a whole, which describes intuitive consciousness. Killing the god of left-brain consciousness (ego) creates the Divine Child of intuition or returns one to the child god or goddess.

Russell (1979) says:

> The left hemisphere may not be dominant in the sense that it is any more important than the right, but in Western culture at least, the faculties associated with the left do take a more dominant position in our lives. We tend to lay greater emphasis on rational thinking, the ability to express oneself verbally, read well, and generally excel in analytic thinking. We place less emphasis on the spatial ability, artistic appreciation, creative processes, and intuitive thought—the faculties more often associated with the right hemisphere (pp. 54-55).

This certainly appears to be true. However, if the left brain is seen as the god and the right brain is the goddess or if active thinking is the god and intuition is the goddess or Divine Child, it appears, at least in science (and, perhaps, to the early Hebrews), to have gone unnoticed that there would be no god or active thinking without the goddess (or intuition). There would be no rational thought or archetype, without the irrational instinct (the reptilian "serpent" brain) which necessarily precedes it. Montanaro (1991) describes the importance of being aware of the two forms of consciousness in the following: "It is very important to be aware of this double human reality in education. A new educational system will not appear until we give serious consideration to the fact that we have a 'double mind'" (p. 82). I would add that connecting our Western mythology, besides other mythologies of the world, to the human biological child and the human body appears essential if we are to understand either from a depth perspective. Science and art may be the new Divine Parents that give birth to a Divine Child who expresses both parents as one archetype.

The church represents the symbolism of the mother's womb, which is where the function of intuition begins. Jung (1956/1912) describes the underlying meaning of the church:

> It can scarcely be doubted that the underlying meaning of the Church is the mother's womb. The Tantric texts interpret the interior of the temple as the interior of the body, and the adyton is called "garbha griha," the seeding-place or uterus (p. 345).

Ego consciousness occurs when unconscious physical sensations, identical with the function of intuition, become conscious. This is represented in mythology as a death or a birth depending on which form of consciousness one is describing. The birth of soul consciousness is a death for ego consciousness, just as the birth of ego consciousness is a death for the soul. The myths are describing the physical and psychological relationship between the two sides of the brain, which ideally speaking, should be communicating in harmony.

Russell (1979) describes Tantric writings saying:

"The Tantrists also claim that when a person gains enlightenment, that is to say, when he is fully aware both inwardly and outwardly, the breath is found flowing equally in both nostrils. This presumably reflects the fact that such a person would be using both hemispheres of the brain in balance, rather than temporarily suppressing one in order to make full use of the other" (p. 62).

The left/right brain theories are another archetypal scheme for the Divine Syzygy archetype, describing in quasi-scientific language what mythology and religion have always described metaphorically. As a biological construct, however, the theory may come the closest to providing what Campbell (1979) describes: "the new and very promising approach opened when it [mythology] is viewed in the light of biological psychology as a function of the human nervous system" (p. 42).

The ancient Sumerian archetype of twin serpents that appear to represent the functions of intuition and sensation are particularly apt because they represent the most archaic and fundamental instincts of man. That may be why they still exist in present-day society as an emblem for medicine. The image can be seen in two ways: One way is the division of the oneness of intuition (the basic instinct) or the right brain into two serpents or two functions; the other is to see the Serpent Lord as the last symbol given before a return to the Self. One comes out of the center (Self) and the ego develops and differentiates, or one goes back into the center and the ego is shed, like the skin of the serpent. This describes the rhythmic process of the human brain working in harmony. The center can be seen as the corpus collosum, the bridge where the two sides of the brain meet and communicate. If conscious sensation is the serpent that bites and poisons, conscious intuition is the snake that bites and cures. On a depth level, sensation and intuition or body and soul are connected, constantly coming apart and coming back together again in the flow of life.

Mundkur (1983) says the following concerning primitives:
> Oppositional pairing in general is well documented in Levi-Strauss's writings on the myths of primitive peoples, whose choice of animal species as metaphors in such pairings is quite idiosyncratic. Psychoanalytic anthropology can offer no convincing theory as to why different ethnic groups so very often conceptualize the bird, the only prominent denizen of the sky, as the antagonist of the serpent (p. 272).

These two animals appear to be opposites; the bird (angel symbol) is close to Heaven and flies, while the serpent is close to the earth and crawls. One describes man's spiritual nature, and one describes man's instinctual nature; the two are often in conflict. The elusive reason might be because the winged bird and serpent taken together as one animal represent both sides of the brain working together in God-like harmony. As separate creatures, the symbolism is that of opposition and conflict.

The cosmological myths are describing the biological, as well as the soul and spiritual qualities of the human child and the eternal ebb and flow of psychic energy. The Divine Child, who is also the human child endowed with the function of intuition, can be seen as the creator and the image created. Jung (1971/1921) expresses something similar when he says, "The idea of a creative world-principle is a projected perception of the living essence in man himself" (p. 202). The "living essence" is that still-point place of Being, where God and the human soul are one.

If intuition is unconscious sensation, as I believe it to be, it would not be located simply on the right side of the brain; it would necessarily exist in every part of the body or in every human cell. The spinal cord as the transmitter of messages is the tree or the angel that delivers them to the left or right brain, which has become a metaphor for two modes of consciousness.

Montanaro (1991) expresses my own conclusions considering the left/right brain metaphor and two kinds of consciousness:
> When we consider the physiology of the nervous system, we can appreciate that both ways of thinking are of great value and that each represents only half of a human being. In the past we have put these different expressions of our brain in opposition but now education must recognize that the work of both hemispheres is

good and beneficial. Only from their satisfactory collaboration can we expect a better understanding of the life around us and within ourselves (p. 83).

In summarizing the Paradise myth of Genesis, I believe that the four major archetypes of Genesis: God, the Serpent, Eve, and Adam, represent the four psychological functions of primal consciousness contained within the brain and body of every human child. Jung (1963/1955), says:

because of its four rivers, and because it was the abode of the originally androgynous Primordial Man (Adam), the Garden of Eden was a favourite mandala in Christian iconography, and is therefore a symbol of totality and—from the psychological point of view—of the self (p. 210).

I would add that the creation myth can also be seen as a double metaphor for the physical and psychological birth process, energy which appears to cycle in the same general way. The cosmological myth is the cumulation of that experience given form and voice by symbols and archetypes that are the natural outcome of basic instincts. Thus, human children create the world that they experience, by the use of the four psychological functions of consciousness: intuition, sensation, feeling, and thinking, attributes of the creative Living God image contained in and perceived by every human and Divine Child.

Chapter 7
Conclusion

McLean (1989) reflects my own view in the following:
> The ancient mythologies, being derived in part from the mystery religions and initiation traditions, projected the inner structure of the psyche outward into the world; the Gods and Goddesses were pictured as being forces in the outer realm of Nature. One of the most important developments of this century is the unfolding of a "psychology" that recognizes the formative energies of such mythological pictures, and realizes that by contemplating the ancient mythologies we can, indeed, look at the fabric of our own souls (p. 9).

The original and primary question of this work is the following: If psychological functions exist, is there an implicit order in the development of the four functions in the individual, infant human psyche, as described by Carl Jung? Conclusions drawn from my investigation indicate that an order of the psychological functions can be seen, identified, and made explicit. The order postulated is: intuition, sensation, feeling, and thinking. This order appears circular in nature, describing psychic energy as it occurs in what appears to be a spontaneous experience of the human child. The cosmological myth of Genesis is also the ontogenesis and can be seen as a description in slow motion, of that physical, psychological, and phenomenological experience, allowing the infinitesimal details to be enlarged and categorized by the personifications of the four functions (psychic energy) contained in every human child. The individuation process that appears to commence at conception emerges as the same process continuously used, constant and repetitive, describing the basic spherical nature and flow of psychic energy. This process is best described in analytical psychology by Fordham (1970):
> The primary or original self of the infant is radically disrupted by birth in which the psyche-soma is flooded by stimuli which give rise to prototypic anxiety. Following this, a steady state re-establishes itself and the first clear sequence of disturbance followed by resting or steady states has been completed. The sequence repeats again and again during maturation and the motive forces behind them are called deintegrative and integrative (p. 103).

It has been my purpose to show how Fordham's description of deintegrative and integrative forces can be linked to the Genesis cosmological mythology in a meaningful way, if seen in the light of the psychological functions, assuming that intuition is a reflection of the Self that can be called soul and begins in the womb. In addition, it is clear that prototypic anxiety is the function of conscious subjective, or introverted sensation, called devil and doubt in the religious literature of Genesis.

Fordham (1989), describing his earlier thoughts, states them most clearly in the following:

> If the theory of the ego is unsatisfactory to account for the complexity of infant life, is there then a larger self present at birth? I thought that an infant could be looked upon as a self in Jung's sense; as an agency of the psyche that transcends the opposites. A fetus begins life from a condition of primary unity in which consciousness and the unconscious are not differentiated. *I deduced that the primary state of an infant was as an integrated being, and that the integrator was the self and not the ego* (emphasis Fordham's, p. 64).

My emphasis in this paragraph would be on the idea that the fetus "begins life from a condition of primary unity in which consciousness and the unconscious are not differentiated." This statement implies to me that Fordham (unlike Neumann) does not see the Self in the infant as being a state of total unconsciousness and if that is so, I agree with him. I also believe that Fordham's attitude regarding this concept is significant for understanding the numerous insights and discoveries he made concerning individuation in children.

I believe that the Paradise myths, Genesis as well as other myths of Paradise, support the idea that psychological experience begins in the womb with the function of intuition. Intuition is the function of the soul complex, which contains ego and soul as one. Sensation introduces the child to the world of opposites, beginning consciousness and unconsciousness, creating the infamous split in the super consciousness of the Self. The human child is born with ego and soul, thereafter apparently divided, which is a description of the birth of consciousness and the birth of the unconscious, as the Self differentiates.

The irrational functions of intuition and sensation are apparently opposed of necessity, allowing each function to be experienced sequentially in time, and allowing the experience of knowing two ways of being in the world, separateness and oneness, two opposites that can be re-experienced as unity. In this way intuition and sensation complement one another. Jung described the opposition of these two functions, but made no attempt to describe the point where they converge.

The rational functions of feeling and thinking, described by Jung as opposites that are complementary, also have a point where they converge and can be seen as reflections of one another that accomplish the same purpose by a different means. I see feeling, among other things, as the phenomenological experience of the thought in its unmanifested form. Feeling is the function that makes value judgments, as Jung described. In addition, I see the function as more than that, and ultimately as the function where all value judgments are withdrawn, where all phenomenon is experienced as Being. From my understanding of the myths, feeling is the unconscious thought, just as thought is the unconscious feeling, each containing the same information in a different form.

Von Franz (1972), in her discussion of creation myths and the fourfold division of the universe, states that:

> We can say that the number four, from our practical experience, always points to a totality and to a total conscious orientation, while the number three is a creative flow and four is the clear result of the flow when it become still, visible and ordered (p. 168).

This, I believe, describes the thinking function as the fourth function (when intuition is seen as the first, in the womb), a total conscious orientation that is a result of the number three, the creative flow of the feeling function. Thinking appears as the last in the evolution of the functions as they turn, and appears to be the picture of what has previously taken place in the other functions, via the archetype which is later expressed as images, ideas, or language. Thinking is not the experience, but the copy, stamp, imprint, or image of the experience. On the other hand, it is an experience of the experience, like Adam is an image of God. Thinking is the Divine Child of mythology, the method by which human experience is expressed in its final form as one of the functions. From my reading of the Genesis mythology, it appears possible to me that the first representation of the human infant may occur shortly after birth in the form of an archetype that may be abstract in nature, yet express in simple terms that the circle of unity experienced in utero has been shattered; the "I" and the "other," that is, the world, have both been born.

In addition to the questions that I initially asked, what appears to me as significant possibilities seemed to offer themselves as answers to questions that I had not originally asked. Although I assumed that the ego, consciousness, and unconsciousness begin at birth, it did not occur to me how the myth might be describing this process by the use of the major archetypes, especially as personifications of the four psychological functions. Although I believed that the so-called split in consciousness was a universal and phenomenological experience of all people in all cultures, I did not see clearly what I believe to be the pristine truth and beauty of our own Western cosmological myth of Genesis, when viewed as a metaphor for the beginning of consciousness and unconsciousness as it differentiates.

I initially did not think to ask if introversion or extraversion came first, but what appears now as a major possibility, began to unfold and present itself as I proceeded. Introversion or a subjective attitude appears to be the first one known by human infants, with extraversion introduced by the human mother. The Divine Child archetype is the transcendent symbol that connects and separates both. Divine love is the double-edged sword of ego and soul, consciousness and unconsciousness. The feeling and intuitive functions appear to be the least known in psychology, possibly because the transition into language always falls short of the experience, which is silent like the goddess. Campbell (1991b) says that "the psychological functions chiefly involved in the outward-turned, "objective" order of cognition, "common to all men," are sensation and thinking. Feeling and intuition, on the other hand, lead inward, to private spheres" (emphasis Campbell's, p. 649). These private spheres may be contained in the idea of the first transference, which is only briefly described in Chapter 2. This was also not an original question. I believe, however, that it has significance as material for future research, especially the archetypes of the Virgin Mary and Divine Child as the images depicting the first exchange of soul and ego between mother and child. Campbell (1990c), also says that "woman with her baby is the basic image of mythology" (p. 1). This basic mythological image often describes the experience of the first transference.

Further conclusions are the following: Myths depicting a return to Paradise are describing what is necessary to reunite ego and soul or soul and body, allowing for the experience of oneness to be re-experienced in life, presumably to prepare (from the beginning) the individual for the experience of actual death and the knowledge that death is only a cycle of life. The human child experiences all functions in the first moments of birth, although there is an explicit order; the human child does not suffer in the womb; and the desire to return to the womb or Paradise is universal and describes a desire to return to the innocent state of Being that was experienced in the womb, and that can be experienced again on a conscious level, a state of Being that Jung referred to as the individuated Self. The archetypes are patterns of phenomenological experience, clearly expressed by Jung (1967/1929), who said "the figures of Christ and the devil are both based on archetypal patterns, and were never invented but rather experienced (emphasis Jung's, p. 246). It is the psyche of the human child that first experiences the archetypal patterns.

Identifying general structures of significant archetypal energy patterns and their personifications in mythology seems to be an important step toward demonstrating that the cosmological archetypes are universal psychic energy patterns contained in every human psyche. Campbell (1993) describes this in his own approach to myth: "What I would suggest is that by comparing a number from different parts of the world and differing traditions, one might arrive at an understanding of their force, their source and possible sense" (p. 26). This has been my own approach to understanding various myths as universal psychic energy related to the four psychological functions.

Marshall (1968) states the following:

> A great work of science or art is great because it contrives to operate on several levels at once: it is general without having a host of exceptions, or it describes an individual case without being ephemeral. But in areas where such unifying works have not yet been accomplished, one has to operate with a combination of more general and more particular partial answers, modifying each as seems fitting (p. 14).

Marshall's statement appears to apply to Jung's description of the four psychological functions, which are general in their scope and necessarily capacious in the categories they seek to define. If, however, they are defining a four-fold structure of the human psyche, which I believe is so, it is necessary first to match them with cosmological archetypes of the same general nature. Identifying the general archetypes from both perspectives appears essential before a depth analysis of the myth can take place.

It was not possible to give a complete analysis of each of the various myths mentioned as related to the four functions. For that reason, I have attempted to show how and why the general symbols and archetypes of divergent myths and antecedent mythologies can be compared with the myth of Genesis, which I have attempted to describe in more detail. The large mythological categories can then be compared and identified as the same or similar archetypal energy patterns contained in the four psychological functions. Various cosmological archetypes can be seen as relevant to the four functions and developmental psychology. I have done this repeatedly to establish the validity of the hypothesis put forth here: An order to the functions can be seen and intuition (in the womb) is the first function used by human infants (represented in the Genesis mythology as the creating God), followed by the function of conscious sensation (represented in the Genesis mythology as the Serpent), which begins at birth.

If the beginning connection can be established as a valid assumption, it is then possible to analyze the complete myth concerning its particulars, which may yield new insights that have previously gone unnoticed. It is not essential for other mythological archetypes to match those given in Genesis. The interpretation of Genesis as a representation of the functions could contain just as much validity or none at all, without other mythological themes that match. If, however, the myth of Genesis and the four functions describe universal experience, a link with even one other significant myth would strengthen and support the idea that cosmological mythology in general is describing the universal experience of beginning human life.

I have stressed the idea of intuition as the function for containing the other functions in undifferentiated form (the three-in-one motif) because I believe this is an important key that must be used before patterns in the archetypes can be established as psychic energy. Montanaro (1991) describes intuition as "unconscious absorption" when she states:

> Every act of learning occurs in a special way. Everything that comes from the environment is received, processed and stored in the brain cells with no effort using a form of unconscious absorption. This intense mental activity is always going on, even in prenatal life, and it characterizes "the absorbent mind." (p. 83).

Montanaro's words express, in my interpretation of them, a new movement in developmental psychology, which is towards the understanding of the human infant in a more complete manner. Jung's contributions, enormous as they were, need to be linked with other minds and other possibilities. And it is my belief that one of his most important contributions, the description of the four psychological functions, needs to be extended and used in a creative manner.

Lovin and Reynolds (1985) define cosmogony:

> A cosmogony, as the etymology of the term suggests, is usually an account of the "generation or creation of the existing world order" *Oxford English Dictionary* 1971, 568). The term includes the connotation that this account has implications for understanding the present human condition, and so it applies well to those classical and biblical accounts of the origins of the physical world that seventeenth-and eighteenth-century English writers first classified together as "cosmogonia" (p. 5).

Linking Jung's psychological functions with cosmogony may have implications for understanding the present human condition. In addition, it may supply us with a new understanding and respect for the mythology of Genesis as a powerful metaphor, yielding new insights not previously brought to collective consciousness.

There is no previous map given for this journey. No one, to my knowledge, has asked this specific question concerning the possibility of an order in the appearance of the functions in humans or attempted to link them with cosmological mythology. Therefore, the answers may be partial and, indeed, even contain error, but this appears to be the risk inherent in research that attempts to contribute anything new. Concerning the newly created idea, Jung (1971/1921) said:

> Current collective values can certainly be measured by an objective criterion, but only a free and individual assessment—a matter of living feeling—can give the true measure of something newly created. It also needs a man who has a "soul" and not merely relations to objects (p. 189).

Insights gained worthy may justify possible errors and be seen as significant for further research.

Research concerning the psychological function of intuition and its role in developmental psychology is just beginning to be explored. It is just beginning to be noticed that infants appear to know things they could not have acquired by learning (Stern, 1985, p. 51). Speaking of future science, the eminent physicist Francis Crick (1994) states: "We can hope to understand more precisely the mechanisms of such mental activities as intuition, creativity, and aesthetic pleasure, and in so doing grasp them more clearly and, it is to be hoped, enjoy them more" (p. 261). Obviously, our understanding of intuition as a psychological function is not precisely understood, which does not undermine its importance for the field of psychology. On the other hand, there are those who have (now, not in the future) a working definition of intuition, such as Zukav (1990), who describes the function of intuition as a "multisensory" system: "Our five senses, together, form a single sensory system that is designed to perceive physical reality. The perceptions of a multisensory human extend beyond physical reality to the larger dynamical systems of which our physical reality is a part" (p. 27).

What Zukav is calling the "five-sensory" or "single sensory system" is what I am calling the ego complex; what Zukav is calling the "multisensory" system is what I am calling the soul complex. For Zukav, the multisensory system is what is used by the soul. We appear to be describing the same process, although Zukav (1990) believes soul consciousness, a term he also uses (p. 185), is evolving in the human race, while I would describe it as a consciousness that is present in the beginning of life and used continuously whether we have total ego consciousness of it or not. Archaic humans were probably no less intuitive than modern humans, if anything they probably used the function of intuition more, attributing their increase in knowledge to gods or angels or other, which Zukav is still doing. The question of who provides the answers when ego consciousness departs or the question of what is the initial force of life has many answers from A to Z, and the answers are the topics of religion, mythology, and even science in its search for the beginning cause of the universe. Does an unseen and not completely known Supreme Power, which we are a part of, support all life in the universe or, are we physiologically designed to experience "other," which is that power in us, as God? It is not my purpose to presume an answer to this question, since I believe it can only be known by individual and subjective experience, but to suggest that the function of intuition is essential for that individual experience, whatever it may be, to take place as a return to the Self. I think it also necessary for the field of psychology (at least Jungian psychology attempting to use the four functions as a frame of reference) to understand intuition as the source out of which the other functions flow and the one to which they return. In the beginning (in the womb) we are in Paradise with no awareness of that experience; (Innocent) a return to that perfect state of Being is a return to Paradise with this difference: this time we are conscious and awake and aware of the experience (Wisdom).

Spence (1994) tells us that some American Indian tribes adopted the serpent as a symbol of time. "They reckoned by 'suns,' and as the outline of the sun, a circle, corresponds to nothing in nature so much as a serpent with its tail in its mouth, devouring itself. This may have been the origin of the symbol" (p. 111). This symbol was used by many divergent cultures, all expressing a similar and universal theme. The symbol of the Uroboros (see Neumann, 1993, p. 33), the image of the Birth of Vishnu as he bites his toe (see Neumann, 1993, frontispiece), or the Serpent Tokch'i eating an egg, all appear to be describing what Freeman (1995) calls the "solipsistic brain" (p. 3). Freeman's (1995, p. 2) conclusion that the only thing we can "know" is what we ourselves create supports my position by scientific data. The creation myth describes how the human child experiences and creates the world, by a subjective and introverted consciousness that eventually learns the extraverted or objective method, which is never, as Jung so often described, totally objective.

Crick (1994) in the preface of his book presents Stuart Sutherland's definition of consciousness (The International Dictionary of Psychology), which parallels my own:

> Consciousness. The having of perceptions, thoughts, and feelings; awareness. The term is impossible to define except in terms that are unintelligible without a grasp of what consciousness means. Many fall into the trap of equating consciousness with self-consciousness—to be conscious it is only necessary to be aware of the external world (quote in preface).

Infants, indeed, appear to be aware and conscious of the external world. This idea, apparently, is only beginning to be accepted in developmental psychology, whereas cosmological mythology appears to describe, by the use of archetypes and symbols, how the actual event takes place. Art often anticipates science, and this appears to be the case in cosmological mythology, which attempts to describe origins of human life and the universe as they occur simultaneously.

Edinger (1986a) states that "the process of division into four is a primordial cosmogonic image" (p. 15). I believe this cosmogonic image is described in the four major archetypes of Genesis, each of which can be seen as an archetype for the undifferentiated functions and the beginning of the individuation process as consciousness begins. I consider Jung's division of the four functions of consciousness to be an important representation of that primordial cosmogonic image. Even though the implications of the connection were not brought to completion by Jung, he appeared to know that his description of a four-fold structure of consciousness was related to primordial cosmological archetypes of the same nature.

Baring and Cashford (1993) reflect my own conclusions concerning the cosmological myth of Genesis as an element of universal psychic energy:

> A symbolic reading of the story may restore it to its rightful place at the beginning of our cultural tradition as a myth of the birth of consciousness. What is important is that an experience of a sacred dimension is found in all cultures whether their organization is simple or very complex. This suggests that the sacred is not a stage in the history of consciousness but an element in the structure of consciousness, belonging to all people at all times. It is therefore part of the character of the human race, perhaps the essential part (pp. 8-9).

In addition, the Genesis myth describes not only the birth of ego consciousness, but the birth of the unconscious soul as super consciousness (Self) ceases.

Taken as a simple but powerful metaphor, the myth simultaneously describes the birth of the Divine Child, the psychological child, and the biological child; at the depth level these three can be seen as one Divine and human Child. Jung (1971/1921) says that "the divine birth is an event altogether outside the bounds of rationality. Psychologically, it proclaims the fact that a new symbol, a new expression of life at its most intense, is being created" (p. 189). It is possible that Jung was describing his own Divine Child—his idea of the fourfold structure of the human psyche—from a psychological perspective.

Jung, when asked by a member of the Vision Seminars about consciousness and individuation, uses the analogy of a flower to symbolize consciousness. He refers to the flower as a symbol of consciousness and individuation:

> Dr. Jung said: "Living consciously is our form of individuation. A plant that is meant to produce a flower is not individuated if it does not produce it, and the man who does not develop consciousness is not individuated, because consciousness is his flower, it is his life… All that a man does, whatever he attempts, means his individuation; it is the accomplishment, the fulfillment of his possibilities; and one of his foremost possibilities is the attainment of consciousness. That really makes him man; so to man, life should be conscious." (Jung, 1976, "The Vision Seminars," p. 297, Vol. 2, NY: Spring Publications).

If there was one word only to describe Jungs goal for the human race, I believe it would be "Consciousness." Jung's statement above appears to me to represent the epitome of his entire psychological orientation and to him, the path for humanity, if mankind is to advance to a higher level of consciousness. Consciousness would not be possible, however, without the experience of unconsciousness, the root and leaf of that flower, which is there when consciousness begins.

The four psychological functions represent a circular and sacred pattern, like the hands of a divine and extraordinary clock going round and round in the moments of our everyday, ordinary life. Each function is designed to complement the other, and each contributes to the birth and death of the other, wired with an invisible and indestructible thread that connects us to the ground of our Being, which was always there and will always be there. Cognitive thinking is the result of the archetype, which would not come into being without the primal, instinctual energy of intuition, which contains it in potential. The instinct contains the archetype and the archetype contains the expressed instinct, just as the Father God contains the Serpent, Eve, and Adam in Paradise, and Adam is the expression and the image of the creating God.

There had to be a beginning place where the psychological functions were first connected—a place where they first emerged. The beginning place was the Self, the center where the four functions unfolded, like the four petals of a divine, wondrous Rose, as intuition, sensation, feeling, and thinking—the soul, body, heart, and spirit of the human and Divine Child.

FIGURES

Fig 1: Newborn — 18

Fig 2: Psychological Functions of Child in the Womb — 43

Fig 3: Psychological Functions of Child at Birth — 47

Fig 4: The Four Psychological Functions as Psychic Energy — 48

Fig 5: Four Creating Gods of the Sumerian Pantheon: An, Ki Enlil, and Enki — 126

Fig 6: Serpent Lord: The Copulating Vipers — 127

Fig 7: Myth of the Fallen Angel: Lucifer, the Bringer of Light — 135

Fig 8: Moses (Child) Taken from the Water — 141

Fig 9: The Four Archangels as Archetypes of Neutral Psychic Energy — 164

Fig 10: The Four Apostles as Archetypes of Psychic Energy — 165

Fig 11: The Cosmological Myth of Genesis - Level 1 — 209

Fig 12: The Psychological Level - Level 2 — 210

Fig 13: The Biological Level - Level 3 — 211

Fig 14: The Union of Instinct and Archetype - Level 4 — 212

Fig 15: The Genesis Myth of Paradise — 213

Fig 16: The Bhagavad Gita Rope Image — 221

Fig 17: Serpent Mound: Tokchi'i, Guardian of The East — 224

Fig 18: Philosophorvm: King is Ego, Queen is Soul — 228

Fig 19: The Morning Star: Symbol of Love — 235

Fig 20: The Maria Axiom or: The Feminine Principle — 236

Fig 21: Dante's Rainbow — 242

REFERENCES

Abraham, F. D. (1995). Chaos, courage, choice, & creativity. <u>Psychological Perspectives</u>, 31, pp. 65, 70.

Alighieri, D. (1977). <u>Divine comedy</u>. (John Ciardi, Trans.) Franklin Center, PA: The Franklin Library.

Andersen, H. C. (1974). The garden of Eden. <u>The complete fairy tales and stories</u>. (Erik Christian Haugaard, Trans.), (pp. 132-144) New York: Anchor Press/Doubleday.

Arguelles, M., & Arguelles, J. (1977). <u>The feminine: Spacious as the sky</u>. Boulder, CO: Shambhala Publications, Inc.

Balint, M. (1992). <u>The basic fault</u>. Evanston, IL: Northwestern University Press.

Bancroft-Hunt, N. (1992). <u>North American Indians</u>. Philadelphia, PA: Courage Books.

Baring, A., & Cashford, J. (1993). <u>The myth of the goddess</u>. New York: Penguin Books USA, Inc.

Beebe, J., & Wheelwright, J. (1987). (Speakers). <u>Psychological types</u>. [Audio tape]. San Francisco: C. G. Jung Institute.

<u>Bhagavad Gita, The</u>. (1960). (M. M. Chatterji, Trans.). New York: Causeway Books.

Blake, W. (1980). <u>Songs of innocence and of experience</u>. Franklin Center, PA: The Franklin Library.

Blakney, R. B. (1941). <u>Meister Eckhart: A modern translation</u>. New York: Harper & Brothers Publishers.

Bucke, R. (1948). <u>Cosmic consciousness: A study in the evolution of the human mind</u>. New York: E. P. Dutton & Co., Inc.

Burnham, S. (1990). <u>A book of angels</u>. New York: Random House, Inc.

Campbell, J. (1964). <u>The masks of God: Occidental mythology</u>. New York: The Viking Press, Inc.

Campbell, J. (1973). <u>The hero with a thousand faces</u>. Princeton, NJ: Princeton University Press.

Campbell, J. (1976). <u>The masks of God: Oriental mythology</u>. New York: Penguin Books, Inc.

Campbell, J. (1979). <u>The masks of God: Primitive mythology</u>. New York: The Viking Press.

Campbell, J. (1988a). The inner reaches of outer space. New York: Harper & Row, Publishers, Inc.

Campbell, J. (1988b). An open life: Joseph Campbell in conversation with Michael Toms. New York: Larsons Publications.

Campbell, J. (1988c). The power of myth. New York: Doubleday.

Campbell, J. (1989). Historical atlas of world mythology. Vol. 11: The way of the seeded earth. Part 2: Mythologies of the primitive planters: The northern Americas. New York: Harper & Row, Publishers.

Campbell, J. (1990a). The flight of the wild gander. New York: Harper Perennial, Harper Collins Publishers.

Campbell, J. (1990b). The mythic image. Princeton, NJ: Princeton University Press.

Campbell, J. (1990c). Transformations of myth through time. New York: Harper & Row, Publishers, Inc.

Campbell, J. (Speaker). (1990d). The way of art [Audio tape]. San Francisco: Sound Horizons Audio.

Campbell, J. (1991a). The Mystery number of the Goddess. In all her names. (Joseph Campbell & Charles Muses, Eds.) New York: Harper San Francisco.

Campbell, J. (1991b). The masks of God: Creative mythology. New York: Penguin Books, Inc.

Campbell, J. (1993). Myths to live by. New York: Penguin Books, Inc.

Chetwynd, T. (1982). A dictionary of symbols. New York: Granada Publishing Limited.

Chopra, D. (1993). Ageless body, timeless mind. New York: Crown Publishers, Inc.

Cirlot, G. E. (1971). A dictionary of symbols. New York: Philosophical library, Inc.

Connolly, D. (1994). In search of angels: A celestial sourcebook for beginning your journey. New York: Berkeley Publishing Group.

Cooper, J. C. (1984). Symbolism: The universal language. Wellingborough, England: The Aquarian Press.

Cooper, J. C. (1988). An illustrated encyclopedia of traditional symbols. London: Thames and Hudson, Ltd.

Crick, F. (1994). The astonishing hypothesis: The scientific search for the soul. New York: Charles Scribner's Sons.

Davidson, G. (1971). A dictionary of angels, including the fallen angels. New York: The Free Press.

Dennett, D. (1991). Consciousness explained. Toronto, Canada: Little, Brown & Co.

Denney, N., & Quadagno, D. (1988). Human sexuality. St. Louis: Times Mirror/Mosby College Publishing.

Dickinson, E. (1960). The complete poems of Emily Dickinson. (Thomas H. Johnson, Ed.) Boston: Little, Brown and Company.

Drachnik, C. (1985). Symbols of psychopathology: Children. Belmont, CA: College of Notre Dame.

Edinger, E. (1984). The creation of consciousness. Toronto, Canada: Inner City Books.

Edinger, E. (1986a). The Bible and the psyche: Individuation symbolism in the Old Testament. Toronto, Canada: Inner City Books.

Edinger, E. (1986b). Encounter with the Self. Toronto, Canada: Inner City Books.

Einstein, A. (1979). The world as I see it. (Alan Harris, Trans.) Secaucus, NJ: Citadel Press.

Eliade, M. (1975). Myths, dreams, and mysteries. New York: Harper & Row.

Eliade, M. (1991). The myth of the eternal return. Princeton, NJ: Princeton University Press.

Eliot, T. S. (1976). T. S. Eliot: Collected poems. Franklin Center, PA: The Franklin Library.

Evans, R. (1976). Jung on elementary psychology: A discussion between C. G. Jung and Richard I. Evans. New York: E. P. Dutton & Co., Inc.

Fontana, D. (1994). The secret language of symbols. San Francisco: Chronicle Books.

Fordham, M. (1957). New developments in analytical psychology. London: Routledge and Kegan Paul.

Fordham, M. (1958). The objective psyche. Great Britain: Routledge & Kegan Paul Ltd.

Fordham, M. (1970). Children as individuals. New York: G. P. Putnam's Sons.

Fordham, M. (1972). Note on psychological types. Journal of Analytical Psychology, 17(2), 112.

Fordham, M. (1976). The self and autism. London: The Society of Analytical Psychology Ltd.

Fordham, M. (1979). The self as an imaginative construct. Journal of Analytical Psychology, 24(1), 27.

Fordham, M. (Speaker). (1982). *Reflections on infant and child development*. Taped lecture to the Hilda Kirsch Children's Center, C. G. Jung Institute, Los Angeles.

Forham, M. (1988). *Jungian child psychotherapy*. London: The Society of Analytical Psychology, Karnac Books.

Fordham, M. (1989). The infant's reach. *Psychological Perspectives, 21*, 64.

Fuller, R. B. (1972). *Intuition: Metaphysical mosaic*. New York: Doubleday & Co., Inc.

Gayley, C. M. (1939). *Classic myths*. Boston, New York, San Francisco: Gin and Company.

Godwin, M. (1990). *Angels: An endangered species*. New York: Simon & Schuster.

Goldman, K. (1993). (Speaker). *Angel voices* [Audio Recording]. New York: Simon & Schuster.

Graves, R., & Patai, R. (1989). *Hebrew myths: The book of Genesis*. New York: Bantam Doubleday Dell Publishing Group, Inc.

Grimm, & Grimm. (1992). *The juniper tree and other tales from Grimm*. (Lore Segal & Randall Jarrell, Trans.) New York: Farrar, Straus and Giroux.

Guntrip, H. (1989). *Schizoid phenomena, object-relations and the self*. Madison, CT: International Universities Press Inc.

Hall, C., & Lindzey, G. (1978). *Theories of personality*. New York: John Wiley & Sons.

Harrison, B. (1994). A meditation on Eve. *Out of the garden*. (Christina Buchmann & Celina Spiegel, Eds.) New York: Ballantine Books.

Heinberg, R. (1989). *Memories and visions of paradise*. Los Angeles: Jeremy P. Tarcher, Inc.

Hillman, J. (1978). *The myth of analysis*. New York: Harper Colophon Books.

Hillman, J. (1991). *A blue fire*. New York: Harper Perennial edition.

Holy Bible, The. (1953). (Translated from the Latin Vulgate). New York: The Douay Bible House.

Holy Bible, The. (1924). (King James Version). Philadelphia: A. J. Holman Company.

Jackson, J. F., & Jackson, J. H. (1979). *Infant culture*. New York: New American Library.

Jacoby, M. (1985). Longing for paradise: Psychological perspectives on an archetype. Boston: Sigo Press.

Johnson, B. (1988). Lady of the beasts: Ancient images of the goddess and her sacred animals. San Francisco: Harper & Row, Publishers.

Jung, C. (1933). Modern man in search of a soul. (W. S. Dell & C. F. Baynes, Trans.) New York: Harcourt, Brace & World, Inc., (Original work published 1933).

Jung, C. (1953). Two essays on analytical psychology. (In R. F. C. Hull, Trans.), The Collected Works of C. G. Jung (Vol. 7). Princeton, NJ: Princeton University Press (Original work published 1943).

Jung, C. (1954). The psychology of the transference. (In R. F. C. Hull, Trans.), The Collected Works of C. G. Jung, extracted from The Practice of Psychotherapy (Vol. 16). Princeton, NJ: Princeton University Press (Original work published 1946).

Jung, C. (1956). Symbols of transformation. (In R. F. C. Hull, Trans.), The Collected Works of C. G. Jung (Vol. 5). Princeton, NJ: Princeton University Press (Original work published 1912).

Jung, C. (1957). The undiscovered self. (R. F. Hull, Trans.) Boston: Little, Brown & Company.

Jung, C. (1958). Aion. Researches into the phenomenology of the self. (In R. F. C. Hull, Trans.), The Collected Works of C. G. Jung (Vol. 9). Princeton, NJ: Princeton University Press (Original work published 1952).

Jung, C. (1959). The archetypes and the collective unconscious. (In R. F. C. Hull, Trans.), The Collected Works of C. G. Jung (Vol. 9). Princeton, NJ: Princeton University Press (Original work published 1938).

Jung, C. (1959). Mandala symbolism. (In R. F. C. Hull, Trans.), The Collected Works of C. G. Jung, extracted from The Archetypes and the Collective Unconscious (Vol. 9). Princeton, NJ: Princeton University Press (Original work published 1955).

Jung, C. (1963). Mysterium coniunctionis. (In R. F. C. Hull, Trans.), The Collected Works of C. G. Jung (Vol. 14). Princeton, NJ: Princeton University Press. (Original work published 1955)

Jung, C. (1964). Man and his symbols. New York: Doubleday & Co., Inc.

Jung, C. (1967). Alchemical studies. (In R. F. C. Hull, Trans.), The Collected Works of C. G. Jung (Vol. 13). Princeton, NJ: Princeton University Press (Original work published 1929).

Jung, C. (1971). <u>Psychological types</u>. (H. G. Baynes, Trans., revision by R. F. C. Hull), <u>The Collected Works of C. G. Jung</u> (Vol. 6). Princeton, NJ: Princeton University Press (Original work published 1921).

Jung, C. (1974). <u>Dreams</u>. (In R. F. C. Hull, Trans.), <u>The Collected Works of C. G. Jung</u> (Extracted from "Individual Dream Symbolism in Relation to Alchemy") (Vol. 12). Princeton, NJ: Princeton University Press (Original work published 1953).

Jung, C., & Kerenyi, C. (1949). <u>Essays on a science of mythology. The myth of the divine child and the mysteries of eleusis</u>. (In R. F. C. Hull, Trans.), Princeton, NJ: Princeton University Press (Original work published 1949).

Kaplan, L. (1978). <u>Oneness and separateness: From infant to individual</u>. New York: Simon & Schuster.

Kellogg, R. (1969). <u>The psychology of children's art</u>. San Diego: Random House.

Kerenyi, K. (1990). <u>Hermes, guide of souls</u>. Dallas: Spring Publications, Inc.

Lenhart, G. (1990a). <u>The ultimate foundations of ego-identity</u>. Unpublished manuscript, Pacifica Graduate Institute, Santa Barbara, CA.

Lenhart, G. (1990b). <u>Psyche and Eros: Symbols of transformation leading to the coniunctio and birth of a divine girl/child named Joy</u>. Unpublished manuscript, Pacifica Graduate Institute, Santa Barbara, CA.

Loomis, M. (1991). <u>Dancing the wheel of psychological types</u>. Wilmette, IL: Chiron Publications.

Lovin, R., & Reynolds, F. (1985). In the beginning. (In Robin W. Lovin & Frank E. Reynolds, Eds.) <u>Cosmogony and ethical order</u>. Chicago: The University of Chicago Press.

Margolies, M. (1994). <u>Angels in Jewish life and literature</u>. New York: Ballantine Books.

Marshall, I. N. (1968). The four functions: A conceptual analysis. <u>The Journal of Analytical Psychology</u>. 1-32.

Marshall, R. (1993). <u>Strange, amazing and mysterious places</u>. San Francisco: Collins Publishers.

McLean, A. (1989). <u>The triple goddess: An exploration of the archetypal feminine</u>. Grand Rapids, MI: Phanes Press.

Meier, C. A. (1986). <u>Soul and body: Essays on the theories of C. G. Jung</u>. San Francisco: The Lapis Press.

Merrell-Wolff, F. (1973). The philosophy of consciousness without an object. New York: The Julian Press, Inc.

Merrell-Wolff, F. (1976). Pathways through to space: A personal report of transformation in consciousness. New York: Warner Books, Inc.

Meshberger, F. (1990). An interpretation of Michelangelo's creation of Adam based on neuroanatomy. Journal of the American Medical Association, 264, 1837-1841.

Milton, J. (1981). Paradise lost. Franklin Center, PA: The Franklin Library.

Molyneaux, B. (1995). The sacred earth. London: Duncan Baird Publishers.

Montanaro, S. Q. (1991). Understanding the human being: The importance of the first three years of life. Mountain View, CA: Nienhuis Montessori USA.

Moolenburgh, H. C. (1992). A handbook of angels. (Amina Marix-Evans, Trans.) Saffron Walden, Essex, England: The C. W. Daniel Co. Limited.

Moore, T. (1994). In R. Hauck (Ed.), Angels: The mysterious messengers. (pp. 201-211) New York: Ballantine Books.

Moustakas, C. (1990). Heuristic research: design, methodology, and applications. Newbury Park, CA: Sage Publications, Inc.

Mundkur, B. (1983). The cult of the serpent: An interdisciplinary survey of its manifestations and origins. New York: State University of New York Press.

Neumann, E. (1956). Amor and psyche, the psychic development of the feminine. (Ralph Manheim, Trans.) New York: Princeton University Press (Original work published 1952).

Neumann, E. (1966). Narcissism, normal self-formation, and the primary relation to the mother. Spring (pp. 81, 107).

Nietzsche, F. (1989). Beyond good and evil: Prelude to a philosophy of the future. (Walter Kaufmann, Trans.) New York: Vintage Books (Original work published 1966).

Nilsson, L. (1993). A child is born. New York: Bantam Doubleday Dell Publishing Group, Inc.

Ornstein, R. (1975). The psychology of consciousness. New York: Penguin Books Inc.

Pagels, E. (1989). Adam, Eve, and the serpent. New York: Vintage Books.

Pearce, J. C. (1980). Magical child. New York: Dutton Publishing Co., Inc.

Peterson, J. (1995). The gods of war. (godsofwar @ isr.harvard.edu) [Online]. Available at: http://wjh-www.harvard.edu/~jbp/godsofwar.html.

Phillips, J. (1985). <u>Eve: The history of an idea</u>. San Francisco: Harper & Row, Publishers.

Plato. (1928). <u>The works of Plato, the symposium</u>. New York: Simon and Schuster, Inc.

Ponce, C. (Speaker). (1991, Spring). <u>The ecology of desire</u>. Unpublished lecture, Pacifica Graduate Institute, Santa Barbara, CA.

Radhakrishnan, J. (1988). <u>An idealist view of life</u>. London: Unwin Hyman Limited.

Reason, P., & Rowan, J. (1989). <u>Human inquiry: A sourcebook of new paradigm research</u>. Chichester, New York: John Wiley & Sons.

Regardie, I. (1970). <u>The philosopher's stone</u>. Saint Paul, MN: Llewellyn Publications.

Restak, R. M. (1980). <u>The brain: The last frontier</u>. New York: Warner Books, Inc.

Rilke, R. M. (1962). <u>Letters to a young poet</u>. (M. D. Herter Norton, Trans.) New York: Norton & Co., Inc., (Original work published 1934).

Rilke, R. M. (1978). <u>Duino elegies</u>. (David Young, Trans.) New York: W. W. Norton & Co., Inc.

Roethke, T. (1975). The Waking. (In Allison, Barrows, Blake, Carr, Eastman, & English, Eds.) <u>The Norton anthology of poetry</u>. (p. 1133) (New York, London: W. W. Norton & Company.

Russell, P. (1979). <u>The brain book</u>. New York: Penguin Books USA Inc.

Sagan, C. (1977). <u>The dragons of eden</u>. New York: Random House.

Schneiderman, S. (1988). <u>An angel passes: How the sexes became undivided</u>. New York: New York University Press.

Sexton, L. (1993, April). <u>Israel's birthright, the way of angels</u>. Unpublished lecture, Pacifica Graduate Institute, Santa Barbara, CA.

Shiarella, R. (1992). <u>Journey to joy</u>. New York: Matrika Publications.

Sidoli, M. (1989). <u>The unfolding self: Separation and individuation</u>. Boston: Sigo Press.

Singer, J. (1977). <u>Androgyny: Toward a new theory of sexuality</u>. New York: Anchor Press/Doubleday.

Spence, L. (1994). <u>Myths of the North American Indians</u>. New Jersey: Random House Value Publishing, Inc.

Springer, S., & Deutsch, G. (1981). <u>Left brain, right brain</u>. San Francisco: W. H. Freeman and Company.

Thompson, K. (1991). <u>Angels and aliens</u>. Reading, MA: Addison-Wesley Publishing Co., Inc.

Travers, P. L. (1993). *What the bee knows: Reflections on myth, symbol and story*. New York: Penguin Books Inc.

von Franz, M., & Hillman, J. (1979). *Jung's typology*. Irving, TX: Spring Publications Inc.

Westman, H. (1991). *The structure of biblical myths: The ontogenesis of the psyche*. Wilmette, IL: Chiron Publications.

Whitman, W. (1981). *Leaves of grass*. Franklin Center, PA: The Franklin Library.

Wickes, F. (1988). *The inner world of childhood*. Boston: Sigo Press.

Wolkstein, D., & Kramer, S. (1983). *Inanna: Queen of heaven and earth*. New York: Harper & Row, Publishers, Inc.

Wordsworth, W. (1888). *The complete poetical works of William Wordsworth*. New York: A. L. Burt Company, Publishers.

Zukav, G. (1990). *The seat of the soul*. New York: Simon & Schuster, Inc.

ABOOKS

ALIVE Book Publishing and ALIVE Publishing Group
are imprints of Advanced Publishing LLC,
3200 A Danville Blvd., Suite 204, Alamo, California 94507

Telephone: 925.837.7303
alivebookpublishing.com

www.ingramcontent.com/pod-product-compliance
Lightning Source LLC
Chambersburg PA
CBHW061125010526
44115CB00025B/3002